Untangling a Red, White, and Black Heritage

Untangling a Red, White, and Black Heritage

A Personal History of the Allotment Era

DARNELLA DAVIS

University of New Mexico Press ∎ Albuquerque

Library of Congress Cataloging-in-Publication Data
Names: Davis, Darnella, 1949– author.
Title: Untangling a red, white, and black heritage: a personal history of the Allotment Era /
    Darnella Davis.
Description: First edition. | Albuquerque: University of New Mexico Press, 2018. |
    Includes bibliographical references and index. |
Identifiers: LCCN 2017060737 (print) | LCCN 2018025969 (e-book) | ISBN 9780826359803
    (e-book) | ISBN 9780826359797 (hardback)
Subjects: LCSH: Davis, Darnella,—Family. | Cherokee Indians—Mixed descent—Oklahoma. |
    Creek Indians—Mixed descent—Oklahoma. | Indian allotments—Oklahoma—History. |
    Thornton family. | Bowlin family. | Adams family. | Racially mixed people—Oklahoma—
    Biography. | Oklahoma—Biography. | BISAC: HISTORY / United States / 19th Century. |
    HISTORY / Native American. | SOCIAL SCIENCE / Discrimination & Race Relations.
Classification: LCC E78.O45 (e-book) | LCC E78.O45 D38 2018 (print) | DDC 976.6/03—dc23
LC record available at https://lccn.loc.gov/2017060737

Cover photograph courtesy of Beverle Lax
Designed by Felicia Cedillos
Composed in Minion Pro 10.25/14.25

From seven generations to Rebecca and Charlotte

Honor thy father and thy mother: that thy days may be long upon the land which the LORD thy god giveth thee.

—KING JAMES BIBLE, EXODUS 20:12

CONTENTS

ILLUSTRATIONS

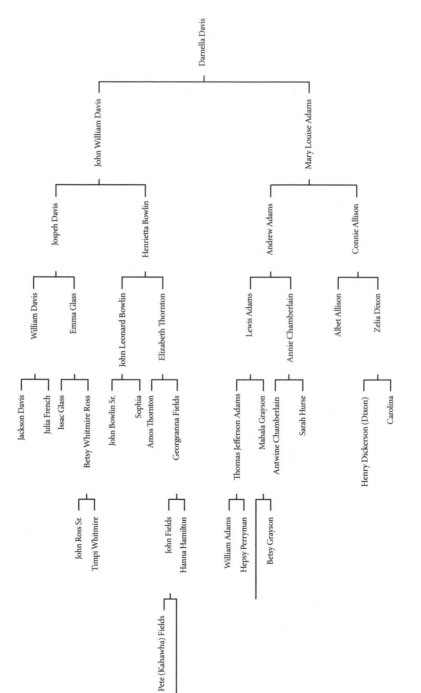

Figure 1. Family tree.

VOICES

I dreamed of Grampa Crugee,
Night after night,
He told me to care for the graves of our ancestors,
Not to let them remain neglected.
I hear his voice, even now.

I hear my grandmother, Henrietta,
Gone now these 40 years.
Through the slow unfolding leaves of my life,
I finally see the muted message only her eyes conveyed,
As I, just a small child, lay afraid with suffering.
She soothed my flushed forehead
With her cool, sure hands.
She was fretting then over many things,
But finally folded her heavy arms over her ample chest,
As much to calm me as herself.
I hear her now.

Here is the voice denied you.
Here is our rising strain.

ACKNOWLEDGMENTS

For many years I paddled along, working when I could on this dubious enterprise. In W. Clark Whitehorn, University of New Mexico Press executive editor, I found a steadfast believer and unwavering champion. My gratitude for his guidance is deep. Thanks to the Ford Foundation, Zanice Bond de Pérez, Venida Chenault, and their colleagues at the University of Kansas and Haskell Indian Nations University encouraged my early work and provided a small stipend for me to vet it with like-minded individuals. I am grateful that the Ford Foundation supported the Shifting Borders of Race and Identity initiative. At its February 2004 meeting, A Research and Teaching Workshop on the First Nations and African American Experience, Quintard Taylor and Don Fixico, among others, stimulated our thinking and made helpful suggestions for moving forward with my project.

The 2006 capstone conference for the Ford Foundation project, "The First and the Forced": Indigenous and African American Intersections, brought together a talented group of researchers. The opportunity to share preliminary findings and to vet ideas for completing my work with a large number of participants was invaluable. I am also grateful of the opportunity to present earlier versions of this work in 2006 at the 27th Meeting of the American Indian Workshop, Place and American Indian History, Literature, and Culture, which took place at the University of Wales, in Swansea.

My dear friend, the late Catherine Royce, edited early versions of the manuscript. She also wholeheartedly believed in my ability to see it through, never stinting in her encouragement. Among many experts in the field and early readers, I owe thanks to the comments and encouragement of Ron Welburn, Robert Collins, David Wheeler, and Heriberto Dixon. A special note of gratitude goes to Elizabeth Patterson, who reads the stones and understands that blood knows blood. Her conviction that I needed to tell this story never wavered. I am, nonetheless, solely responsible for the content of this work. Any errors or omissions are mine alone.

Innumerable family members have shown both interest and support. My incomparable Aunt Hazel's legacy of safeguarding the family's memories was carried on by her daughter, Frances Lax-Wooten, who lovingly preserved and shared many family photos and mementos. Thanks are due to the late Phyllis Bowlin, who answered many questions as she perused Elizabeth Bowlin's family Bible.

On the Adams side, I spent time with Uncle Leo, who enjoyed reminiscing about the family. My cousin Andrew was helpful in pointing out a number of resources as we each conducted research on Thomas Jefferson Adams. Among the elders, Marcelle Douglas (nee Adams) took time to provide edits on an initial draft but was even more helpful in the many conversations she and my mother, Mary, had over details about the family that I sought to uncover. I have benefitted mightily from their vast font of knowledge.

I also owe thanks to the little town of Cromarty, to Jenny Henderson, owner of the Royal Hotel, and to the residents, artists, performers, and tourists who complemented the perfect natural setting (complete with harbor seals, Moray Firth dolphins, pasturing cows, and fragrant forests) that enabled me to make key changes at a crucial stage of this project.

Time is a great master. I strove to get this all down by 2010, though I only completed an initial draft by that year, when my mother turned eighty. It seemed only fitting that she should enjoy a written memento of the events and people who shaped her youth and launched her out into the wide world. I thank her now for her unfailing delight in answering my endless questions.

Versions of the work were greatly enhanced by the thoughtful comments of Catherine P. Bell and Oliver Sinclair Franklin. Their interest in the relation of the personal to the broader issues of the Allotment Era prompted me to develop those features more fully. As I returned to sources I'd checked long before, Francis Flavin urged me to invest in yet another examination of the primary sources available where I began, at the National Archives in DC. Anne Pemberton lent her aesthetic skills to enlivening the faded photographs of my forebears, while Tina Manousakis and her Washington Creative Writers

Club members' kind and trenchant comments spurred me on. Despite these many helping hands, again, I am solely responsible for this effort.

Still, nothing I do seems mine alone. There are many forces at work that are far beyond my understanding. I do know that each day is fuller, richer, deeper because of the presence in my life of our two daughters, Rebecca and Charlotte, and of my partner, Brendan, my companion through the highways and byways of this brief splendid existence.

Allotment

This is the story of my people, a people whose racial, economic, social, cultural, and political identity was forged during the Allotment period. It is an authentic American tale of how our government divided up Indian Territory, assigning acreage according to a dual system of blood quantum. In 1887, the Dawes Act launched policies that would eventually parse land using a sliding scale for Indians of varying purity and another for those associated with the tribes whose blood was tinged with Black.

The legacy of this era, the long shadow of racial categorization, hangs over us to this day. Appeals for the removal of members of the Five Civilized Tribes with Black blood are being contested in our highest courts by families whose forebears served as stalwart tribal citizens for generations. Nearly 130 years later, I'm called to tell this story. It is the story of my family, my people, the Reds, Whites, and Blacks who converged during the Allotment Era and survive today.

Allotment was nothing less than a master plan to curtail the racial integrity of indigenous peoples. Its antecedents lay in an earlier grand scheme that sought to redress America's racial dilemma. During his years as an Indian fighter, a popular concept seized the mind of young Andrew Jackson. The future president, hardened by fierce combat with warring Indian nations, was soon steeped in the urge to purge the East of their marauding bands. Jackson believed that the Indians should relinquish the land that Whites sought to make profitable. He championed a vast plan to push the indigenous peoples west, far removed from rapidly developing southern fields and towns.

Under the Jackson administration, the Indian Removal Act of 1830 set in motion events whose impacts were legion. Many know the story of the resulting Trail of Tears, when federal agents rounded up thousands of Indians for a forced march to new settlements beyond the mighty Mississippi. Few know the fate of those who survived the trek. Fewer still ponder the long-term outcomes of Removal.

For the Cherokees, Creeks, Chickasaws, Choctaws, and Seminoles (the so-called Five Civilized Tribes), establishing new communities in Indian Territory meant joining a pitched battle for power along the western frontier. Towns sprang up then disappeared in rapid succession. Rival factions of mixed- and purebloods vied for dominance, creating tribal policies that were quickly struck down by a federal government and its local commissioners that limited the autonomy promised to the tribes as an enticement to quit their native woodlands in the East.[1]

Fragile coalitions were overlaid by shifting military alliances during the Civil War, sparking friction among tribal clans, mixed-bloods, and opportunists of every stripe. Individuals as well as bands of Indians switched sides, sometimes back and forth. A dizzying series of hastily drafted treaties were penned and discarded as less formal pledges were sworn by ragtag bands to self-appointed leaders. Skirmishes with and among Indian raiders threatened the promise of a peaceful coexistence on the western front.

Fifty-seven years after the Indian Removal Act, a further master plan emerged to address America's uneasiness with the indigenous people in their midst. To accelerate the assimilation that officials deemed a prerequisite to full citizenship in our burgeoning democracy, tribal lands were parsed into family units to farm homesteads in imitation of White settlers. The year was 1887 when the Allotment Era began. It would end in 1934, leaving behind the refuse of broken promises, racial divides, and tribal shifts that are little understood and for decades were scarcely touched upon in our historical canon. My people remember. I will tell you who we are.

Honoring Voices

I remember being roused from sleep in the middle of the night for our journey to Oklahoma. The car had been packed at the end of the previous evening with provisions to minimize the need to stop (fried chicken and biscuits for

Dad and a small pail for the child who might have slowed us down at a gas station's restroom). Our vehicle was already running as we stumbled down the front steps swathed in our warm bedding against any early morning chill. Drowsily we tumbled into the back seats. The goal was to make the trip from Detroit to Vinita in nineteen hours or as close as we could to record time. Dad always tried to best our previous dash down home for Easter, or Thanksgiving, or Christmas as he honed his strategy for arriving by nightfall. No matter the time of year, the weather, or the length of our stay, an early start was essential.

With little traffic as we exited the city, Dad's well-tuned car hummed along making it easy for us to fall asleep again, a mass of young limbs quieted by the still of night. The smell of coffee from the big silver thermos might awaken us sometime after daybreak. By then, we'd be well on our way in our mission to be home, really home, with the folks my parents revered.

It was as though they had been torn away from the source that gave them their sense of place in the world, from a veritable Eden. Their kin were the very sweetness of life. As children, we did not doubt. In examining that strong tie to the land of their origins, I now understand how little of the warmth and competence that they enjoyed there was reflected in the wider world they encountered beyond the family fold. Little did we realize the extraordinary lives our forebears lived or how hard it was to "go home again."

Dad's father, Joseph Davis, had been a veterinarian whose neat house, gardens, and chicken coops exuded both order and bounty. Grampa Crugee, my mother's father, was loved for his humor and warmth. Hunting, riding, and roping skills made him legendary. Make no mistake, these men, their wives, the lives they created were the whole package.

Exactly what that package meant, who and what these people were, and what the land meant to them would lead me to take my own trips back to Oklahoma. In doing so, I uncovered a numinous path leading from the Allotment Era to the present. It is a path that has enriched my understanding of racial diversity and through that greater knowledge endowed me with a calling: to share the histories of these families with those who seek a deeper authenticity about race in America. I am tasked with telling you who we are.

If this story is viewed as a sentimental yarn about the ole days, then let it take its place among those that crowd our recent history, though few are tendered by my people. This work is a modest inquiry, limited in scope, on the legacy of policies that have affected peoples of African American and American Indian heritage and the lands given to them. Its informants are my ancestors, Cherokee Freedmen and Muscogee Creeks. Here are their voices, responding to the opportunities and constraints that America has afforded its people of color. This work explores my family's legacy. It is not a historical account of policy impacts on the Creek or Cherokee Nations as a whole. Still, scholars of history may find some points of interest here; litigants can broaden their scope on the Black Indian debate, while some readers will discover a new leaf in the pages of our nation's saga. For me, finding my voice through the voices of my forebears has justified this more than twenty-year effort. The personal gain, the value, of handing down to my children a true telling of their origins is beyond measure. It offers a glimpse of the importance of "home" in its deepest sense, a glimpse that through words, through voice, through story, I can share.

In telling the stories of my forebears, my duty is to reclaim not only their memory and identity but their unique value as authentic Americans. Beyond revaluing these mixed-blood peoples, their stories challenge us to revisit the idea that America strives to uphold a moral purpose that may yet be realized.

Questions

Two families, alike in many ways, leave starkly different legacies etched on the land that was briefly Indian Territory. Their voices were not raised in loud cries of protest as life shifted under their feet. As mixed-race peoples, their voices have been muted or stilled in the telling of the American myth. But their progeny has endured and their voices have risen again in our time. Perhaps America is maturing. Perhaps it can begin to discern the complex rhythms that course through the veins of its peoples. Some may even be ready to move beyond the simplistic strains sounded for the malleable masses that have more readily embraced contrasts in black and white than hazier studies in shades of gray.

Why do I tell this story? A dear friend, who has passed to the other side, often spoke of a luminous path guiding and lifting her through a rich life and prolonged illness. Grappling for direction in life, we wonder how to live, what to do, when to commit, what is the next right thing. Yet, my friend saw in ordinary events a clear path. Rarely is the path straight. It is replete with twists, turns, and forks in the road. Yet, she felt she always had a choice in advancing to the next step, the one she sensed was right.[2]

Nearly thirty years ago, I set out on the path that has led me here. I didn't know it at the time, but hindsight is 20/20. Now I see that it began with a question for my mother. Growing up in Detroit, we lived in the big industrial city but were not "of it." Instead, our ties to the family's lands in Oklahoma were stronger than those to the community where our men found steady work. Every holiday, Thanksgiving, Christmas, Easter, and a good part of each summer found our family in northeast Oklahoma. The land we came from once formed the end point of the press to move many indigenous tribes west.

As a young girl, I knew little beyond the concerns of our close-knit family. As I grew older, I began to hear the gaps in the stories that my maternal aunts and uncles would tell. They were clearly devoted to their elders and fond of "going home," yet their recollections of coming of age on their farm outside of the small town of Beggs, Oklahoma, carried the unspoken fact that they did not remain there. I wanted to know why.

At family picnics and holiday gatherings, when our family had eaten together and the children had grown quiet in the gathering northern dusk, uncles and aunts would drop their voices, sit back in their folding lawn chairs and reminisce about their days in the country. Laughter would rise from their easy banter, but as the night came on they would soberly recall the feats of their fathers, the proud grace of their mothers, and the bounty of childhoods filled with equal measures of wonder and laughter. Nodding their heads in unison, they were joined by a shared past that was sweet but gone. Often, evening would end with plans to go back to their land, to open a store, or start some other venture.

But none of them returned to live on the land where they were born and raised. I wanted to understand how this could be. I suspected that part of the reason might have had to do with *who* we are, with how our identity was tied to time and place. So, even more pressing for me was the desire to know *what* we are.

I'd heard all my life that we were mixed. I could see that our family didn't look like most others we encountered. More puzzling was the talk about how we were part Indian. Some people called my mother Pocahontas, while my aunts spoke of my dad as growing up a little Cherokee boy. The complicated family ties also were confusing. My mother's cousin had married one of my father's cousins, so we were twice related. Then another of my mother's cousins married the sister of my mother's brother's wife. Figuring out those connections wasn't as challenging as trying to understand the blurring of my maternal grandfather's different sets of children. Crugee had survived two wives and married a twenty-three-year old when he was sixty, spawning six more children to add to the seven he already had.

Despite the close and interrelated nature of our families, we ran the range of colors and features. Although most were fair, they had a dusky cast; some had dark brown skin while others were nearly white with eyes as blue as the sky on a clear, cold December day. Many had bone-straight hair that seemed to skip a generation, or dance from mother to son, then son to daughter.

These puzzling relations all led me to the question I asked my mother: Well, what part Indian are we? The question was not disinterested. Before it became the rage, prior to the search for Native American ancestry brought on by the frenzy of the 1992 quincentenary of Columbus's "discovery," I found myself applying to a master's degree program knowing that my cousins had gotten money to go to college. Being the mother of a young child and wanting to advance my education, I hoped to fill out a form, list my indigenous connections, and tap into the college benefits offered to Native Americans that my extended family enjoyed.

I naïvely thought that by giving the Indian roll numbers of my grandparents, I would be granted monies to continue my studies in Boston, where we were living at the time. When the Commonwealth of Massachusetts asked me to provide my Certificate of Degree of Indian Blood, or CDIB, a document of which I'd never heard, I duly wrote to the Cherokee Nation in Oklahoma. I'd been told that they held all the records for the Creek and Cherokee Nations. This would prove to be a long, slow process accompanied by a steep learning curve.

It took several months just to get all my supporting evidence together. I had many roll numbers for my Cherokee relations and so I started by submitting those. Many more months passed and I heard nothing. When I finally called to find out the status of my application, I was assured that there was simply a huge backlog. About a year later, I was shocked to learn that the Bureau of Indian Affairs could not supply me with a CDIB because all my Cherokee relations were listed under the Freedmen section of a thing called the Dawes Rolls. They therefore had no ascertainable degree of Indian Blood.

That was Round One. That initial foray into the official realm of tribal claims left me empty-handed. Although I had duly copied all the Indian roll numbers supplied by my curious aunts, showed my connections to the tribal members, and written a fairly straightforward cover letter, I soon learned that I would get nowhere without a CDIB. Now, my question took on an unanticipated seriousness. Obtaining this CDIB got more complicated with every step. Eventually, I would have to delve into the Creek side of the family history to unravel claims to indigenous bloodlines. By the time I established that I lacked sufficient documentation to obtain resources reserved for students of native heritage in the state of Massachusetts, it was years later, my master's degree was behind me, and my own family, now with two youngsters in tow, was preparing to move to Washington, DC.

Settling into Washington meant grabbing small patches of time for my own projects between school drop-offs and part-time teaching, or squeezing in a few extra minutes when the babysitter was available. Once our youngest was in half-day nursery, I was faced with the challenge of how to make the best use of the two hours that each morning afforded on regular school days. With too little time to return home and come back again, I wondered how to be productive. Thus, began the second phase of my search for an answer to the question that my mother hadn't satisfactorily provided. Round Two.

Some ambitious mothers get up early to have an hour or two before their children awake. Some manage an impressive orchestration of logistics, materials, and personnel to provide brief snatches of non-child-focused productivity. My friend Catherine, who had two children before we did, wisely advised: Having two children is like having twelve, only fewer, so plan accordingly.

Washington offered an opportunity to delve into the records of Native Americans and I now had the time to access them directly. Armed with a collection of family enrollment numbers arrayed on a color-coded sheet, I queued up each morning to gain entry to the hushed halls of the US National Archives when the doors opened at 8:45, making sure that I left in time to pick up the wee one before lunch.

Although I prided myself in the execution of my clockwork mornings, searching the National Archives was a slow process, one that over many years (and long before easy internet access) led to my exhaustion of the Washington collection covering the Muscogee Creek and Cherokee Nations, my maternal and paternal tribes. Years later, my day job would enable me to spend an intense few hours copying every document I could from the National Archives in Fort Worth, that vast stretch of buildings that lined the railway sidings where the Western Collection housed all Indian Land Allotment documents.

In the interim, and as my career centered more on research, I was collecting other archival documents, oral histories, and family records. Thanks to luck and opportunity, I was able to sharpen my thinking about this story—this giving voice to a silenced people—among others who were grappling with revisiting American history. In recent years, a number of authors, academicians, and tribal officials have noted the dearth of information about racial mixing, especially among American Indians.

While I pieced together archival documents, amassed family photos, and talked with relatives whose lives had taken them far from our ancestral home, historians, anthropologists, and waves of genealogists were beginning in fill gaps in the historical record. Since I began my search, a new generation of scholars has been advancing the study of racial identity as it relates to the pivotal moment marked by Allotment in Indian Territory. They are tendering theories that reframe the intersection of race, culture, politics, and gender, offering new perspectives on the dynamic interplay of Red, White, and Black lives in social constructions of identity. Shifting through extant materials, they are bringing to light neglected facets of the record, while my objective has been to weave the documented trail of my family's history with the family's personal stories and reflections. As scholars grappled with racial categorization, my concern was with race and self-identity. I was delving into the 130-year legacy of my family's experiences as people of color and beginning to realize the uniqueness of our story, a story that might elucidate and humanize the reclamation of racial identity that so many others were seeking.[3]

As I squeezed in time to clarify familial views on racial identity, I also looked to my own upbringing. Growing up as a skinny little colored girl, shy and afraid of the menacing forces embodied in unsympathetic Whites and unsavory elements within the Black community, I wondered if I would live to see the twenty-first century.[4] These were not the idle musings of a neurotic teenager. By the time I'd graduated from high school, more than a couple of my middle-school classmates had fallen in drug-related violence while an equal number had taken to lives on the streets. Several of my fellow high-school graduates would succeed in academia, the arts, in the medical arena, or on the bench, but they did so lumped together without regard to any nuance in their racial history; they did so as exceptions against a broad-brushed stereotype. I couldn't help but wonder if the day would come when America's backstories on race would be told.[5]

As we move into the twenty-first century, we appear poised to unpack racial stereotypes. Not every person of color is descended from southern sharecroppers or newly arrived from south of the border. Even among descendants of slaves, distinctions go further than field and house slaves.[6] And not every person seeking to establish ties to indigenous forebears is a wistful wannabe.[7] At this moment in our nation's history, as polarizing factions self-indulgently engage in "a poisonous dialogue," any hope of retaining our stature in the world makes it essential to tack closely to the truth. As de Tocqueville noted in the 1830s, America was built on many spurious assumptions about the land, its peoples, and the sacred nature of their associations. In its brief two-hundred-year history, the American experiment has acknowledged some self-serving distortions of fact and even confessed to some abuses of power.[8] Recent years find the United States at a crossroads where declaring its moral commitments may either shred a thinly woven unity or guide the nation into a truly inclusive democracy. A full and unvarnished telling of our history would do much in enabling us to realize a true democracy.

Bringing to light the story of these ancestors and their neglected place in forging this nation should strengthen the image of self-reliance and resolve that are hallmarks of America. The story is both richer and more complex than the narrative of any one race. It questions the basis of such outmoded terms as "poor mulatto," which fail to capture who we are today.[9] Through this tracing of family history, we hear the larger and perhaps more somber saga of the shifting racial identities found on our shores. A more factual examination of where we have been may lead us to a greater authenticity and perhaps a glimpse of where our civilization may be heading.[10]

The Thornton family, its descendants (the Bowlin and Davis families), and the Adams clan help reveal the forces at play in the forgotten racial policies of our evolving nation. Their story is one of how race was tied to land, and land to opportunity. It's a tale about how race, land, and hope were twisted, distorted in a crucible of our American morality. It is worth revisiting the little understood but fluid frontier of the post-Reconstruction era to set the record straight.

2

The Thorntons and the Bowlins

The status of Cherokee citizens, and the freedmen associated with the tribe, was at issue following the Civil War.[1] Under Reconstruction, some federal policies pursued an ambitious arc of restitution but soon fell prey to less lofty concerns as opportunists, bureaucrats, and disgruntled Southerners scrambled to reshape the national agenda.[2] An entire generation would witness the country's dithering over laws that might address the troubling legacy of slavery. The Freedmen's Bureau, established in 1865 to aid former slaves in a transition to gainful employment, withered quickly as Southerners gutted its funding. Although it left burgeoning educational institutions devoted to schooling Blacks, by 1872, its well-meaning efforts were largely crushed.

As the South reasserted dominion over the fates of former slaves, Indian Territory had its own share of problems.[3] The 1830 act, signed into law under Andrew Jackson, that removed Indians to lands beyond the Mississippi was revisited in a new set of federal policies governing their land.[4] One such policy would conveniently open new settlements for Whites while making individual parcels of land available to American Indians and, in some cases, smaller parcels to the freed slaves associated with the tribes.

Tribes quickly saw this move as a further constraint over their autonomy to construct lifestyles that would safeguard their cultural integrity. Others grasped the notion that land could be had for those with ties to Indian communities. Some ties were rock solid while others were literally marriages of convenience. In either event, the stage was set for contentious claims of tribal affiliation. The prize was measured in acreage.

My paternal great-great-grandmother, Georgeanna Thornton, and her daughter were the subjects of a hearing that began in 1901 to establish their claim to Cherokee land. The transcription of the proceedings takes up nearly fifty pages preserved on microfiche in the National Archives in Washington, DC.[5] This fascinating trove of racial history has been there all along, mutely describing the contours of the policies that shaped relations among Blacks and Indians. Long before the Civil Rights Movement began to raise public awareness of the fetid roots of racial prejudice in America, before the quincentennial marking European contact sparked interest in mixed-race heritage, lawmakers tangled over who qualified as Indian. Those records of Red, Black, and White comingling lay silent but ever ready to be brought to light.

Tantalizingly, Georgeanna Thornton's files trace a path to her tribal affiliation and the land to which she laid claim. To decode these records we need to travel, to reconstruct the climate at the turn of the nineteenth century, in what is now northeast Oklahoma. That climate serves as a backdrop for deconstructing the Thornton case, just as the archival documents unearthed from musty files provide a contrast to the family's oral and recorded histories.

Untangling claims to birthright following the Civil War cannot be approached without tackling social taboos, political shenanigans, and the mangled accounts of "authorities." Despite its constitutional assertions of equality, in its early history, the United States embraced a view of citizenship that (at least in Thomas Jefferson's mind) saw only property-owning White males as worthy of full participation.[6] The constraints on access to education during slavery would ensure that generations of people of color could give little consideration to their franchise.[7] Only the willfully ignorant would fail to connect the dismal performance of our children with the antebellum imposition of illiteracy on millions who dared not protest.

A new generation of writers is finding a general audience interested in the fate of minorities looking for equality in America. Douglas Blackmon and Ira Katznelson have described how the brief promise of equality embodied in Reconstruction and later, in the New Deal, quickly dissolved in the face of prejudice against former slaves and non-White veterans, as well as others perceived as forming a lesser class of citizens.[8] Yet, even in the time before Oklahoma became a state, the uncertainty of racial hierarchy among non-Whites was a matter of concern for the federal government, former slaves, and for indigenous peoples bent upon defending their tribal integrity.[9] What would be the impact if Indians were to trade their sovereignty for US citizenship? Should emancipated Blacks really be given a vote? Suddenly, it seemed that some people of color might be more equal than others.

In hindsight, the Thornton application for Cherokee Freedmen status before the Commission to the Five Civilized Tribes can be viewed in terms of this racial uncertainty, that is, in the many and varied categories in which Georgeanna's descendants, and the Cherokee Nation, might have identified her and themselves: as Cherokee citizens (or not), by virtue of blood, previous ownership, amorous liaison with a respected full-blood, as an independent but peripatetic washerwoman, or by her loyalty to the tribe. For Georgeanna's descendants, any current sense of racial identification is intimately linked to her claims to the land that came to be known as Bowlin Spring. The development of that land reflects the cultural values that have led to the family's uninterrupted possession of it for over one hundred years. To understand those values, it helps to re-examine some accepted notions about interrelations among the races that have both mingled and spilled blood on US soil over the last five hundred years. It helps to go beyond the notion that Blacks, Whites, and Indians have maintained pure-blood pedigrees and that readily distinguishable boundaries exist for the chattel slave, immigrant settler, and innocent indigene. It helps to take a closer look at government actions, at how folk responded to or resisted those policies and practices aimed at controlling the American narrative on race.

The Land in the East

What most of us retain about Native Americans and the lands they occupied often derives from the sketchy plots of B movies where drama trumps fact. Yet, early scholars were not immune to romanticizing or vilifying indigenous peoples. Many tomes penned by "authorities" on one tribe or another now show bias, exposed like old bones by the winds of time. In reviving the voices of my forebears, I slowly learned first about the facts of their lives then about how they came to live as they did. That meant tracing their stories back as far as I could go, while navigating many twists and turns along the way. Luckily for me, their lode runs deep.

The checkered past of my forebears goes back centuries. There is evidence that the first Cherokee encounters with Europeans occurred when the Spanish reached the interior from the Southwest in the 1500s.[10] Even then the Spanish reported that the people they encountered ran the gamut of colors from dark brown to pale tan. Generations later, when Whites arrived on the eastern shores of what is currently called the United States, it is true that they were met by some of the tribal peoples who lived along the seacoast. But these coastal peoples were well acquainted with other tribes, tribes that, in their journeys from the interior down along the waterways leading to the sea, would also eventually meet the White men. Trading goods from their woodland homes for the materials produced by the coastal peoples was a long-standing tradition among the Cherokees. In the early 1600s, when word traveled inland of many people with skin like ghosts, some Cherokees must have looked forward to their trips to the coast to see if these tales of men with fire sticks and pale skin were true.[11]

Although the tale has largely been told from a Eurocentric perspective, there is no doubt that the tribes inhabiting the coastal areas and eastern woodlands grew to know, engage in commerce with, and even befriend and marry Whites.[12] As Cherokee, Creek, Choctaw, and Chickasaw tribes adopted many of the White ways, and later as the Seminoles coalesced into a unified community, these groups of woodland Indians came to be known as the Five Civilized Tribes.[13] Though the term is now viewed as problematic or even pejorative, these "Five Southeast Tribes," or "Five Tribes," played a vital role in bridging cultural divides, as racial blending naturally occurs whenever one people encounters another. Among the practices that the Cherokee peoples emulated were European ways of speaking, dressing, and farming. Completing the image of the landed White, many prosperous Indians and mixed-bloods began to buy slaves to cultivate their large estates of cotton and tobacco.[14]

Despite the adoption of these Eurocentric practices among the Five Tribes, concepts of property and its possession or ownership differed markedly from those of the White settlers. The Indians' reciprocal relation to the land made it sacred and the reverence for "place" was deeply ingrained. No matter how Indians' dress, lifestyles, or skin colors echoed those of Whites, their claims to the land were devalued by would-be settlers who felt a greater right to rich terrain that lay largely unexploited.[15]

In tandem with the White press to cultivate the fertile soil that indigenous peoples simply occupied, well-meaning humanists formed civic and religious groups that argued for their eventual assimilation. To prepare the native peoples to become active participants in the democratic republic, the reformers urged policy makers to create educational programs to teach Indians the agricultural and domestic arts and to school them in Christianity. In contrast to those who sought to remove them from their midst, the reformers embodied a belief that with a Christian education, one day Indians could take their place as fellow citizens.[16] That conviction did little to ease the standoffs over land as tribal factions fought to maintain a toehold in their ancestral lands. Time and again, with each defeat on the battlefield or at the negotiating table, if one faction refused to vacate land, another tribal contingent seemed poised to cede land as long as the terms gave them some advantage.

When the 1803 Louisiana Purchase nearly doubled the size of the United States, Thomas Jefferson's administration broached the idea of exchanging Cherokee land in the coveted East for the wide-open spaces beyond the Mississippi.[17] Congress would not entertain any large-scale, systematic migration plan until the culmination of the War of 1812, when prospects of a British territory west of the Great Lakes were extinguished and debate resumed over whether Indians should be acculturated or segregated entirely from any proximity to Whites.

From the republic's very beginnings, the pattern emerged; treaties struck after military conquests routinely divested indigenous people of their land.[18] At the end of the eighteenth century, a series of land cessions in the state of Georgia increased the flow of White incursions as settlers dug in from east to west. In 1823, in the first of a trio of decisions that would shape laws governing Indian lands, the Supreme Court declared that it had no jurisdiction to consider the case. At issue were state laws declaring that Indians could not hold title to the land they occupied. In asserting authority over their own land, in 1827, the Cherokees adopted a constitution mirroring US sovereignty rights only to see the state of Georgia deny the legitimacy of their tribal boundaries. Instead, the state declared the area occupied by Cherokees as "state land." Despite the fact that the US Supreme Court upheld the Cherokees' right to sovereignty and ownership, Andrew Jackson's administration refused to honor the court's decision. On that decision, President Jackson is said to have remarked, Chief Justice "John Marshall has made his decision. Now let him enforce it."[19] Jackson's stance was that the federal government could not guarantee Indians' protection from the onslaught of land-hungry Whites. The contest between state and federal jurisdiction left Indians vulnerable to marauding Whites as well as officials at both levels of government consumed with driving them out of the East.

Jackson's thoughts on Indian rights grew from firsthand experiences. In a number of military campaigns, he proved himself a dauntless Indian fighter. During the War of 1812, when the British battled US troops over territory east of the Great Lakes, along the Canadian border, and in the South, each campaign was aided by Indian warriors loyal to one side or the other. For example, in what was viewed as a virtual civil war, large numbers of Creeks had been fighting in hopes that the winning side would offer more favorable terms for maintaining the integrity in their southern homesteads. The battle against British troops and the fight to retain what land remained to the southeastern tribes converged in 1814, when Jackson led an army with six hundred Creek auxiliaries against the Red Sticks. The Red Sticks, a British-backed contingent of Creek warriors, were roused by a visit from Tecumseh, the visionary Seneca who imagined a land belonging to all Indians. Tecumseh's eloquent message resonated with Creeks convinced of their hereditary rights to their homelands. They fought valiantly, as Jackson was twice driven to retreat, but on March 26, Jackson's third assault brought a decisive end to the battle at Horseshoe Bend on the Tallapoosa River.[20]

Although Creek fighters fought valiantly at his side on the southern front, Jackson had little patience for efforts to forestall White settlement on indigenous lands. Following the rout at Horseshoe Bend, Jackson dictated a treaty of peace that ceded twenty-three million acres of Creek land as an indemnity.[21] The cession would eventually serve Jackson's larger scheme of corralling the Indian tribes.

Andrew Jackson shared the view of many southerners that Indians had only a slight claim to land that would be better utilized in the service of White farmers. His military campaigns against Indians were a natural extension of his beliefs, as were his acts as president.[22] Pressure from White farmers eager to expand and secure cotton plantations only hardened Jackson's conviction that a grand scheme was needed to remove all Indians from east of the Mississippi river.[23] Under his administration, the intent of the 1830 Indian Removal Act was to engineer the elimination of Indians from their homelands, particularly those in the rapidly developing southeastern states. Removal to land west of the Mississippi effected a separation of the races. There, Jackson was convinced that Indians would be able to govern themselves as they saw fit.

With the Indian Removal Act, Jackson may have expected that Indians would be eager to exchange their strife-ridden land in the East for land west of the Mississippi. History has recorded the poor response of those few Indians who made the trip voluntarily.[24] Instead, Jackson's policy initially led to more negotiations for treaties that native peoples hoped would slow the loss of Indian farms and settlements, then to bloodshed as tribes fought for their lands.[25] The losses from these skirmishes paled in comparison to the numbers who would perish under forced removal.

In the face of escalating tensions, the response to federal efforts to encourage voluntary removal ebbed and flowed along with hopes for a negotiated solution, until wholesale removal came to be considered a necessity. Like the Creeks, factions within the Cherokee Nation were often at odds, especially where traditionalists vied with progressives. The fate of the Cherokees was largely determined by the 1835 Treaty of New Echota, signed by a group of progressive, slaveholding "leaders."[26] A letter from John Ross, the legitimate chief who embraced a more traditional view, condemned their duplicity: "This spurious Delegation, in violation of a special injunction of the general council of the nation, proceeded to Washington City with this pretended treaty, and by false and fraudulent representations supplanted in the favor of the Government the legal and accredited Delegation of the Cherokee people."[27] Although the popularly elected tribal leaders launched a protest, federal officials sided with the sham delegation.

Anticipating the end to peaceful coexistence, an early vanguard of Cherokees voluntarily had removed from the Southeast in 1828. By the end of two years, only a couple of thousand Cherokees had resettled in the West while an estimated fifteen thousand remained.[28] Several hundred members of the pro-treaty faction, led by Major Ridge, departed with their slaves following the New Echota deal, which, despite vehement protests from Principal Chief John Ross, had ceded the Cherokees' homeland for $5 million and land in the West. The pressure increased on those who remained as families hesitated to leave the only land they had ever known. Eventually, thousands of "laggards" were forced to leave. The tragic tale of forced removal is a shameful chapter in this nation's history. Rounded up and held in filthy stockades with woefully inadequate supplies, as many as 1,500 died during their confinement.

Once forced removal began, the journey from the East was about eight hundred miles long. Beginning in June of 1838, a few families made the trip while others waited out the worst drought in recorded history. After weeks of scorching heat, many were forced to start out in the fall knowing they would soon face the onset of winter. Some four thousand Cherokees, or one in four, died on the trail.[29] Weary from the long, sad journey across land and over water they arrived in the territory and tried to take up a semblance of their former lives. The proud Cherokees, rarely reduced to public weeping, called it *nv no hi du na tlo yi lv,* "the trail where they cried."[30]

By 1839, the last group of Cherokees arrived in the West where they recast the "old settlers," pro-treaty faction, and more recent arrivals from the East. With a working constitution, the nation strove to rebuild public facilities and developed an impressive educational system.[31] Though distinctions were made between the early settlers and those newly arrived, differences were more or less resolved through the incorporation of various factions in the General Council, and John Ross was acknowledged as principal chief of the Cherokee Nation.[32]

Amazingly, although John's Scottish-born grandfather, John McDonald, was connected to the Cherokees through marriage to a mixed-blood woman, his grandson rose to become their powerful chief.[33] Freedom from religious strife and relief from virtual servitude led waves of Scots to set sail for America, where their relative poverty found many gravitating to the potential opportunities afforded far from the Eastern Seaboard. There, they were welcomed by the Cherokees and were readily integrated into the tribe, intermarrying and prospering.[34] In the East, many mixed-bloods, well-schooled in the ways of Whites and recognized as effective intermediaries and keen negotiators, became prominent leaders in a number of the southeastern tribes.[35] Then, mixed-blood unions between Indians and Whites were recognized, if not wholly welcomed, in polite society. A narrower view would have been taken of Indian mixtures with Blacks. Soon enough, laws would follow the one drop rule, and these mixtures would only produce a "Negro"—the colloquial term of that era—one who was subject to the policies dictated under chattel slavery.[36] In practice, greater proximity to the bustling frontier may have blurred the distinctions of Black and Indian progeny imposed in more established communities.[37] Whether White and Indian, Indian and Black, or some combination of the three, for a time, racial mixture was more fluid than is often acknowledged.[38] Before and after Removal, the one-eighth blood quantum of the Cherokee leader clearly mattered less than his absolute devotion to preserving the nation and upholding its traditions. Ross was respected for his keen negotiating skills and his tireless efforts to maintain unity in the face of continuous efforts to sow dissent among rival factions.

Life in the West

With a written language, a widely circulated newspaper (the *Cherokee Phoenix*), and a network of schools, the Cherokees experienced a period of relative peace in the years after Removal and before the Civil War.[39] Despite a history of many broken promises by the federal government, in the West, the Cherokees gathered in Indian Territory with their tribal sovereignty intact. Their ability to govern themselves on the land designated for them was to serve as a buffer against the kind of assaults on their cultural integrity instigated under Jackson who, with Removal, promised their perpetual autonomy in the West.[40]

Once settled, the tribes may not have imagined themselves constrained by new federal dictates governing their ability to transfer land, hold mineral rights, and police themselves without oversight. Indeed, they would, in relatively short order, be fighting to retain what autonomy had been granted to them. Given their distaste for Jacksonian-style policies and their ongoing distrust of federal government treaties, it is little wonder that ill will toward Washington led many of them to side with the South in the "War between the States."

Arguably, there was no greater threat to Cherokee unity than Ross faced at the onset of the Civil War. As with other tribes concerned with threats to their continued existence in Indian Territory, the Cherokees were divided internally, with some favoring the prospects offered by a proslavery South, while others allied with Northern abolitionist sentiments. Wishing to remain neutral, the principal chief initially resisted Confederate overtures promising greater autonomy and more generous annuities for the tribe. Ross entertained sympathies with the North but struggled to retain unity among the tribe's various factions. He agonized as impatient Cherokee citizens took up arms to fight loyally by the sides of troop commanders for both the North and the South. Confronting a potential schism among his people, after much hesitation, Ross was pressured to side with the Confederates rather than have an opposing faction strike a deal that would have cleaved the nation in two. Before a year had passed, he would reverse his allegiance when the South failed to honor its promises to protect and support his people. As supplies dwindled and funds grew scarce, the Cherokees again suffered the hardships wrought in broken promises. By July 1862, federal troops arrived in Tahlequah offering relief for the Cherokees as Ross accepted what little they could spare for his beleaguered people.[41] In the midst of adversity, Ross had served his people nobly, always fighting to maintain unity despite the diverse opinions, traditions, and political leanings represented among the tribe's citizens.

Having shifted allegiances, Ross had placed Cherokee loyalty into question. Along with many other tribes, the Cherokees found themselves out of favor with the war's victors.[42] For a time, the air was rife with rumors of retaliation in various guises. In the nation's capitol, there was much talk about how land would be apportioned to its newly recognized citizens—talk that would profoundly impact Indian Territory.[43] There was no shortage of would-be farmers, ranchers, prospectors, pioneers, and entrepreneurs massing at the borders of Indian Territory, awaiting word on the outcome of the land under dispute. The Cherokees' brief allegiance to the Confederacy would, indeed, cost them additional lands and other concessions to the freedmen among them at war's end, even before the Dawes Commission undertook the work of dividing their land among enrolled members of the tribe and eventually enabling the government to sell off the remaining acres.[44]

Part of the congressional dialogue about redistributing Indian lands at the end of the war concerned former slaves. During Reconstruction, attempts to provide reparation to newly emancipated slaves came in a number of proposals that offered some variation on the allocation of five to forty acres of land. As the question of relocating former slaves became more public, sending freedmen west, along rail lines, or into "unsettled" land appealed to policy makers as well as former slaves. In Civil War Special Field Order No. 15, General William T. Sherman sought to compensate those freedmen who had served valiantly under him by conferring forty-acre plots to their families. This order, issued January 16, 1865, was overturned by the end of that year and neither this nor any other reparation was made to former soldiers or other "Negroes" emancipated following the Civil War. Putting aside General Sherman's intentions, stated in his field order as including the retirement of a few old army horses or mules, there never was a *federal* provision of forty acres and a mule for emancipated heads of households. Without resources, "Negroes" had no alternative but to seek any advantage they could find to better their lot.[45] When rumors were heard that Indian lands might be turned over to freed slaves, many adventurous "Negroes" went west in hopes of finding their fortunes. Despite tribal restrictions on non-Indian intruders, many became squatters on Indian lands that they intended to claim.[46]

Among the Cherokees, prosperous landowners must have worried that they would pay dearly for their brief Confederate alliance. Indeed, proposals were heard on the floor of the nation's Congress that both the land and annuities of Indian tribes should be handed over to emancipated slaves. While tribal members were eager to return to the relative tranquility of their homesteads following the war, Whites once again saw—in the natives' postwar disfavor—opportunities for further westward expansion.

At the close of the Civil War, the Cherokees resisted the Union's insistence that former slaves belonging to the tribe be given citizenship in their nation. As an autonomous nation situated in Indian Territory, the Cherokees only acquiesced in negotiating a new treaty with the United States in the spring of 1866.[47] It is likely that for some Cherokee, admitting citizenship for their former slaves meant drawing the same color lines embodied in the all-too-convenient "one drop rule" that has shaped racial categories from the early days of miscegenation to the present day. As noted, under the one drop rule, any racial mixture was ignored and the individual in question was deemed "Negro" and prior to emancipation, subject—conveniently for Whites—to chattel slavery. The intermingling of races was beneficial for slave owners but may have played out differently among Indians, as suggested by Tiya Miles in her 2005 book, *Ties That Bind*.

Just as restitution to slaves was the focus of intense debate, plans for more effective use of Indian land were hotly contested. Once again, Indians were seen as too-reluctant participants in the new democracy. Their insistence on retaining their languages and cultures was disdained, and even those who fully adopted Eurocentric lifestyles were grouped with those who did not, and all were similarly distrusted. That distrust was justification enough for Whites who felt a greater legitimacy in claiming land.

The Dawes Act

On February 8, 1887, the Dawes Severalty Act, or General Allotment Act, put an end to speculation about the fate of Indian lands. The act spelled out a plan to allot each eligible Indian a plot of land to be cultivated in the style of the individual farmer so esteemed during the colonial era, while extending US law over the allottees.[48] While members of the Five Tribes were exempted from the 1887 act, with passage of the Curtis Act of 1898, they too were included in the scheme to adopt commercial farming as a means to assimilation. The objective was to eventually forsake former tribal practices and governance in favor of citizenship in the United States. After allotment, surplus lands would then be available to non-Indians with the means to become settlers.[49]

After separate negotiations with individual tribes who did not fall within the specifications of the Dawes Act culled millions of additional acres, the Curtis Act ended *all* tribal authority. Placing all Indians under the jurisdiction of the United States forced the Five Tribes, among others not relegated to reservations, to relinquish tribal lands and submit to the allotment process.[50]

The Commission to the Five Civilized Tribes was led by former senator Dawes and thus took on his name.[51] The Dawes Commission spent years surveying and appraising the fifteen million acres that was to be allotted to members of the Cherokee, Creek, Choctaw, Chickasaw, and Seminole tribes, with the bulk of the work only completed at the beginning of January 1903. A smattering of contested claims and other delays extended the process until 1906.[52] As tribal policies fell under the increasing scrutiny of regionally appointed government representatives, the Commission to the Five Civilized Tribes became the arbiter over a number of legal issues governing property rights. When the allotment process was complete, tribal communities had lost 90 million of the 140 million acres reserved for them less than fifty years earlier.[53] The 1934 Indian Reorganization Act would end such allocations and with it bring the Allotment Era to a close.

In the meantime, most applicants made their requests for plots worth the equivalent of 160 acres of average land with 40 acres designated as a homestead. Eligibility was established for members of the Cherokee Nation through prior listing on the following rolls:

1817–1838 Cherokee Emigration Rolls, a list of Cherokees involved in the removal from Georgia and the southeastern United States.

1867 Tompkins Roll, a list of Cherokees residing in northeastern Oklahoma with an index of Freedmen.

1880 Census, Cherokee Nation Citizen Rolls compiled to distribute per capita funds related to land sales but excluding many Freedmen.

1890–1893 Wallace Roll of Cherokee Freedmen in Indian Territory, identifies Cherokee Freedmen entitled to share in annuities and other payments to be divided among Cherokee, Shawnee, and Delaware tribes.

1896–1897 Kern-Clifton Roll for Cherokee Freedmen, a list of those eligible for payments to fill the omissions of the Wallace Roll.

Inclusion on these rolls was not the only criteria for eligibility on the final Dawes Rolls, the definitive list of allotees. That list permitted only three categories of allotees: full-blood, mixed-blood (including Whites by intermarriage), or freedmen. Under the Commission of the Five Civilized Tribes, field-workers established the blood quantum of "full-bloods," the legitimacy of mixed-bloods (if the mixture was White), and the worthiness of those with African blood to claim ties to the Cherokee Nation. This process was fraught with arbitrary decisions that, given language barriers as well as cross-cultural ineptitude, sometimes led to different designations among siblings.[54]

As tribal land was divided into plots, speculators clamored for any advantage in claiming part of Indian Territory. Hysteria ensued when two million acres of unassigned land was opened to settlers in an early Oklahoma Land Rush. On April 22, 1889, thousands of settlers rode, drove, walked, or ran to claim a plot of "surplus" land. Despite widespread violence and general mayhem, the government would allow a series of land runs as the Cherokee Outlet and unassigned land from other tribes were claimed.[55] As Whites flooded the region, their grab for land would shape resentments among Whites, Blacks, and Indians for decades to come. At the turn of the century, it prompted tribes to give even greater scrutiny to those claiming affiliation with the Cherokee Nation and to the annuities and increasingly scarce land being dispatched by the Commission of the Five Civilized Tribes.

Thus, the stage was set for the events that played out in the lives of my people, those who identified themselves as Cherokees and Cherokee Freedmen living in and around Fort Gibson in the early years of the twentieth century.

The Testimony

Imagine gaining admittance to the Greek-columned edifice that houses the Constitution and the Bill of Rights, where you find not just the names and numbers of your forebears but their words and deeds. Maintained in the National Archives in Washington, DC, are pages of testimony in the application for enrollment as Cherokee Freedmen of my great-great-grandmother Georgeanna Thornton and her daughter Elizabeth.

Contained within the microfiche pages are the words of the people who knew these women, spoke of their actions, and commented on their position within the Cherokee Nation. But much of their story is necessarily left out. What must be pieced together is what they thought of themselves, how they identified themselves, and what can be learned now from the applications to be recognized as Cherokee Freedmen that they filed on May 31, 1901.[56] What became of Georgeanna and Elizabeth as they sought to define a life based on land ownership? On the basis of testimony provided during the hearings, it appears that their lives came to be greatly influenced by one very enterprising man.

Georgeanna Thornton was long in years when her daughter Elizabeth Bowlin's application for Cherokee Freedmen status was considered by Commissioner C. R. Breckinridge that May. Though Georgeanna's energy might have been ebbing, the family holds that John Bowlin, Elizabeth's husband, urged the women to apply for land.

In the testimony preserved in the National Archives, members of the

Commission questioned the legitimacy of Georgeanna and Elizabeth's claim to land when their names were not found on the 1880 Freedmen of the Cherokee Nation Rolls or the 1896 Census Rolls.[57] However, Elizabeth's name did appear on the Kern-Clifton Roll, along with those of four of her children: Henrietta, Will, Eunice, and Doda—all with their last name spelled B-o-w-l-e-n. And, on examination of the Wallace Roll, both Elizabeth and Henrietta were found under B-o-l-y-n.

Finding Elizabeth's name on the rolls, the Commission's decision was to place Elizabeth, her husband (who was applying for Cherokee Freedmen status by intermarriage), and their seven children on the "Doubtful" list until a decision had been made in their case.

On the same day, testimony also was heard in the application of Elizabeth's mother, Georgeanna Thornton. The various rolls were again searched and her name was found as G-e-o-r-g-e-a-n-n Thornton on the Kern-Clifton Roll and as G-e-o-r-g-i-a-n-n-a Thornton on the Wallace Roll. She too was listed as a Cherokee Freedman on a Doubtful card while the Commission deliberated her case.

Three Cherokee citizens gathered on October 7, 1901, providing supplemental testimony on Georgeanna's behalf. The Commission heard them testify that Georgeanna was owned by Judge Amos Thornton and lived at Fort Gibson during the war. Patsy Johnson, Aleck Nivens, and L. D. Daniels agreed that her whereabouts followed the activities of the regiments both during the war and after peace resumed. The statements of these initial witnesses were grouped together with the application for citizenship by marriage of Elizabeth's husband and, thus, filed under John Bowlin et al.[58]

A few days later, Lewis Ross Thornton, the son of Amos Thornton, testified. Lewis was a butcher who had served the troops in Fort Gibson. He was also identified as Georgeanna's former owner. On the day he testified, Lewis gave little help in establishing Georgeanna's links to the tribe or her whereabouts during and after the Civil War.[59] Some time passed before more information would come from others who knew her during that period.

It was over three years later, June 18, 1904, before Elizabeth and Georgeanna were scheduled to further argue their claim as Cherokee Freedmen. In all, nine more witnesses came forward to testify on their behalf, while Cherokee attorneys sought to cast doubt on their claims. The 1904 hearings lasted several days with the final testimony transcribed in July.

Of the many voices heard in the testimony, absent are any words spoken by Amos Thornton—master, father, landowner, and a well-known judge presiding throughout the Civil War for the Cherokee Nation.[60] However, John Bowlin is a palpable presence, giving the most colorful and spirited testimony and reportedly engineering the entire process as part of an ambitious plan to make his fortune.

Judge Amos Thornton

Judge Amos Thornton was among the relatively prosperous Cherokee land-holders in the West. Born in the East on November 10, 1810, historical documents refer to him as a prominent Cherokee judge at Fort Gibson. He and three brothers—William, Charles, and Riley—are listed on the Cherokee Emigration Rolls of 1817–1835. Amos was entered as number 29 on the September 22, 1833, count. He's described on the Sugar Creek, Tennessee, portion of the rolls as having a family of five. Genealogists suggest that he was married in the East and brought his wife, Mary Louisa McAdams, a White woman, and their children on the Trail of Tears. However, his name appears on the 1851 Old Settlers census among those Cherokees who were already in the West before the majority of tribal members arrived in 1839.

An item in the *Fort Gibson Post*, from February 3, 1898, lends credence to his long standing in the community. It makes note of an exceptionally bountiful crop of pears from a "tree planted by the late Judge Amos Thornton" that was about fifty years old. The flavorful fruit was propagated by gourmands and horticulturalists alike for "its great productiveness, excellent quality, and great adaptability to this climate. . . . A notable addition to the horticultural products of this section." The article declares, "It will be called the Thornton pear." When Judge Thornton planted the pear tree in 1848 near the Fort Gibson railroad depot, his wife may have been ailing. By 1849, Mary Louisa was dead.

A Civil War veteran, Thornton served in the 2nd regiment of the Indian Home Guards as a private in Co. E., attached to the Kansas Infantry. He served from November 11, 1862, until he was mustered out with a gunshot wound on July 6, 1863.[61]

Evidence of Amos Thornton's professional career appears in the August 17, 1881, Official Directory of National Officers in *The Cherokee Advocate*. He is listed as a circuit court judge for the Illinois District. On the personal side, he may have been married a few times. At some point, he wed a woman named Minerva (or Menerva) Foreman.

Less is known about Minerva, or about when and why she and Amos separated. She did go on to marry Conan Vann, a Cherokee, and to live long after Amos Thornton died. But in this instance, Amos Thornton is of interest for two other roles that he played: that of master and that of squire. For he was the master of Georgeanna Thornton and she was his slave. According to family lore, Georgeanna was a parlor maid who never worked in the fields. In 1863, from Georgeanna's own testimony, we learn that at the age of fifty-three Amos fathered Georgeanna's daughter, Elizabeth. Records show that Georgeanna was born in 1831, making her thirty-two when she gave birth to Elizabeth. However, the Shady Grove Cemetery, the Bowlin family's burial site, records her birth date as 1845, which would have made her only eighteen. For the Commission, Georgeanna's few recorded words speak volumes:[62]

Q. You have a daughter who just applied?
A. Yes sire that was my daughter.
Q. What is her name now?
A. Elizabeth Bowlen.
Q. Give me the name of her father?
A. Amos Thornton, that was my master.
Q. There was never any marriage between you and this woman's father?
A. No sir.

John Leonard Bowlin

Born in Bolivar County, Tennessee, in 1850, John Leonard Bowlin proved an ambitious man. His obituary describes him as a prosperous farmer who made the most of the opportunities open to a "Negro" willing to stake his fortune in Indian Territory. But his beginnings were humble and few would have described his prospects as anything other than bleak.[63] He remembered his mother as a mulatto, a cook who was owned by his father, John Bowlin Sr., originally of Cork County, Ireland. No great affection could have resulted from the union, as John recalls seeing his mother, Sophia, and sister, Eunice, being sold on the block when he was six years old. Family lore holds that his mother

Late Craig County Pioneer Once Wild Game Hunter

John Leonard Bowlin, Who Died Recently, Came To This Country In 1880

John Leonard Bowlin, 85-year old county pioneer who died at his home in the southwestern section of the county last Friday, once made a livelihood by trapping and killing wild animals in Tennessee.

Bowlin had been in poor health for several months at the time of his death. He had been confined to his bed for one week. Old age was given as the cause of his demise.

He was born in Boliver, Tenn. in 1850. He was a trapper during his early years but came to Oklahoma in 1880, where he married Elizabeth Thornton and settled down to live on the farm. He became one of the most successful farmers in the county but recently retired. He died August 24, 1934, at 3 p. m.

Funeral services were held in Shady Grove cemetery, with Rev. A. C. Starr of Vinita officiating.

Survivals are the widow, one son, Leonard, and four daughters, Mrs. Henryetta Davis, Chelsea; Eunice C. Starr, Coffeyville; Mrs. Doda Christine

JOHN BOWLIN

Johnson, Los Angeles, California; and Mrs. Sophia A. West, Chelsea; 19 grandchildren and nine great grandchildren. Three childen, one son and two daughters, preceded him in death

Figure 2. John Bowlin's obituary. From the papers of Frances Wooten Lax. Courtesy of Beverle Lax.

gave John a small bag of cookie crumbs and urged him not to cry. That image was to remain with John Bowlin. It was the last he ever saw of his mother.

Perhaps John Bowlin Sr. harbored greater affection for his son, who appeared to be a free agent long before emancipation. Some say John's father took him to hand following the war, some say it was his half-brother. In any event, he traveled to Saginaw, Michigan, where he acquired a good bit of education. As an unfettered youth, John Bowlin worked in hotels in the North, saving money and planning for his own investments in the West.

Fort Gibson

Much of the testimony about Georgeanna Thornton concerns activities that took place in the once bustling community surrounding Fort Gibson. Like the subjects of the testimony, the town that played many key roles in Indian Territory has since faded from prominence. Like the Allotment Era, few know its history.

In the early 1800s, as both Indians and White settlers moved west, fortified towns formed the locus of trade, growing rapidly during the period preceding the Civil War. For a time, Fort Smith, sitting just within Arkansas's western border, served as the gateway to the frontier.[64] Then in the 1820s, the army was charged with finding another site, further west, from which to monitor conflicts among the rebellious Indian tribes and the growing numbers of White settlers. As a result, Cantonment Gibson was built near the confluence of the Grand and the Arkansas Rivers, east of present-day Muskogee. With Removal, Fort Gibson was headquarters for the Seventh Infantry, which arrived in 1824. The fort quickly became the last stop on the southwestern frontier. Many Indians who had abandoned their eastern ties arrived there by boat, and thousands of Creeks, Cherokees, and Seminoles passed through the town as they made their way to the lands later designated for them.[65]

In 1857, during a period of relative inactivity, troops withdrew from the fort and turned its buildings over to the Cherokee Nation. During the Civil War, the fort changed hands yet again as Confederate then Union troops occupied its position. Although the fort was used as a supply point during Reconstruction, activity waned again until the railroad arrived, bringing a new wave of outsiders who required a military presence to keep the peace. By 1890, the fort had largely fulfilled its military functions and was closed, leaving Indian Territory's oldest community—in what would, in 1907, become the state of Oklahoma—to languish as other towns sprang up around it.

Fort Gibson shared the characteristics of other frontier towns whose populations swelled or ebbed along with a military presence. As a crossroads during Removal, or a market town during quieter times, its population was transient, with many passersby just making their way further west. It is little wonder that witnesses gave conflicting accounts of when Amos or Georgeanna where last seen in that town together.

Claims

Among the many assertions tendered during the citizenship hearings for Elizabeth and her mother, no one disputed that Georgeanna was a slave of the Cherokee Judge Amos Thornton, whose household was located near Fort Gibson in the Cooweescoowee District, later to be known as Rogers County; nor was Elizabeth's paternity denied by any witness, including Amos Thornton's son Lewis and daughter-in-law Ellen. Less clear were the whereabouts of Georgeanna in relation to the Cherokee Nation and her former owner.

During the Civil War, tribal members were expected to stay with the nation, for protection as much as to discourage defections to the other side. The 1839 Constitution stipulated that a Cherokee moving out of the nation lost his citizenship unless readmitted by the Council.[66] The Treaty of 1866 further underscored the value of tribal cohesion. Following the war, it allowed that anyone in the nation or returning to the Cherokee Nation within six months would have all the rights of Cherokee citizens.[67] Tribal loyalty might serve to shore up the credibility of applicants who were absent from the 1880 Census but who asserted their citizenship. At stake for Georgeanna was land for herself, her daughter and son-in-law, and her seven grandchildren. If she could prove her ties to the Cherokee Nation as well as her continued presence among its citizens, she might improve her claim to Cherokee land.

The bulk of the recorded testimony concerns Georgeanna's whereabouts. Then as now, loyal tribal citizens, especially women, showed their allegiance to the tribe by staying within the geographical parameters of the nation. Those who left were seen as espousing other values than the well-being and continued integrity of the community.

Former Cherokee slaves expressed the strength of their tribal devotion when they petitioned in 1897 for full citizenship within the tribe, declaring, "The Cherokee Nation is our country; there we were born and reared; there are our homes made by the sweat of our brows; there are our wives and children, whom we love as dearly as though we were born with red, instead of black skins. There we intend to live and defend our natural rights, as guaranteed by the treaties and laws of the United States, by every legitimate and lawful means."[68] Georgeanna's claim to Cherokee Freedmen status makes no mention of her devotion to the tribe or the nature of her ties to the land. Instead, her claim was argued on the basis of her ownership by a Cherokee citizen and her continued location among the Cherokees after the war ended.

Despite the October 7, 1901, testimony by three Cherokee citizens, affirming Georgeanna's ties to Amos Thornton and her presence in and around Fort Gibson, between June 18 and July 16, 1904, nine other witnesses gave testimony about Georgeanna and Elizabeth. Three were Cherokee Freedmen, two were coloreds married to Cherokee Freedmen, and four were Cherokee by blood. Together they may have represented an attempt by the Commission at a fairer hearing that included Cherokee citizens, freedmen, and people of color who had married into the tribe. Like the first three witnesses (one fifty-two-year-old woman and two men aged fifty-six and sixty), all were in their fifties, except one sixty-eight-year-old. Of those testifying in 1904, three witnesses were women. Collectively the witnesses' words paint a picture of a former slave with ties to Fort Gibson who made a life cooking and washing for the troops during the Civil War and tending to the needs of her only child.[69]

While a number of witnesses attested to when and for how long Georgeanna or Elizabeth spent time in Fort Gibson, Parsons, Kansas, or elsewhere as they followed the troops, attorneys representing the Cherokee Nation tried to cast doubt on Georgeanna's fealty to the tribe. Among them was Colonel R. W. Blue who practiced in the United States courts, the state courts of Kansas, and those of the Indian Territory. Other attorneys included William Wirt Hastings, attorney general for the Cherokee Nation,[70] and James Sanford Davenport,[71] a future congressman who was Cherokee by intermarriage, first to a granddaughter of long-time Cherokee Chief John Ross. Davenport's second wife was also a member of the Cherokee Nation. As an intermarried citizen, Davenport acted as an attorney for the tribe and was instrumental in placing freedmen on allotment rolls.[72]

Among those who testified, there is consensus that Georgeanna grew up in the Thornton household. Whatever her ties to Amos may have been, at the outbreak of the war, Georgeanna, along with the rest of the family and slaves, followed Amos Thornton out of Fort Gibson and into the "states." When Amos was wounded in 1863, the household returned to Fort Gibson where Thornton was mustered out of his regiment.[73]

As the Civil War drew to a close, the Thornton household appears to have scattered. Georgeanna continued to live in or near Fort Gibson, while Amos himself seems to have moved on, settling further south in Cherokee territory near the lake at Greenleaf. Amos's son Lewis testified that Amos moved there before he and his own wife joined him "on the bayou" in the winter of 1867.[74] Lewis's widow, Ellen, would testify that there, not far from the Illinois River, Amos lived out the remainder of his days.[75]

After Amos moved to the country, Georgeanna may have worked for a time for his estranged second wife, Minerva.[76] Sometime after the cholera outbreak of 1867 sent the population out of the area surrounding the fort, Georgeanna also took leave of Fort Gibson. According to one witness, "Cholera broke out there and the government hauled them out from town four miles and give them tents, and I got missed of this woman then . . . the government people scattered the people out from town on account of being too thick."[77]

Georgeanna went west to either Fort Sill or the town of Arbuckle, where she continued to cook and wash for troops. Some witnesses said that Georgeanna's father, John Fox Fields, came to take her somewhere off in the country, but both the location and the dates were uncertain. Meanwhile, Georgeanna had sent Elizabeth to a school in Parsons, Kansas. Although conflicting stories about Georgeanna's romantic liaisons may never be resolved, she is reported to have married several times, but it appears that she had only the one child by Amos Thornton.

Many have speculated about the criteria used to decide claims of citizenship such as Georgeanna's and Elizabeth's. The record does not reveal what swayed the Commission to decide in their favor. However, a change in regulations regarding the eligibility of intermarried non-Cherokees to claim land put an end to John Bowlin's application, which was denied in 1906.[78] By then, John Leonard Bowlin was already a prosperous man, and with the allotments granted to his mother-in-law, wife, and seven children (between 1905 and 1908), he owned much of the green fields surrounding Bowlin Spring.

John Bowlin named these lands for a source of clear water that spilled from a fissure in two large rocks and fed into the Pryor Creek watershed. The name Bowlin Spring eventually took hold in the county. Previously, people had spoken of settling up on Pryor Creek (which included the many tributaries feeding the watershed as opposed to the town itself, which spread farther south along the creek's wider banks). Despite Pryor Creek's importance as the site of the last meeting in Indian Territory between the Federalists and the Confederates, today's residents speak devotedly of their community of Bowlin Spring, the area named for the enterprising man, my paternal great-grandfather, whose family's general store would become the anchor of the farming and mining communities for miles around.[79]

Who Owns the Narrative?

The testimony set forth in the Thornton/Bowlin case is both rich and rare. Few Americans can trace their pedigree much past their grandparents. Fewer still can reach back over a hundred years. That far back, the number of African Americans or those with mixed racial backgrounds whose lineage can be documented is heartbreakingly sparse. Given so much information—when formatted in standard text, there are over fifty pages of testimony in the Thornton case—one might be eager to embrace the record as fact. Nonetheless, family lore calls into question what the witnesses said in their sworn testimony.

Eliza Andre and Frank Smith, well-known Cherokee citizens and long-time residents of Fort Gibson, were both witnesses for a number of other applicants for Cherokee citizenship. Yet nothing is known about their credibility. As frequent "witnesses," they might have found the task of vouching for Georgeanna and Elizabeth in some way advantageous, for who knows what the enterprising Mr. Bowlin might have used to entice them to testify.[80] By his own account, Mr. Smith, a former soldier who had fought with Stand Watie for the Confederacy, was not engaged in any business. In answer to whether he was simply at leisure following his military service, Mr. Smith replied that he was "just loafing around the town."[81] Another Cherokee Freedman witness, Blue Thompson, agreed with the assertion that "any number of [applicants for citizenship] claimed one thing and actually did another with reference to their home."[82]

Apparently, hearings such as those granted to Georgeanna and Elizabeth also were rare, particularly for women.[83] So, one may speculate—as the family believes—that John Bowlin might have assisted in locating sympathetic witnesses in seeking a favorable outcome. Indeed, another witness, William Hudson, appears to have been pressed into service when John Bowlin ran into him at the Muskogee Courthouse on the morning of July 16, 1904, the day that Mr. Hudson's testimony was taken.[84]

The credibility of these witnesses may never be established. However, doubts about their testimony serve to underscore the limitations of historical research that relies on records that, for any number of reasons, have undergone selective archival and selective retrieval, first by the appointed Commission and then by additional anonymous bureaucrats. A closer reading—between the lines—helps us in piecing together different historical threads.

For example, throughout the hearing it seems astounding that not even Amos's son Lewis, or Lewis's wife Ellen, denied that Elizabeth was Amos's daughter. In fact, the testimony makes clear that she was a well-known member of his household and even hints that Elizabeth was the reason for which Amos and his wife Minerva parted. There are many ways that we could interpret the testimony of one witness, Arch Carter, who asserted that people "claimed to be that old Amos Thornton was the father; that is what hurted Mrs. Vann and old man Thornton."[85] Ellen Thornton, his daughter-in-law, does say that when Amos Thornton returned from the North with the slaves who had followed him, Minerva—who had stayed in Fort Gibson—no longer lived with him. Even Ellen referred to Minerva as "Mrs. Vann," recalling her by the name she took when she later married Canon Vann.[86]

With relatively few firsthand accounts of the era, what life must have been like at the time for these coloreds, Cherokees, and mixed-bloods is hard to imagine. For many, the option of either aligning themselves with former slave owners or striking out on their own into the unknown might have seemed equally daunting. With the North victorious and the Cherokees, after internal divisions and much indecision, having aligned themselves temporarily with the wrong side, they might have asked, who was the preferable ally? Where was the best place to settle? Without the structure of slavery, what community would emerge, as newly enlisted citizens, settlers, and scoundrels all jostled for land in Indian Territory? One thing is sure: President Lincoln's successor could hardly have been worse for people of color than Andrew Johnson. As a former senator from Tennessee, Johnson was sympathetic to the South. When Congress authorized a provision that allowed the Freedmen's Bureau to assign confiscated land to freedman and Black war refugees, Johnson rescinded it.[87] Countering Congressional intent, his administration rapidly restored Southern lands to their previous owners (who quickly indentured former slaves through sharecropping), leaving Martin Luther King Jr. to suggest that reparations could still rectify—even decades later—the shameful treatment of freedmen under Reconstruction.[88]

Although Amos Thornton and his legal wife parted company upon his return to Fort Gibson, family lore agrees that Amos was devoted to little Elizabeth. Her descendants have no doubt that he was her father and that he had a great deal of affection for the child. A number of Elizabeth's grandchildren claim that a will exists, written by Amos Thornton, bequeathing part of his estate to little Lizzie. My late cousin Frances had it tucked away amid piles of her family keepsakes that may well be unearthed someday. But according to Elizabeth's granddaughter, my late Aunt Hazel, Lizzie's husband (the proud Mr. Bowlin) would not let her accept the inheritance.[89]

Other puzzling bits of information tease our curiosity. One wonders, for example, about the land referred to in the testimony as owned by Mr. Hunt but previously occupied by Amos Thornton.[90] Had Amos Thornton intended to leave that land to Elizabeth? In his testimony on June 28, 1904, John Bowlin seemed to imply that his wife had some claim to Hunt's land, but he could not secure it for lack of Cherokee citizenship. Indeed, one archived document shows a transaction for land settled by Mr. Hunt with a payment to Elizabeth for twenty dollars.[91] In 1904, Amos's daughter-in-law testified that Mr. Hunt resided on the land that "belonged to Mr. Thornton."[92] Perhaps additional research can bring to light whether Mr. Hunt occupied land that Elizabeth had claimed from her father or bought with assets that he had left to her.

According to one account, at the close of the Civil War, Amos wanted to keep Elizabeth and raise her as his legal daughter. But Georgeanna wanted to exercise her newfound freedom and, fearing that Amos would take her daughter away from her, hid little Lizzie in a basket of clothes on washing day and simply walked out of the yard never to look back. Whether weary from the strains of war or ailing in body and spirit, Amos would soon repair to the peaceful waters of Greenleaf Lake and any ties he had to Georgeanna would grow weak and eventually fade.

It seems reasonable enough that if Amos moved away from Fort Gibson, and his son moved to the country, they and anyone else might lose track of the independent Georgeanna as she made her living washing and cooking, in Arbuckle, or Fort Sill, or elsewhere. Only when John Bowlin saw the advantage of pressing Georgeanna and her daughter Elizabeth's claim to Cherokee land did her whereabouts matter.

That the testimony may have been entirely trumped up is a possibility, as well as the idea that what the witnesses said didn't matter. Years ago, one of the family elders recounted that Georgeanna wanted no part of the garrison life she'd seen at Fort Gibson. So the story goes that she actually took Elizabeth up to Canada—far from the Cherokee Nation—to wait out the unpleasant war. As recalled, the two returned only when all conflict had ceased. Eventually, John Bowlin would meet Elizabeth in Parsons, Kansas, where he'd worked as a porter at the Belmont Hotel and where she had spent time at school.[93] Though no record remains of the type of schooling Elizabeth received, the fact that this girl attended school beyond the primary grades sets her apart from other coloreds, indicating once more some elevated status or source of support above the washerwoman's pay that her mother could muster.

John Bowlin was clearly a man of vision and action who planned to make the most of his resources. John saw a future in Indian Territory and found ways to make the most of the opportunities available to him. Family members who knew her describe Elizabeth as very sweet and quiet, whereas John was outgoing and a real presence wherever he went. Despite a difference in their ages of thirteen years, Elizabeth and John were married in Parsons in 1880 before moving to Fort Gibson to set up house.[94] John may have chosen Elizabeth for her sweet nature, her claim to land, and her pedigree as the daughter—although illegitimate—of a judge, someone with a certain stature in the community. One might wonder which aspect the ambitious John Bowlin found most appealing. Was it the exotic mixture of her Indian blood, her pedigree as the daughter of a feisty woman, one who refused any abuse—actually sewing one of her later husbands up in a sheet and beating him? Or, was John enamored of the experience Lizzie gained from schooling and travel? Perhaps John longed for the stability that a sweet-natured woman could provide for him after such a peripatetic youth.

John and Elizabeth Bowlin would enjoy a long marriage and live to see their land bear fruit. Together they had seven children, two boys and five girls. Once established at Bowlin Spring, John farmed over three hundred acres of land but also started a business in trade, traveling once a week to Tulsa to buy thread and tobacco for the women and men living along the headwaters of Pryor Creek. In the photo that accompanies his obituary, he wears a bowler hat tilted at a slight angle that frames a face with dark eyes and a well-groomed mustache. At ease in a high white collar and jaunty coat and vest he has the swagger of a man confident of his success.[95]

The trade he began was consolidated when his eldest son, Leonard Elmer, built a store next to his father's house on the unpaved main road that linked the farms owned by a handful of families in the area. Though the store was Leonard's, it was actually inspired by his baby sister Sophie. As a young girl, Sophie loved baking sweets and making candy. She sold her goods so successfully that Leonard expanded the trade started by his father by building the Bowlin Spring Grocery Store.

John Bowlin's vision and legacy have stood the test of time. Through hard work and shrewd investments, his lands prospered while the Bowlin businesses enjoyed a market niche as the only source of provisions for their largely rural corner of Craig County. His children's children now stand behind the counter at the Leonard E. Bowlin General Store. They fry chicken in the back room that over the years served as the juke joint bringing together young revelers from as far away as Tulsa to dance to music that wafted over the rusting pickups and roadsters parked in the nearby clearing. On Saturday nights they continue to slather on the succulent secret sauce handed down from generation to generation. Their annual calf fry still brings in the crowds.

Uncle Leonard's store has been expanded twice. As family members gathered from all over the globe for Thanksgiving in 2004, they sat around the red-and-white-checkered oilcloth-draped tables working on designs to once again remodel the store that serves the folks who work the ranches nearby as well as people from the surrounding farms, many of the older ones remembering its heydays.

Even today, the operation is a family one. In 2004, nine of John Bowlin's grandchildren were still living on the plots allotted to the family beginning in 1908. That year, as family and in-laws admired the newly hung Christmas ornaments, one of the extended family remarked that he loved being out at Bowlin Spring, being able to get away from the pressures of his high-tech urban existence to this place that in many ways reminds him of Southfork, the vast lands held by the close-knit fictional family made famous in the old TV series *Dallas*. Indeed, the neat houses nestled in the rolling hills are just within sight of each other but enjoy their own spacious grounds, stretching

Figure 3. The Bowlins, 2004. Photo by the author.

collectively as far as the eye can see. In this respect Bowlin Spring forms as legitimate a dynasty as any in America, less well known but an important chapter in our history.

The Davis Connection

Just as John Bowlin recalled the sale of his mother, there would be other links to slaves among the Thornton descendants. Indeed, sometime in the 1830s or 1840s, a ship from Scotland would bring a woman named Tempe (or Timpi) to these shores. Whether Tempe was an indentured servant or a slave with African origins is lost to the passage of time. What is known is that she was a slave of Daniel Ross, the father of the John Ross who would later become the principal chief of the Cherokee Nation. The elder Ross reportedly sold Tempe to a man named George Whitmire. It is uncertain whether Tempe's daughter Betsy was fathered by Daniel Ross, George Whitmire, or someone else. Whatever her racial mixture might have been, her name is sometimes hyphenated as Ross-Whitmire.

Tempe's daughter, Betsy, would marry a freedman named Isaac Glass. Their daughter Emma was born in 1858. In time, Emma would marry a fair-skinned man named William Davis. William was the son of Jackson or James Davis—who reportedly was Cherokee and "Negro." Although family members described Jackson as a "Doubtful" man because of his muddled bloodlines and the fact that he lived part of the time around Fort Sill in Kansas, he received strip payments based on the 1896 Cherokee Rolls. His payment number was thirty-nine, although no land was allotted to him in 1907. Jackson married a woman named Julia, who apparently was owned by Robert and Margaret French. Julia also appeared on the Old Settlers Cherokee Census, although she was thought to be part Dutch. Jackson Davis died in 1915. As far back as the mid-1800s, this branch of the family was as racially mixed as the Thorntons and Bowlins. The story of who we are racially goes back a long way.

There is some intriguing but inconclusive evidence that Julia had a sister named Mary who also married a man named Davis. These two couples may well have traveled together from the East on the Trail of Tears, for they both settled in the Cherokee Nation and had cousins nearby named Bowlin. The story goes that one branch of the family was so near to being White that they kept moving west to California in pursuit of a more promising existence. I owe this tantalizing conjecture to Julia Kidd, whose genealogical search I noticed on a Native American professors listserv. The encounter was especially striking because it held the promise of a possible link to what for me was the shrouded time before Removal, a time when Creek names were primarily in a Muskogeean language. While I could trace the Anglicized names of my ancestors, most of my efforts to find their origins in the East all led to dead ends. Julia, a retired writer and librarian of my mother's age, not only shared her family's history, she generously gifted me with her frank assessment of how her family had come to pass for White. Her efforts to reclaim her heritage were eloquently laid out in our email exchanges, an outpouring of information I treasure. I include some of them here, even though in my final push to complete and defend my doctoral studies, Julia's initial posting, the one that prompted the exchange, was lost.[96]

To Julia:
Your post caught my eye because my great grandfather on the Cherokee side married a Julia French at Fort Scott. His name is Jackson Davis. He died in 1915. . . . There is some recollection that the French family was part Dutch.

To Darnella:
My grandfather was Daniel Davis . . . an interpreter on what is now the Qualla Reservation. He married a Cherokee. . . . My great grandmother was Mary T. French, Cherokee #1243, born in Alabama, 1825, who married John Murphy Wood, born in Alabama 1827. . . . As you know, it wasn't unusual for families to have several members marry other families. We may be related in two ways.

Julia:
I have long wondered about the period when Jackson Davis married Julia French. . . . Jackson and Julia had two girls and two boys. One of the girls was named Mary Ellen and one boy, William, was my great grandfather. He married Emma Glass and they had eleven children including Joseph Davis, my grandfather and a veterinarian in Vinita, Oklahoma. Joseph had eight children with Henrietta Bowlin. . . . Their son John Davis was my father.

Darnella:
I feel humble tonight. My family came from Texas to New Mexico in the 1880s and then another group in 1904. After I was born to a Kentucky father and a New Mexico mother, we moved to a small town named Cloudcroft. . . . There was a family in Riodoso named Bowlin whom we visited frequently. Mother said they were her cousins. My family claimed to have no Indian blood, but I have discovered, quantitatively, more Tuckahoe, Cherokee, and perhaps Creek than 'anglo.' We must remember that I was born in 1930, and until 1900 people were paying $5 a braid to decimate the Indian population from Texas.

The Wood family went to Texas in the 1830s and 1840s. Mary French Wood was very dark and John Wood had a sallow skin and very coarse hair that he kept until he died in 1933. I would go to the Mescalero Reservation with my dad (they called me the little girl with white hair), and I would feel the drums, later in Scottsdale, something would well up inside and I would be in the round dance. I think they made the move from the East and felt they could 'pass' in Texas. I believe they tried to protect us, but I am very proud of my background and the courage they had to make a new life. . . . My children and grandchildren will know the truth!

Julia:

My hair is standing on end. I just talked with my mother who was born in 1929. She remembers a Creek family named Kidd living in Beggs, Oklahoma when she was young. . . . The Bowlins were very fair skinned. We were told that many moved west, possibly to California, to pass. . . . I am stunned by the possible connections.

Darnella:

Another French family member is telling me her father was Cherokee-Creek. (Last email, May 4, 1998.)

It seems amazing that both our families' French and Davis descendants might have found their way to Texas where they were later joined by some of their Bowlin cousins, all presumably passing for White. The likelihood that these French/Davis/Bowlin Cherokee connections are coincidental seems slim given the synchronicity of times and places, the shared paths that the families took as they traveled westward, and the uncommon moniker of Bowlin being associated in both cases with the Davis and French surnames.

Unfortunately, correspondence with Julia Kidd lapsed and with it any hope of readily verifying the facts about these branches of the family that redefined their racial identity far from the Cherokee Nation. Interestingly, a French family website makes mention of a Robert Mosby French married to Margaret Wilson Fields, a Cherokee woman of Oklahoma. Their son, Robert Mosby French Jr., born 1877, is associated with Muskogee, which is exactly thirty miles south of Bowlin Spring and thirty miles east of Beggs, the town where my mother passed her youth. As even the greenest genealogist knows, there are many dead ends in the search for forebears, especially if they had reason to leave no trace.

Among those members of the Davis family who had settled in the Cherokee towns of Nowata and Vinita, some may have appeared no different from those passing for White in Texas. The Dawes Roll policies governing racial identification admitted only Indians by blood, intermarried Whites, or freedmen. In the words of Angie Debo: "Apparently at the time of the enrollment the Dawes Commission regularly enrolled all with apparent 'Negro' blood as freedmen. If any of them had Indian blood they were not recognized as Indians by tribal law, for there was no way by which a valid marriage could be contracted. Illegitimate children of White fathers and 'Negro' mothers are, of course, uniformly classed as 'Negroes' by White Americans, and the Indians had followed the same rule."[97] These practices left nearly White mixed-bloods with the choices made by family members who stayed among their own, passed for White, or just suddenly disappeared.

The hegemonic policy of denying slaves a designation of degree of Indian blood makes it nearly impossible to speculate on what racial groups the Davis family actually represented.[98] Counter to popular perceptions, racial mixing has been occurring since the first contacts of indigenous peoples with Whites and then Blacks. From more recent photos, we can see that the Bowlin descendants and the Davis families represented a racial rainbow, from those with blue eyes to members with rich brown skin. Their hair ranges from coarse to super fine and from raven black to a straw-hued blond.

Sharing their racially mixed backgrounds, William Davis and his wife, Emma, would have nearly one child every year between 1882 and 1901, for a total of eleven. Joseph, their eldest son, would marry Henrietta, the eldest daughter of Elizabeth Thornton and John Bowlin. Joseph became a veterinarian, caring for farm animals as well as household pets from his home in Nowata. He kept a neat kitchen garden and chickens for fresh eggs to feed his large family of six girls and their youngest child, a long-awaited son.

Joe Davis was a stern man with steely blue eyes. He was respected as a professional whose brush with the famous came when he treated Will Rogers's lame horse. Will Rogers was only passing through the small town of Nowata, but his horse needed care, and his inquiries led him to seek out Joe Davis. Joe treated ailing animals under a portico at the rear of his house. An observant child, I can recall the pungent smells of disinfectants as he patiently stitched up the wounds of dogs or cats using an array of large carpenter's needles.

The Davis clan was also listed on the Cherokee Freedmen Rolls and their land allotments were a stone's throw away, just north and west, from the Bowlin's spread. One Bowlin parcel actually abutted Davis land. Joe and Henrietta's children also ran the spectrum of colors from honey brown to pearly white. There's a family story that their daughter Hazel was so light-skinned that with her blue eyes, she had to return to Indian Territory to marry her dark-skinned beau, Sam Armstrong. At the time, Cherokee laws governing interracial unions were recalled as being more liberal when it came to

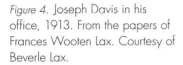

Figure 4. Joseph Davis in his office, 1913. From the papers of Frances Wooten Lax. Courtesy of Beverle Lax.

wedlock between Blacks and Whites than the laws in Kansas, which at the time made such marriages illegal. Those who actually caught a glimpse of the attractive young Hazel Davis were convinced that she was White.

It turns out that the story is a myth. Although miscegenation laws were not always strictly enforced in Indian Territory, Hazel and Sam's wedding took place long after Oklahoma became a state.[99] Counter to numerous accounts of the tale, they wed on July 28, 1928, in Oswego, Kansas. Still, the Black and White marriage was remarked on in the local newspapers, but no copy remains among the family's possessions.

Born on St. Patrick's Day, Hazel's brother, John, had greenish-gray eyes and was both serious-minded and inquisitive. He left high school to learn candy making in Bartlesville, eventually finishing a GED before heading off to Britain and World War II. He'd enlisted in the US Army Air Corps, serving as an aircraft mechanic in Wharton, England. John was honored for taking part in rescuing children from the Holy Trinity Church School in Freckelton, England, when the buildings caught fire as a plane crashed into the primary school in bad

Figure 5. John William Davis, in uniform. Collection of the author.

weather. With sixty-one dead, it was the worst civil disaster of the war. The rescue effort is acknowledged in an engraving commending all of the American heroes who raced to help that day.[100] Interestingly, the army recognized John as a member of the Cherokee Nation and placed him among a squadron of Whites and Indians rather than with the "Negro" troops.

Back in Oklahoma, John played football and at one game caught the eye of Mary Adams, the great-granddaughter of Thomas Jefferson Adams. The two would marry and set up house in Vinita, Oklahoma, starting a family that would produce five girls as well as one stillborn and one healthy boy. Their union would produce the most fascinating aspect of racial mixing and ties to Allotment land, one that helps me to tell who we are.

The Bowlin Legacy

One of the first questions that arise out of this slice of history is: Why didn't my great-grandmother, Elizabeth, claim Cherokee citizenship by blood? Was she embarrassed by her illegitimacy? Did she fear that a claim of blood might have been more robustly refuted than a claim to Cherokee Freedmen status?

Pursuing a claim to Cherokee citizenship as a function of her father's blood might have secured 160 acres of land, while her claim, as a Cherokee Freedman, might only yield 40 acres.[101] Yet, at the time, the Cherokee alliance to the Confederacy might still have negatively influenced the decisions of the supposedly neutral Commission of the Five Civilized Tribes. Perhaps Elizabeth felt that Freedmen status was, or would soon become, preferable to blood ties with her father's tribe. Perhaps, for a time, coloreds—especially those with money—held more sway than Cherokees. Following the Civil War, Black towns financed by wealthy "Negroes" fleeing the prejudices of the South or the stultifying class structures of the North were springing up all over Oklahoma—replete with banks, newspapers, churches, schools, and bustling businesses.

Who knows what factors may have affected the positive response to the Thornton claim. Certainly, Georgeanna and Elizabeth were lucky. Between 1898 and March 4, 1907, when the application process ended, the Commission received more than two hundred thousand applications for enrollment. Of those who applied for the citizenship that would make them eligible for allotments, about two-thirds were turned down.[102]

If John Bowlin cared about his racial identity or that of his wife, he was not deterred from fulfilling his dreams of using his money, earned in the North, to claim and work the land around Bowlin Spring. He flourished. It seems there were few obstacles to slow the Bowlins as they garnered wealth in their community of Black, White, and Indian farmers, miners, and ranchers. Yet, as divisions and hatred solidified following the Allotment Era and as Jim Crow laws gripped the South, John Bowlin's children's children, as well as his mixed-race in-laws, would have been more likely to be concerned about their racial status.[103]

In truth, Elizabeth's racial "identity" could have been composed of any combination of races, since her mother Georgeanna's slavery did not necessarily equate with the "Negro" race as our tendencies to oversimplify racial categories might tempt us to believe. Among the Cherokee by blood witnesses, Patsy Johnson states that she and Georgeanna were first cousins.[104] Tangling the Red and Black with White strands in the family, more than one of Elizabeth's grandchildren would claim an Irish forebear. Of Georgeanna's pedigree, we know only that her father was a slave and that she was born near Fort Gibson. If the record is accurate, John Bowlin was himself a mixture of slave and Irish—again, with no indication of his mother's pedigree. Yet, here we find an application for Cherokee Freedmen status and can only wonder what that identity meant to Georgeanna or Elizabeth, for during their hearing, even Judge Amos Thornton's Cherokee blood ties were questioned.[105]

The testimony given during the hearing sheds scant light on these questions of racial or tribal identity. Applicants are referred to in terms of the position they hold or are seeking: full blood Cherokee, freedman, or Doubtful. There is no discussion during the hearings of phenotype. However, for many years, the Bowlins—just like the Ewings of Southfork—were highly selective as to who married into their clan or who was buried in the family cemetery, Shady Grove. All but one of the ten children of John's son Leonard Elmer Bowlin and his fair-skinned wife Mary (nee Mayhew) would marry either Whites or Indians. Only Phyllis would wed a Black man. Some hold that initially no Blacks would be tolerated in the Bowlin burial grounds, and great care was given to whose names were entered in Elizabeth's family Bible, which has been lovingly preserved by her grandchildren.

Today the Bowlin family contains a full spectrum of colors, yet is frustrated that recognition of their Indian blood has been denied. They would reject the notion that establishing blood ties means reaching back to a time and place before the Five Tribes found utility in such a term. Instead, they would look to the social myopia that failed to acknowledge biracial unions and the comingling of races among servants and masters on the western frontier. They would recall the times when decisions about racial identity and tribal association lay in the hands of census takers whose judgments were based sometimes on guess work, sometimes on physical appearances, or who sometimes disregarded facts in deference to policy.[106] The result was that "those with any African blood were put on the Freedmen roll, even if they were half-Cherokee. Those with mixed–White and Cherokee ancestry, even if they were seven-eighths White and one-eighth Cherokee, were put on the Cherokee by blood roll. [Today] More than 75 percent of those enrolled in the Cherokee Nation have less than one-quarter Cherokee blood, the vast majority of them of European ancestry."[107] During Allotment, as census takers determined blood quantum, they also ordained the mixed-bloods who could claim land.

For the Cherokees, it is ironic that the federal rationale for placing Indians on allotments was to discourage communal farming in deference to White ways. This policy proved redundant for the many Cherokees who had already adopted the manners and habits of the settlers.[108] In contrast, few tribal values and practices among the Five Tribes could have been as out of keeping with the pioneers as were the values and practices of nomadic tribes from the plains and points further west who'd had relatively minor contact with Whites. Although history acknowledges the role of the mixed-blood trader or negotiator, as the frontier moved westward there appears to have been relatively little recognition of just how long the association of members of the Cherokee Nation with Whites and "Negroes" had endured.

US society generally is uneasy with mixtures that do not fall readily into categories of—might we say—black and white. Indeed, since the phrase "pity the poor mulatto" passed out of usage in the early years of our history as a comment on the lamentable state of marginalized "half-breeds," mixed-race peoples do not and have not fit readily into a simple category in public discourse. Even now we struggle with how to describe the racially mixed man who occupied the White House. If we say he is Black, what do we mean? Of the two Davis sisters, Alberta and Nellie (both attractive girls as seen in a photo from the late 1930s that shows one very light- and the other much darker-skinned), would we say that they are the same color?

In the United States, legal definitions of multiracial peoples with African heritage go back to the one drop rule.[109] That rule made a slave of anyone with "any known black ancestry."[110] In contrast with other countries, this rigid definition undercuts the myriad paths that people of mixed heritage take in their pursuit of personal identity formation or their ties to multiple cultures.

However society may have described them, as with most cultures, for the Bowlins, the family provided the core, a refuge against the vicissitudes of adversity. More broadly, whether an individual member embraces or rejects it, the family serves as a fixed point from which ever-widening circles of community radiate. At the center is the nuclear family of mother, father, and children, while another would be a clan or a village of a few men, their wives, and their progeny. Beyond these immediate core groups are the grandparents, aunts, uncles, and cousins, and beyond those the neighbors, community, town, region, and so on.[111] In theory, complications arise not when an individual accepts the group without question or rejects it absolutely but rather when the individual is torn between alliances with the culture of

Figure 6. Alberta and Nellie Davis. From the papers of Frances Wooten Lax. Courtesy of Beverle Lax.

origin and the conflicting demands of gaining acceptance from other groups.[112]

In practice, these considerations are further clouded by the messy actions of men. As we have seen, the Cherokee had been mixing with both Whites and "Negroes"—not to mention other tribes—for generations. Amos Thornton's identity as a Cherokee judge can only be interpreted—without evidence to the contrary—as reflecting citizenship or culture rather than a purely Cherokee blood quantum. Establishing "full blood" status for almost anyone of that era would sorely test any Indian's claim to an untainted bloodline running back nearly three hundred years, beyond contact with outsiders. At some juncture, choice enters the picture, either in acceptance of social labels or in the rejection of conventions that misrepresent one's true colors.

Given the nested nature of communities, multiracials might either identify with one "admired" group or reject groups altogether.[113] In a 1995 research article on Navajo youth, Deyhle reported that healthier youth tend to be those who either identify with the group or totally reject it.[114] The troubled youth are those who are torn between their alliances with family and the "other." In a study of immigrant assimilation, Gibson found that the healthiest youths are those who can successfully negotiate separate and distinct cultural groups. Hence, the benefit of mixed-bloods as bridges among different communities.[115]

It follows, then, that the family cohesion found at Bowlin Spring has, perhaps, less to do with color or race than with history and land or culture. Identity formation may not be linked to race so much as it is to cultural heritage. Yet, that identity may not be largely recognized or reflected in the larger social circle, given the dominance of the White national narrative. The pressure to be included in a given racial sphere may be at play among those who have "chosen" an oversimplified racial group with which to identify.[116]

The inability of the Bowlins to gain recognition of their blood ties may have prompted a pragmatic commitment to keeping their family's integrity unsullied. Without formal recognition by the Cherokee Nation, they may have felt the threat of further diluting their tribal claims through marriage with Blacks, a dilution that likely would have dimmed any hope of establishing future claims to Cherokee citizenship.

It is interesting that the Bowlins speak less of the high-spirited Georgeanna, who in the end went on to marry seven times, once to a captain of the army named Hamilton and lastly to Ducky Williams of Pantha Creek. But they think the world of Elizabeth. They are clearly proud of their Cherokee heritage, even though many family members recall times when to be Indian was worse than being identified as "Negro." Still, there has been no effort from the branch of the family that moved west to reunite with the cousins who guarded their tenancy at Bowlin Spring.

Long after the Commission designated Georgeanna and Elizabeth as Cherokee Freedmen, a category that carried no recognition of Cherokee bloodlines, members of the Thornton and Bowlin families would come to refer to themselves as Cherokees, Cherokee Freedmen, "Negroes," and Whites. Although their own choices appear to have been prompted more by social or political motives, they lack the legal standing that might restore their birthright of shared Cherokee blood. They have no CDIBs. If adherence to a cultural identity led some to stay on the land while others sought to escape it, that culture remains largely familial but decidedly nebulous.

Cherokee Uprising

Surprisingly, this chapter of history isn't closed. In 1983, would-be voters discovered that the Cherokee Nation had stripped the voting rights of its "Black" members. The tribe's actions have led to suit and countersuit as the Descendants of Cherokee Freedmen movement has attempted to reinstate their former stature.[117]

To understand the Cherokee stance, it helps to know that for decades following the Allotment period, many disenfranchised Indians entered a shadow world as their tribal bonds weakened. They lived in a kind of no-man's-land of racial ambiguity. When Oklahoma became a state, in 1907, it superseded Indian Territory as a social and ideological construct. Accepting Allotment land had meant abandoning traditional tribal practices in favor of becoming US citizens, subject to the laws of the federal government and the state of Oklahoma. The 1934 Wheeler-Howard Indian Reorganization Act then reversed previous policy. While it ended the Allotment Era, returning undesignated land to the Indians, it also restored a measure of tribal auton-omy by allowing tribes to opt for reconstituting local self-governing councils. This return to autonomy was meant to spur economic development as well as self-reliance within tribal communities. Although Alaska and Oklahoma were largely exempt from the initial act, the Oklahoma Indian Welfare Act of 1936 extended the reach of the policies enacted two years before.[118] Less than twenty years later, tribal autonomy fell from favor as a return to assimilation appealed once again as a solution to the Indian problem. This time around, legislators desired a final solution in the termination of all federal responsibil-ity for Indian affairs. Termination policies would decentralize the Bureau of Indian Affairs, transferring some services to other agencies or the states.[119] But the press to curtail the federal trust agreement and the piecemeal nature of implementing termination in the settlement of land claims proved onerous as each tribe's readiness for termination was argued and assessed. The move-ment actually served to rally Indian cohesion as communities united against oppressive federal policies. If this makes your head spin, imagine the mixed-bloods of that time trying to decide where a slight advantage might lie. Stick with the tribe? Move on? Assimilate? Cling to the past? Blend in?

For Indian nations, land held in trust by the federal government sustained the paternalistic relationship of the Great Father, meting out funds to peoples unable to fully govern themselves. In 1975, the federal government sought to loosen tribal dependency with passage of Public Law 93–638, the Indian Self-Determination and Education Assistance Act. The act provided funds for some social services to federally recognized tribes, plus authority over their administration.[120] Clearly a response to the Civil Rights Movement, the act sought to value Indian rights. The tensions surrounding protests and acts of civil disobedience, sometimes instigated by organization such as the American Indian Movement (AIM) or the Indians of All Tribes (IOAT), were part of a larger demand for a more positive public view of our nation's diversity.

The revival of interest and pride in claiming native ancestry following the 1992 quincentennial of Columbus's landing in the "New World" led to a huge jump in the number of "Indians," including those with legitimate claims. Census figures for birth rates alone would not account for these leaps.[121] A newfound pride in even small but legitimate ties to indigenous peoples seemed to account for the surge. And it was a surge.[122] Suddenly tribes were inundated with claims for benefits and services by anyone with a slim belief that their great-great-grandfather might have been part Indian. This greater awareness coincided with the rapid construction of casinos following the 1988 provisions allowing Indians to establish gaming operations on tribal soil.[123] Suddenly, all manner of folk were double-checking their pedigree.

Factions within the Cherokee Nation had always been unhappy with the notion that acceptance of the freedmen associated with the tribe as full-fledged citizens had been forced upon them after the Civil War. As the number of "wannabes" expanded, these animosities could be inflamed in the service of political expediency when the time came around to elect the next governing coalition. Stripping the freedmen of voting rights in order to win a runoff for principal chief seems to have sparked the initial disenfranchisement.[124] Subsequent suits and countersuits hung on the 1866 treaty of peace and criteria for Cherokee citizenship: inclusion on the Dawes Rolls either as blood citizens, intermarried Whites, or freedmen.

Among the many plaintiffs in the Cherokee Freedmen's controversy was Bernice Riggs (Riggs v. Ummerteskee, JAT 97–03-K). Her 2001 case could clearly document her Cherokee blood ancestry, but she did not qualify for a Certification of Degree of Indian Blood because her forebears did not appear on the Dawes Roll as other than Freedmen. No Cherokee by blood designation on the Dawes Roll meant no Cherokee citizenship.

On March 7, 2006, Justice Stacy L. Leeds of the Judicial Appeals Tribunal of the Cherokee Nation handed down a decision in the case of Lucy Allen v. the Cherokee Nation (JAT-04–09). Lucy Allen is a descendant of individuals listed on the Dawes Commission Rolls as "Cherokee Freedman." Her petition sought to declare unconstitutional legislation (11 CNCA No. 12) that limits citizenship to those "who possess Cherokee blood." In 2006, the court agreed with Allen, in a two-to-one decision, and irate groups of Cherokees vowed to overturn the ruling.

By 2017, the back and forth of court rulings in the restoration of voting rights followed by their withdrawal was well into its fourth decade. For years, Marilyn Vann (Vann v. Salazar et al.), leader of the Descendants of Freedmen movement, worked tirelessly to expose the technical glitches and short-sighted views that hampered the legal proceedings.[125] Meanwhile, jurisdictional wrangling pitted the most recent case (Cherokee Nation v. Nash et al.) against the Vann litigation in a first-to-file action that looked more like venue shopping: hear the case in Oklahoma or the District of Columbia? Making the controversy even more complex was the apparent violation of the Bureau of Indian Affairs approval process and the Congressional House Resolutions that sought to impose some order on this chaos.

It seems incredible that one hundred years after the fact, the tribe was still contesting the "forced" adoption of their former slaves as an unjust imposition on their sovereignty. It was willing to accept members from other Indian tribes and intermarried Whites as citizens but bristled at the acceptance of former slaves, even those with incontestable proof of Cherokee bloodlines. Meanwhile, the long court battle was alienating a younger generation of freedmen, leaving their elders to fight for the forebears whose lives were intimately joined with the tribe's. Each faction argued for the justice of their claims, their right to self-determination, and, above all, for recognition of who they are.

Astonished by the animosity of the tribal purity debate, I was equally struck by its apparent lack of grounding in historical fact. Tirades about and by Black Indians were often emotional and righteous, clouded by dissimulation and half-truths. As a researcher who has spent decades arriving at an understanding of race's place in America, I found the obfuscation in the ongoing litigation deeply disappointing. Some tribal litigants admitted they had not examined the long history of Black participation in the tribes, dismissing claims without considering that in some cases freedmen's blood quantum might have been identical to, or even exceeded, that of "blood" citizens. Instead, they focused solely on the distinction that one had a CDIB and the other did not.

On August 30, 2017, US District Court Judge Thomas F. Hogan handed down his decision in Cherokee Nation v. Nash et al. (Case No. 1 13-CV-1313). Hogan's ruling was based on the substance rather than the technicalities of the decades-long litigation. His seventy-eight-page decision reaches back to pre-Removal days and the antecedents of slavery among the Cherokee. It traces the tribe's movements out of the South and into Indian Territory, its inner turmoil as factions sided with both the Union and the South, and the presence of people of color at every juncture along a shared path. With the judgment, the time for bickering over jurisdictional venues and the configuration of plaintiffs reached an end. In a victory for freedmen, Hogan's decision affirms their rights to citizenship within the Cherokee Nation based on the 1866 treaty of peace. In a nod to tribal nations, it acknowledges the sovereignty of the Cherokee over their constitution. Satisfied with the Court's decision, Marilyn Vann is happy to move on.[126] Cherokee Attorney General Todd Hembree sees a win/win situation and vows not to appeal the decision, even as similar litigation among the Creeks and the Seminoles is ongoing.[127]

Hogan's decision may well set a precedent, but the appeasement of plaintiffs and defendants should not obscure the Court's reliance on the contested racial categories embedded in the Dawes Rolls. The Court's silence on the biases of hypo-descent and White privilege contained in that "definitive" list of Cherokee citizens should not mask, enshrine, or erase the fuller accounting of the Cherokee's racial legacy, an accounting of which this story forms but a slender thread.

Motivated by the many patterns of injustice that emerged as I studied my family's history, my modest quest began to take on the trappings of a crusade. Here were decent, hard-working people, wanting only to maintain a modicum of dignity and respect in the face of policies designed to undermine them. From the farm to the frontlines and on to the factories, they put their trust in American ideals. Like so many others, they pinned their hopes on jobs that would deliver them from the hardscrabble existence offered on Allotment land. What united them was that land and the ties to native peoples that placed them there. As people of color, with or without Cherokee citizenship, they would retain pride in the fact that their families owned their own place even as its bounty dwindled.

3

Tom Adams and His Descendants

hile the history of the Cherokee is relatively well documented (even if, at times, slanted and misunderstood), fewer know much about the nation's tenth largest tribe, the Muscogee Creeks. In her 1941 preface to *The Road to Disappearance: A History of the Creek Indians*, Angie Debo writes: "The history of the Creeks since the Civil War has been almost a complete blank. Indian agents, journalists, and travelers all center their attention upon the more 'progressive' Indians, and historians in the absence of convenient data have observed the same bias."[1] When, twenty-five years later, the book was reissued, Debo noted that little new information about the Creeks had come to light: "Unlike more articulate tribes . . . the Creek Indians were a conservative people who lived their own lives and kept their own counsel, and their inner history was hidden."[2]

More recent studies show that from the vantage point of White settlers, missionaries, and especially policymakers, seeing the myriad communities inhabiting the Southeast as unified nations served to facilitate communications as well as negotiations in the early days of European expansion throughout the current states of Georgia, Alabama, and Florida. In truth, the confederation of tribes that came to be known as the Creeks was a mishmash of towns and villages composed of peoples speaking a variety of languages

and representing different lineages and clans.³ As with any diverse community, "normal" infighting was leveraged by Whites to advance their expan-
sionist agenda, leaving divisions that still run deep. Indian treatises on tribal
configurations among those dwelling in the Southeast, however, are markedly sparse.

Today, the lack of new information has not deterred scholars from sifting
through extant documents in attempts to provide the points of view missing
from earlier histories: Recent works strive to reconstruct the perspectives of
those who were previously marginalized. Their focus has been to re-evaluate
the historical record, free from the biases of the past that skirted race but
privileged White points of view.⁴

Despite the relative dearth of information from Creeks themselves, their
early history shared much in common with their southeastern neighbors, the
Cherokees. From colonial times, for both of these tribes whose traditional
homelands nestled in verdant woodlands, racial mixing and identity would
become a practical function of optimizing economic opportunity and social
capital. Although they came to form different political groups and occupied
different regions, the Cherokees and Creeks shared parallel fates.

Among the Creeks, my family's experiences may be typical of an important chapter in our nation's history. Following removal to the West, the

Figure 7 (opposite page). The Adams spread in the vicinity of the town of Beggs.
During the Allotment Era, the township and range system was used to parcel land
in six-mile-by-six-mile squares. Each of these segments consisted of thirty-six subsec-
tions of one square mile, which were further divided into NW, NE, SE, and SW
quadrants totaling 160 acres. Thomas Jefferson Adams was allotted the entire 160
acres of subsection 26 NW, Township 14 North, 12 East, for farming or ranching.
His wife, Mahala, was allotted 160 acres in the abutting subsection 23 SE. The
forty acres granted as their homestead adjoins Tom's acreage. The map shows
4,300 acres but is only a portion of the land allotted to the Adams clan, which
almost completely surrounded the town of Beggs. The map supports the assertion
that the Adams family owned land that stretched from Beggs to Okmulgee, following the southerly direction of Adams Creek, whose curving line is visible on the
map. The black square, directly south of Beggs, indicates the few acres that remain
in the family. Based on Hastain's Township Plates of the Creek Nation, pages 127
(the eastern half of Township 15 N, Range 11 E), 150–51 (Township 14 N, Range
12 E), and 152–53 (Township 15 N, Range 12 E). Graphic design courtesy of
Brian Barth.

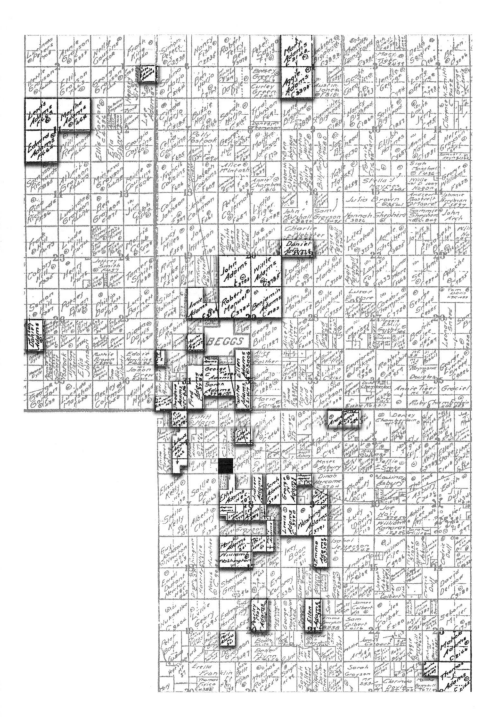

events surrounding the Muskogeeans[5] as they sought to rebuild their culture in Indian Territory affords a backdrop for giving voice to the members of the Adams family, whose history provides a poignant view of the frontier. Luckily for me, the lives of my Adams forebears were noteworthy.

Documents from the National Archives, land records, and family oral history, taken together, describe the allocation and subsequent reduction of the once vast Adams's land allotments. The various sources form telling markers of the family's identification with or rejection of the tribe. Tracing the history of the Adams family is an exercise in redefining race and culture as both refuge and compromise for my people whose land once stretched the ten miles from Beggs to Okmulgee, Oklahoma.

The relative value of being White, Black, or Indian continued to shift following the Allotment period as members of the Muscogee Nation fought to maintain their integrity and their livelihoods. As with the Cherokees, the 1898 amendment of the Allotment Act sought to divide communally held Muskogeean lands into 160-acre parcels to encourage the adoption of yeoman farming. And, again as with the Cherokees, the lengthy process of surveying and allocating the tribal lands had barely begun before Oklahoma became the target of prospectors and hordes of "settlers." Like members of the Cherokee, Choctaw, Chickasaw, and Seminole tribes, many land-rich and cash-poor Muscogee Creeks were soon burdened by property taxes and fell prey to unscrupulous speculators. In the years following Allotment, laws enacted to protect Indians' land rights influenced some, including members of the Adams family, to abandon tribal identity for ready cash.[6]

The racial identification of the Adams's family (my mother's side), across six generations, is a study in the context of federal, state, and tribal policies that alternately eroded and supported tribal cohesion. That story is more than an oral history; it benefits from many files preserved in the National Archives in Washington, DC, and in Fort Worth, Texas, along with materials from the Oklahoma Historical Society. From the patriarch, my great-great-grandfather, Thomas Jefferson Adams, who as acting chief of the Muscogee Nation signed the Red Fork Oil Lease in 1904, to descendants who identify themselves as White, African American, Indian, and mixed-bloods, the family serves as a microcosm of the forces that continue to define or contest racial purity and tribal alliance in the legal battles making headlines today.

The Muscogee Creeks

After first contact with Europeans and their pathogens in the sixteenth century decimated legions of southeastern Indians, tribal communities relocated and regrouped. When the French, then the English, formed a second wave of foreigners pushing into the interior, they encountered from fifty to one hundred distinct tribes occupying the land that eventually became known as belonging to the Creeks. Through a tangled conflation of terms, the people who traveled by boat to trade with settlers on the coasts came to be known by the name of the waterways that facilitated their commerce. The British referred to communities clustered along the Chattahoochee River and those along the upper braches of the Alabama River as Lower and Upper Creeks, respectively. Among these groups were a smaller number thought to form the core or founding towns of the Creek Nation. The language they spoke was Muskogee.[7] Today, the tribe refers to itself as the Muscogee (Creek) Nation, merging the geography and linguistic roots of the people who occupied the southern woodlands of what would become the states of Georgia, Alabama, and the Carolinas.[8]

Their easy access to the southeastern shores coupled with their frequent contact with Europeans placed the Muscogee people, or Creeks, among the tribes that quickly learned the languages and manners of Whites. As the colonies developed and the republic grew, close contact with non-Indians produced both mixed-bloods and purebloods schooled in European ways, who played key roles as representatives of Creek communities in negotiations with the US government as well as other tribes.

Generations of close contact and familiarity with European culture resulted in the adoption of so many White ways that Creeks along with Cherokees, Seminoles, Choctaws, and the Chickasaws eventually became known as the Five Civilized Tribes. Still, the benefits accrued in embracing White ways were eschewed by many Creeks, leading early on to major fissures between those who could speak eloquently in English on behalf of the Muscogee Nation and those who held tight to traditional ways that minimized contact with outsiders. However, both factions were devoted to the lands that had provided so abundantly for their livelihood.

The circumstances that led to the push for elimination of the indigenous peoples from the Southeast during the 1800s left many Creeks torn between the hope for continued coexistence among Whites and the fear of upheaval from their ancestral homes. The demand for land split tribes, communities, and families, as some chose the option to leave while others held on. This dismal chapter of US history is usually glossed over, sparing educators the task of explaining to schoolchildren the details of Jacksonian-era policies aimed at the total removal of all Indians from the East.

During the early 1800s, tensions intensified as the growing population of southerners viewed the eastern woodlands as underutilized and under inhabited. Those anxious to possess land held by populations that they esteemed less worthy inhabitants were abetted by state legislatures and by Andrew Jackson, who refused to enforce those rulings that did favor Indian landowners.

Given the lack of federal regard for their lifeways, it is amazing that between Removal and Reconstruction, the Creeks were able to establish themselves in Indian Territory so effectively, building settlements, towns, and a sense of order amid the uncertainty of the oppressive policies that continued under Jackson. Despite these signs of progress, it is clear that the tribe was far from unified when the Dawes Act articulated a plan for land use designed to accelerate acculturation. Although the Creeks were among a dozen tribes exempted from the act, they uniformly rejected its tenets. Yet, civilized or not, the tribe's lands were to be similarly allotted under the Curtis Act of 1898.

By the 1880s the demand for land grew. Population growth had doubled in the East as well as the West and the press for acreage was exacerbated by freed slaves who, on the heels of the Civil War, were cast out with no place to go and no money to get away. The 1890s would see a tide of western movement with the waning of the Indian wars as the Five Tribes sat, in Indian Territory, like an island in a rising stream of settlers. The reality set in among politicians as well as more astute citizens that stealth methods would be required to make the most of the meager opportunities available during and after the brief and unsatisfactory period of Reconstruction. The historians Angie Debo, Daniel Littlefield, and Grant Foreman, before them, all have contributed to vivid descriptions of the Sturm und Drang among the various factions of the Five Tribes as they faced Removal and the construction of new lives west of the Mississippi.[9] Less has been authoritatively written about what it took to endure these tribulations into the twentieth century, especially as lived by the tribes' descendants. Here and there we find native voices. Unfortunately, many echo the prejudices prevalent in popular discourse.

Writing at the turn of the century, Alexander Posey, the Creek humorist and editor for the *Indian Journal*, satirized the sociopolitical times. With his series of Fus Fixico letters, Posey poked fun at the stereotypes of the "uncivilized Indian" as well as those who would too readily embrace the values of a Eurocentric culture.[10] Yet Posey, like fellow Creek journalist George Washington Grayson, had little goodwill toward "Negroes," believing that they had no place among Indians.[11] The fear of tribal dilution was real. Littlefield notes, "From the middle of the eighteenth century on, blacks played a significant, and sometimes dominant, role in Creek affairs. . . . Any study of the Creeks must take their blacks into account."[12] The number of people of African descent living in Indian Territory add weight to his assertion. According to one estimate, at one time, 10 percent of Creeks owned slaves.[13] Despite many inaccuracies, when the rolls were finally closed in 1907, the Creeks counted as many freedmen as full-bloods among their numbers.[14]

The Allotment period served to reconfigure the landscape for Indian settlement as well as the tenor of discourse between Washington and Indian Territory. Indians wishing to retain their land or benefit from an allotment had to comply with the rules set out by local commissioners, even as those rules were bent and frayed. Like the Cherokees, the Creeks had escaped the dictates of the 1887 Dawes Act, but, eventually, through the 1898 Curtis Act, the long process of surveying, claiming, and allotting land would engulf them too, tainted by speculation, fraud, and a thousand ways around the laws for those with the means to circumvent the allotment process.

The intentions of the Allotment acts were the "Americanization" of indigenous people through individual ownership of arable land that could sustain a "family" and if properly cultivated provide a crop for sale. Those who had previously worked plots on the tribe's common land were to adapt settler practices on farmland to be developed by the homesteader, his wife, and their children.[15] Such practices represented attempts not so much to assimilate Indians as to press upon them the values associated with land ownership. In effect, these values would serve to weaken ties to traditional ways in thinly disguised attempts to generate a monoculture of "Indians" rather than distinct subgroups or tribes. The assumption was not that Indians and Whites would become one big family but that distinct tribal cultures would dissolve in a kind of red bean stew. The more that White values took hold, the more the coterie of eastern reformers hoped that Indians would loosen tribal ties, leaving few interested in claiming "full blood."[16]

Originally laid out in Section 5 of the Dawes Act, allotment policy declared that the land would be held in trust and would not be saleable, but exemptions abounded and were curiously linked to the degree of Indian blood. Section 6 of the act granted US citizenship for those who accepted the plan. Yet, Section 8 exempted the Five Tribes.[17]

A little-remarked-upon aspect, in initial accounts of the allotment process, was the transfer of land along patriarchal lines, with the family established in a homestead with a male head of the household. This turned traditional matriarchal lines of descent upside-down, substituting a contrasting set of hierarchies for traditional Muskogeean affiliations through the mother's clan.[18]

The Creeks saw through the heavy hand of Washington and the eastern reformers in the Dawes Act. Its ploys to control the land set off a storm of controversy but ultimately led to an allotment act that included the Five Tribes. The Curtis Act of June 28, 1898, would dissolve all previous agreements covering Creek land use. Its constraints on the actions of the Creek National Council would affect the infamous Red Fork deal signed by Tom Adams.

Thomas Jefferson Adams

Prior to removal from the East, some Creeks had taken Anglicized or Scottish names but also retained the names given to them in their youth. After Removal, most Muskogeeans used popular names, with many men taking names of US presidents. Thereafter, children often were given the names of their grandparents, aunts, or uncles. An overrepresentation of the names of the founding fathers is therefore not unusual among the Muscogee.[19]

Although his family's links in the East are shrouded, Thomas Jefferson Adams was born around 1845. According to the 1899 Creek Nation Census (Card no. 651), he was fifty-seven and affiliated to the town of Ketchapataka. His mother, Hepsey, came from a prominent Creek family, the Perrymans from Big Spring. Among the many documents where he is featured, Thomas showed no outward signs of embracing traditional ways. Most photographs

capture him dressed nattily in a vest and tie, with a well-groomed mous-
tache, cutting a striking figure as he posed in his official capacity during
events that would prove historical for his tribe.

Thomas Adams merited two pages in O'Beirne and O'Beirne's 1891 publi-
cation, *Leaders and Leading Men of the Indian Territory*. The text reads:

> Born in February, 1848 [*sic*], at the old Creek agency, the eldest son
> of William Adams, by Hepsie Perryman, niece of Louis Perryman,
> Thomas first attended school at Tallahassee Mission, in 1852, and, later,
> moved to Asberry Mission. In 1861 he married Miss Mahala Grayson,
> daughter of Betsy Grayson. During the war he was detailed by the
> Federal government to the commissary department as distributor of beef
> to the various camps. In 1866, when the war ended, he was elected to
> the House of Warriors, which office he has held until the present—over
> twenty-five years. In 1885 Mr. Adams was elected Speaker of the House,
> which office he held for four years. Since 1867 the subject of our sketch
> has been practicing law in all the courts of the Creek Nation. He is also
> on the board of trustees of the New Yarker [Nuyuka *sic*] Mission School.
> Mr. Adams had fourteen children, eleven of whom are living—Isaac,
> Wash, Betsy, Thomas, Hepsie, Lewis, Lee, Mitchell, Lizzie and Mary.
> He has about 600 head of cattle, 40 or 50 head of horses, 40 sheep, and
> some 150 hogs, besides a good farm of seventy-five acres of land. On his
> ranch is a good dwelling-house, out-houses, stables, and every other
> possible convenience. Mr. Adams is considered one of the brightest
> lawyers among the Creeks, and is a successful politician, having, in fact,
> no superior among his people in bringing about such ends as he wishes
> to accomplish. He is about six feet one inch high, weighs 198 pounds, and
> physically, very powerful. He is energetic to accomplish an undertaking,
> and is very popular with his constituency.[20]

The Chronicles of Oklahoma also mentions Tom's appointment as a trustee.[21]
Serving each of the two houses of the Creek National Council, he was
appointed to help in the selection of a site for rebuilding the Tullahassee
School and he oversaw the construction "for the benefit of the full bloods in
the western part of the Muskogee Nation." As speaker of the House of Warriors, Tom was present when the school reopened in 1885.[22] At the time,

Figure 8. Thomas Jefferson Adams (or is it George Washington Adams?). Collection of the author.

J. S. Perryman was principal chief. According to the *Chronicles*, of the seventy pupils in the entering class, only two boys and a handful of girls could speak any English in the English-only program.

Interestingly, the photograph that accompanies Tom's entry in *Leaders and Leading Men of the Indian Territory* is regarded by the family as that of his son George Washington Adams and not Thomas. The confusion may spring from the fact, recalled by my cousin Brenda Hollier, that both Thomas and George wore topknots signaling their status as healers or medicine men. Brenda also recalled our great-grandmother Annie saying that Thomas came to Indian Territory on the Trail of Tears and that his mother died along the way. This seems highly unlikely, even if Thomas was born as early as 1842.

There is no doubt that Adams was a prominent figure among the Creeks and an enterprising one. With an eye to the future, he had articles of incorporation for the Adams and Sepulpa Mining Company drawn up on August 27, 1895, with himself named as the company president. At the time, rumors that oil would soon be found on tribal lands abounded, leaving the group of forward-thinking Creeks headed by Thomas determined to be active participants in any future strikes. All over the Territory, Indian people were scrambling to safeguard any lands or rights from prospectors and squatters, while Whites waited on daily news of any "opening up" of plots, as policies governing the various Nations seemed to shift at a dizzying speed.

Though the articles of incorporation for the Adams mining company were sanctioned by the laws of the Muscogee Nation, no one could tell if, when, or for how long those laws would be honored—not with the smell of oil in the air. Geological surveys reported the area ripe for major oil strikes. With pressure from Washington to expand the frontier, Indian talk was of resisting further dictates from the East. Nonetheless, the Indians lacked the knowledge and skills to tap the resources under their feet. Unschooled in surveying and test drilling, the Creeks needed outside help to assess the prospects of a mineral cache.

Those Indians who were fluent in English, who had some experience with Whites, and in particular with those who dealt with the oft-revised federal treaties played an important role at this pivotal time. Their education, or lack thereof, delineated their abilities to interpret two vastly different cultural philosophies for the sake of the continued prosperity of themselves and their tribes. Not surprisingly, the job often fell to the mixed-bloods.

These biculturals did not always embrace Eurocentric ideals. Often the products of parochial schools whose emphasis was on the indoctrination of Christian values, the mixed-bloods were not ignorant of the double standards applied to Red men. Although there was much to be gained in their capacity as negotiators, the frequency with which that position was abused may have had more to do with a conflict of values than with personal greed.

The need for formal incorporation to protect the mineral rights on Creek land raised questions about education, cultural sophistication, bicultural commerce, and political maneuvering both in a legal and a social sense. Trusting in the written White man's laws to protect their interests, the Creeks resorted to oil leases that sought to forestall the imposition of federal sovereignty over Indian actions.

According to documents on file in the W. H. Heydrick Collection, archived with the Oklahoma Historical Society, Tom Adams was acting principal chief for the Council of Warriors during key events in the land that would shortly become the state of Oklahoma.[23] He played a leading role at a pivotal moment in the nascent exploration for fossil fuel.[24] Excitement over the prospect of striking oil was tremendous. The first lease for oil in Indian

Territory would make the history books, and that lease was signed in 1904 by the acting principal chief at that time, none other than Thomas Jefferson Adams.

Far from naïve (he was a shrewd partner in a law firm he ran with Amos Reed and Charley Ward),[25] Tom hoped that the Creeks could trust the White man to keep his word, respecting the accords that were mutually agreed upon. But, once again, Washington reneged on its promises. In the end, the strictures that relegated all tribal contracts to the scrutiny of the Secretary of State would void the lease.

A handsome photo commemorating the lease signing was among a number of black-and-white glossies tucked into an old tin bread box that for many years held our family mementos. We were told that it gave evidence of our family's stature. Although several family members remembered the picture as appearing in the Oklahoma state history textbooks, no one has a copy, nor do they know of anyone who had kept theirs. Still, the photo remains, reproduced in a newspaper article, noting that the lease "didn't jell."[26]

The group that was photographed represented a microcosm of influences on the Creek Nation in 1901 when the photographer posed the assembled men, each looking earnest and intent—all except for Thomas Jefferson Adams, who wears his vest and silken tie with a degree of swagger missing from the others. Those others included prospectors from Pennsylvania, convinced of the presence of oil in Indian Territory. J. C. Heydrick is identified as a pioneer oilman and his partner, John C. Wicks, as a driller.

Together the White men had surveyed the land around the confluence of the Arkansas and Verdigris Rivers. They were anxious to see their educated guesses play out and certain that oil was likely to be found in abundance in the area. Meanwhile, the US Congress had tied the hands of Indian tribes, requiring any major tribal decisions to be reviewed and approved in Washington. The weeks and months that passed while tribal authorities traveled to the capitol and waited for approval proved impractical, leading local officials to draw up and sign documents they hoped would be viable but later proved untenable. Such was the case with the lease that Heydrick and Wicks drew up for acting Chief Thomas Jefferson Adams.

The enthusiasm that drove their actions was understandable. Many other prospectors were convinced of the presence of oil in the area, but the Red Fork

First Lease Didn't 'Jell'

By SAL VEDER
Of The World Staff

An old photograph, slightly yellowed with age, came to light recently to bring back memories of Tulsa's first oil boom days.

The photo, uncovered by J. I. Belford of Tulsa, former Beggs insurance man, is believed to include men who played a prominent role in the signing of a 500,000-acre oil and gas lease executed by the Creek council at Okmulgee about 1900, shortly before drilling of the famed Sue A. Bland No. 1 well in the Red Fork field, June, 1901.

The lease was never approved, because of difficulty in settling allotments in the Creek nation.

Dr. Fred S. Clinton, who with Dr. J. C. W. Bland drilled the Red Fork Discovery well and brought fame and fortune to Tulsa, made mention of the lease in an article included in "Chronicles of Oklahoma," Autumn edition, 1952.

Wrote Dr. Clinton:

"One fine May morning Dr. J. C. W. Bland sent for me for a consultation at Red Fork about a 500,000-acre oil and gas lease said to have been passed through the Creek council, Okmulgee, subject to approval by the Secretary of Interior Ethan Allen Hitchcock."

Although never approved, the lease is believed to be the first executed by the Creek council under Principal Chief Isparhecher.

Chief Isparhecher is not among the 12 included in the photograph. They are (according to Belford) John R. Yarger, Creek roll No. 4866; Lewis Adams, 3790; John C. Wicks.

a pioneer driller believed to have worked on the Sue A. Bland well; George W. (Wash) Adams, 3780; James Sapulpa, 6442; Timmie Fife, 4653; Legus C. Perryman, 2943; Joseph Henry Land, 1695; William A. Sapulpa, 3281; Thomas J. Adams, no roll number, and J. C. Heydrick, pioneer oil man. The twelfth person is not identified.

Only Land is still living, according to Belford.

The photograph was sent Belford from Wichita Falls, Tex., by the youngest brother of J. C. Heydrick. He knows little about it, he says.

"I'm under the impression," Belford said, "that the photograph was taken about 1899, but I don't know where. Probably at Okmulgee, the Creek Nation capital, and possibly at Sapulpa. However, I have my doubts about the latter."

Belford remembers many of the men in the picture for it was at his father's store and post office at Orcutt, Indian Territory, that many of them gathered.

"I was about 9 years old and I remember when William A. Sapulpa first walked into our store. I didn't know him from Adams, but I found out later who he was."

Belford remembers one incident vividly. It was the first meeting of Sapulpa and Chief Isparhecher at the store. Belford's father, N. R. Belford, had left the youngster in charge of the establishment.

"Sapulpa walked in first and asked where father was," Belford recalled. "Then he wandered about the store. Soon another Indian walked in and said: 'my friend Bill Sapulpa.' It was Isparhecher.

Figure 9. Thomas Jefferson Adams and sons, "Oil Lease Didn't Jell." Collection of the author.

oil strike would be the first. When Wick hit a gas pocket on June 24, 1901, oil reportedly shot thirty feet in the air. Virtually overnight, the town of Red Fork was inundated with all manner of hopefuls looking to cash in on a quick fortune. The brief notoriety of the town that proved the first, if not the most productive, of oil producing wells in Indian Territory gave scant attention to the Creek signers who had made the strike possible. The photo documenting agreement among the White prospectors and the Creeks eventually disappeared from the history books and the full story of the impact the lease had on Thomas Jefferson Adams's descendants long remained buried, overshadowed by the larger place in history occupied by the White prospectors whose continued efforts would eventually lead to the establishment of Standard Oil.

Any authority that Thomas had as acting chief of the Creek Nation to sign off on the Red Fork lease was undermined by federal authorities. There is no documentation showing his response to this denouement, only the reality that life went on at his family's homestead south of Beggs. The cares of farming, raising herds of livestock, and nurturing the next generation were worry enough. Still, another photo shows his physical stature as he stands before the members of the tribe assembled against the backdrop of the Creek Nation Council House in Okmulgee. In a long coat, pipe in hand, he is erect with a proud and solemn bearing. He is both at ease and grounded while the men gathered behind him appear less certain, more tentative—like extras to his soliloquy. (Interestingly, the Muscogee Creek Nation failed to identify Tom when it used the photo on the cover of its official 2008 calendar.)

According to my uncle, Leo Adams, Thomas enjoyed both his power and his wealth. Leo recalls him standing on his front porch at the close of day and surveying his land. Thomas said it was the richest spot on the Creek Nation, prompting the more literal-minded to speculate that money was buried somewhere on the property.

Money was the cause of at least one suit against Tom and his sons. In the 1915 case of Pevehouse v. Adams, Tom was accused of abusing his power as executor and guardian for three minors.[27] Land transactions appeared to leave the minors with the short end of the stick, to the Adams boys' benefit. But the decision, handed down on November 16, 1915, seems to side with the Adams family, leaving their newly expanded properties intact.

Tom was not silent in debates over Creek property. As the tribe debated the potential import of Allotment, Isparhecher, the conservative leader of the

Figure 10. Thomas Jefferson Adams before the Creek Nation Council House. Collection of the author.

National Party, maintained that "Indians" should receive 160 acres of land while "Freedmen" were entitled to no more than 40 acres.[28] As chief justice of the Creek Supreme Court in 1896, Tom Adams counseled Isparhecher that any land taken by adopting people of color as citizens would decrease the land available for rightful members of the Creek Nation. In other words, Tom viewed Creek citizenship primarily as a right to property, to owning, not just improving, land.[29]

Allotment among the Creeks

The intention of the allotment policies was to press Indians to adopt yeoman farming within a relatively narrow period. By the time the land had been surveyed, processed and claimed, homesteads established, and crops planted, there was but a brief window—a mere twenty-nine years—before restrictions were lifted, the land was assessed, and taxes on all categories of land became due.[30]

Much of the cultivation of cash-poor Creek homesteads was achieved through hard work and barter. Milk and butter were traded for hams or flour. Each farmer and his extended family counted on the sons and cousins of neighbors to help bring in the harvest, butcher the hogs, or slaughter the cattle. The women would gather to grind sausage, boil syrup, or feed the many men needed to raise a barn or a new homestead.

Although the Adams-Sapulpa Oil and Mining Company agreement with Heydrick and Wicks did not make the Adams family wealthy, enough oil was found and drilled on their lands to warrant government-appointed guardians to ensure that the Creek citizens were not unduly exploited, a concern that would later prove justified.

The Adams's Land

The Adams's land, its acquisition, development, cultivation, and eventual dissipation, forms a compelling narrative about racial identity in the face of social and economic expediency. Keen to make the most of his large family's opportunities, Tom Adams, like many other Creeks, did his own reconnoitering, selecting plots of land to serve his ambitions for both farming and carrying on his affairs in town as a lawyer and judge, tribal official, and as head of the Adams-Sapulpa Oil and Mining Company.

Acquiring and maintaining his extensive properties likely benefitted from the legal skills that Thomas Adams possessed. On January 13, 1900, at the age of fifty-five, he applied for a 160-acre allotment as a blood citizen of the Muscogee Nation from the town of Hillabe Ketchapataka and the head of the Adams household.[31] At the time of the application, Thomas stated that about 40 acres of the timber land was already cultivated, that it was fenced, and that it featured a small log cabin. It also had an old burial ground, a public graveyard that was no longer used.[32] The applications for 160 acres that he had made on October 5, 1899, on behalf of his wife, Mahala (nee Grayson), and for 159 acres on August 8, 1899, for their nine-year-old daughter Mary were held until Tom had selected his homestead.

Building the Adams land holdings was a slow and deliberate process. On July 12, 1902, Tom applied for 120 acres of land for his fifteen-year-old daughter, Martha. Martha's 160-acre allotment was split among a 40-acre plot adjoining the 320-acre family farm, an 80-acre plot just south of the town of Beggs, and a 40-acre plot bordering the town's western edge.

On March 16, 1903, Thomas Adams filed an Application for Homestead

Allotment to have forty acres from his allotment, Mahala's, Martha's, and an undefined number of acres for Mary "set apart as homesteads . . . the same being a part of the lands already selected by me as allotments for myself and those whom I lawfully represent."[33] Thomas and Mahala's abutting lots made for a large spread dominated by the imposing two-story house they constructed that O'Beirne referenced as "a good dwelling house . . . stables, and every other possible convenience."[34]

Meanwhile, Thomas Adams's grown sons—George Washington, Thomas Jr., and Lewis—had filed for their own allotments and homesteads. From the start, it was evident to Thomas that those with a lesser degree of Indian blood would have greater flexibility in transforming land into ready cash. For full-bloods, the transfer of land was tightly controlled (under the Curtis Act there was to be a five-year restriction on transfer of ownership), ostensibly as a guard against the exploitation of newly landed citizens by outsiders. For those with one-half or less blood, there was no restriction on the sale of the 120-acre "surplus" portion of the allotment.[35] In addition, the government maintained ownership of mineral rights although the treatment of royalties became a topic of contentious debate.

Tom Adams quickly grasped the opportunities and constraints posed in having a large, land-rich family. According to family lore, to affect his plans he simply designated his boys as half-bloods while leaving their sisters with the full-blood status they were all entitled to as the offspring of Tom and his full-blood wife, Mahala Grayson. Indeed, based on the Creek census cards, something doesn't add up. Card number 1172 shows Lewis, the acknowledged son of a full-blood mother (Mahala Grayson) and a full-blood father (Thomas Adams), as one-half. This is a plain contradiction of Card Number 651, which shows the full-blood status of Thomas and Mahala, as well as Lewis's sisters Martha and Mary.[36] Tom's decisions would color our family's racial identity as much as the federal policies that sought to constrain it. This distortion, whether intentional or accidental, would create ripple effects for decades to come as it diluted the Adams's Muskogeean bloodlines and undermined their subsequent claims to tribal rights and services. Meanwhile it enabled Tom to buy and sell land more readily than less astute Creeks, or those unwilling to trade racial purity for greater autonomy over the purchase or sale of their lands.

As the strong male patriarch, Tom Adams worked his plans on yet another dimension. The second-class citizenship of the Adams women, at least under

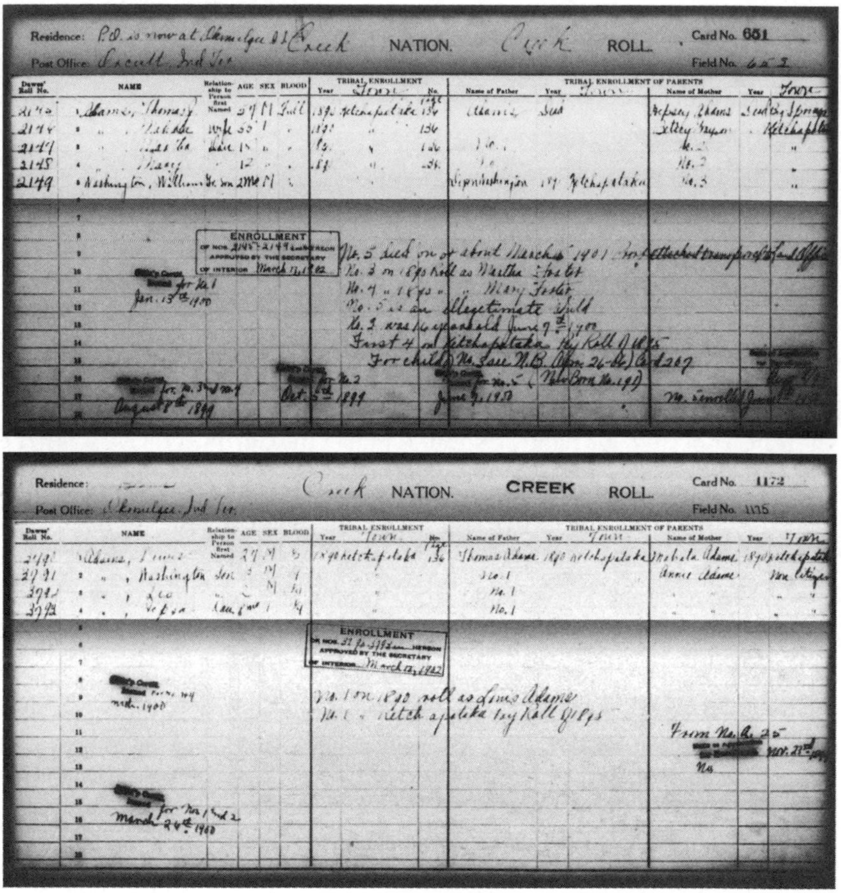

Figure 11. Census cards of Thomas and Lewis Adams, showing the full-blood status of Thomas Jefferson Adams and his wife, Mahala nee Grayson, and the half-blood status of Lewis, with Thomas and Mahala named as his father and mother. National Archives, Washington, DC.

the iron rule of Tom Adams, may have been both a symbol of the pioneering spirit of the new landowners while also marking a shift among the Creeks toward a more male-directed culture. It seems that both his sons and daughters did his bidding, changing their blood quantum or retaining or selling their land as Tom directed them, at least while he was alive.

In the end, the trajectory of the plots that formed the Adams family allotments in and around Beggs suggested an imaginary line between the small, non-Indian town named for C. H. Beggs, the vice president of the Frisco Railroad, and Okmulgee, the regional hub of Muskogeean government and the site of the Creek Nation Council House.

Just as the Adams land spread for mile after mile, the family bloodlines would move in all directions. Some would marry mixed-bloods, some would see promise in liaisons with wealthy "Negros," while some quietly slipped away to pass for White. In some instances, ties within the Creek Nation were reinforced as Adams family members married the sons and daughters of the Creek families whose names are inextricably tied to the tribe's history. The names Grayson and McIntosh affirm its ties to Scottish immigrants, while Perryman, Derisaw, Berryhill, and Harjo signal ties to families of long standing in the Muscogee community. Scottish ties were also evident on the Cherokee side through the Thornton connection, while Bowlin is an Irish name, and Davis is Welsh in origin. As I probed family members for their knowledge of our heritage, I began to understand the forces that shaped "my people."

The Sons and Daughters of Tom Adams

In the photo that had celebrated the Red Fork oil lease signing, Tom Adams's sons look on, solemn, proud, but also deferential to their father who was the clear leader. Despite the strengthening of family ties, Tom's progeny must have carried on at least one tradition closely associated with the tribe's clans: that in which elders were revered and wisdom gained from their greater experience was highly valued.

Although Thomas Jr., George Washington (or Wash), and Lewis did not serve their nation as long or as prominently as their father, they were respected citizens with stature in their community. They were also political actors in their own rights. George Washington Adams, born in 1863, was the eldest son of Thomas Jefferson Adams. He was sought out by members of the local community for his knowledge of plants and herbs that cured many ailments that had resisted treatment by European-trained physicians. His reputation for curing syphilis drew patients from near and far. The braided topknot he wears in his photographs designates him as a traditional medicine man but contrasts paradoxically with the suit he is wearing. That suit represented a different side to Wash and the Adams clan, one that would later send his namesake to the nation's capital as part of official delegations representing the Muscogee people.

George Washington Adams's nephew, Washington Adams, often spoke at council meetings, joining a loose coalition of Whites, Indians, and mixed-bloods who traveled the region. Speaking with neighboring tribes and at regional councils, Washington (who was known as Stripet) and his colleagues tried to rally support for Creek efforts to maintain tribal integrity against an onslaught of government restraints. Stripet may have made more than a few trips to the District of Columbia as part of a group of Creeks who spoke with the Secretary of the Interior. One group was composed of Bill Lovall, a White man; Jack Davis and Charley Ward, who were Indian; and Jim Allan, who was a mixed-blood.[37] Along with Stripet, their multicultural band rode to Washington funded by the generosity of the people who, attending Council House meetings, would put money on a blanket spread out for the purpose of enabling Muskogeeans to have a voice in the nation's capital.

According to one account, Stripet and Willis Ward were received at the White House and spoke with the president about a treaty that had been signed but not honored. Time and again the delegation was promised action but instead encountered delays and postponements. Often, their trips were in vain. Despite careful planning, more than once—having traveled for weeks—no official was prepared to receive them. Deeply disappointed, they would return home empty-handed.

Long before then, the elder Washington farmed the two tracts of land southwest of Beggs that he had applied for in December of 1899. In 1900 and 1901, he made Allotment applications for three of his sons—Benjamin, John, and Robert Manuel—totaling 640 acres extending north and east from the towns' northern edge. The application for Wash's son Fred was for Lot 3 of the NW quadrant of Section 6 Township 14 North and Range 12 East. Fred was born April 1, 1899, and died July 10 of the same year.[38] Altogether, Wash, his wife Sarah, and their sons held 1,140 acres in addition to the 360 acres held by his father. Wash and Sarah prospered on their land, part of which they reportedly donated for the construction of the Phillis Wheatley School in Beggs. The school was named for the woman who, in 1761, at the age of seven, was purchased by the prosperous Boston family whose last name became her own. Soaking up the classical education she received, Phillis would go on to become a poet of international renown. The school in Beggs would honor her legacy, inspiring the Black and Indian youth who passed through its doors.

Oddly, in contrast to the activities of his older brother Wash, there appears to be little information about Thomas Adams Jr. He alone among his siblings has a roll number that appears out of sequence.[39] But, there were also sisters. Thomas Sr. had three daughters: Bett, Mary, and Martha (Sissie), who was born in 1887.

Martha married a well-to-do Indian, Ural Powell, then a second man, Peter Boon. Like every family, there are less savory tales that prove easily forgotten. In piecing together the family tree, I found an anomaly in the links of Tom Adams's children. Two of his daughters, Julie and Pie, appeared to also be listed as his grandchildren. Casting about among the elders for an explanation of this apparent error jogged a few memories. The story was even murkier. Gossip had it that Julie and Pie were Tom's children, their mother being his daughter Bett. Bett's offspring were readily recalled because each had six fingers. Neither Bett nor Julie would ever marry, but Pie married Monroe Brown, a man who would later play an important role in safeguarding the family honor.

My great-grandfather Lewis Adams was born in 1875 when Thomas Jefferson Adams was thirty years old. As an adult, Lewis also made allotment applications for himself and his children on September 13, 1902,[40] and homestead allotments on January 22, 1903. Again, archival documents provided information but not the whole picture. The Fort Worth Archives house Lewis's allotment application where he claims citizenship on the basis of his mother being Indian—not his father.[41] In document 119, he acknowledges that his wife, Annie, is not a citizen of the Muscogee Nation but a United States citizen. These claims were disputed by family members who believed that Annie was part Indian. In any event, Lewis and Annie appear to have eschewed any call to retaining tribal purity, concentrating instead on making their way as farmers, tilling the soil of their own allotment.[42]

Lewis was a hard worker, laboring on his family farm, but he also oversaw the general store in town that he managed with Annie. Lewis and his wife ran their large farm with the help of sharecroppers. They also gained revenue from the land's oil wells until they ran dry. Linda Hogan has vividly captured the ways in which Whites swindled Indians out of their oil in her 1990 fictionalized account, *Mean Spirit*. The high drama that unfolded in Hogan's depiction of the adverse effects of sudden wealth among the Osage Indians living in Indian Territory makes a colorful tale. But I always find truth more gripping than fiction.

As expected, unrestricted surplus land was quickly sold to White settlers and less fungible Indian homesteads were soon surrounded by outsiders. The Adams family found themselves the victims of rustlers who had learned to siphon their oil from just such adjacent plots. Money was indeed hard to come by. Despite their hard work, without the cash to pay taxes, Lewis and Annie would have few options but to sell parcels of the land they had enriched. As family pride replaced tribal fealty, the Adams clan steeled itself against periodic hardships.

Annie and Lewis would have five children between 1899 and 1904. They would name the eldest, Washington, after Lewis's brother, George Washington, but Lewis's son would be called Stripet. From his namesake, Stripet would learn the secrets of medicinal plants. The uncle, Wash, passed on to his nephew, Stripet, the knowledge of herbal cures that he had gained in the surrounding woods and fields.

On December 5, 1905, Lewis was notified that his two-year-old child, Andrew, was entitled to an allotment and urged to make an application without delay as the rolls would soon close for potential allotees.[43] Under Tams Bixby, member of the Commission to the Five Civilized Tribes, on December 8, 1905, Andrew's baby sister, Ethel, was also granted citizenship and the right to an allotment. Her selection consolidated the Adams holding due south of Beggs and would prove that the last Adams allotment may have been the best.

Late in my search for information on the sons and daughters of Thomas Jefferson Adams, another piece of their puzzle fell into place.[44] I found that Tom's son and grandson had echoed their patriarch's leadership, playing a key role at a pivotal moment for the Creek Nation. On March 19, 1934, as representatives of the Supreme Organization of the Unrestricted Indians of the Muskogee Creek Nation, they developed a petition that would become part of the record when, a few days later, Commissioner John Collier visited Muskogee to promote passage of the Wheeler-Howard Indian Bill, later known as the Indian Reorganization Act or IRA.

Stripet's colleague, C. W. Ward, was chair of the Unrestricted Indian Organization, Stripet was the secretary, his father, Lewis, was chairman of the committee charged with drawing up the petition, while Stripet's cousin, Sarah Brown (nee Adams), and his uncle, Thomas Jr., appear as signatories on the submission. Confronting the dilemma of trusting yet another federal intervention or missing a chance at reviving tribal autonomy, Creeks who had held unrestricted allotments hoped to join forces with those with restricted land.

Commissioner Collier saw the damage that allotment policies had wrought. As he traveled the country, he lamented the long history of broken treaties, the loss of millions of acres of land, and then the allotment process that, in its effort to safeguard full-bloods, created a nightmare as Whites grabbed unrestricted lands from mixed-blood Indians and those (largely full-blood) with restricted lands and few resources suffered through the Great Depression. In the Indian Reorganization Act, Collier hoped to mitigate what he termed a "record of absolute catastrophe."[45]

Among the Five Tribes, allotment had fostered another division. Stripet, Thomas, Lewis, and Sarah, as Creeks with less than one-half Indian blood (thanks, perhaps, to Thomas Adams changing their blood quantum), sought to reunite with "restricted" Creeks before contemplating the potential impacts of the Wheeler-Howard bill. The rapid dissipation of Creek land in the wake of Allotment must have prompted the Adams clan to realize the need to strive for tribal unity. They must have known that as Creek land was transferred to White ownership, their tribe's land base, and therefore its vitality, would weaken. C. Ward, Stripet, and my grandfather Crugee were at that Muscogee meeting.

While reservation lands were held in trust and therefore remained protected and free from taxation, under the Curtis Act the Five Tribes continued to hold their land in fee simple. That unique status would set them apart from other tribes, creating a mess of legal claims that have proved impervious to any simple solution.[46] It would also fan the flames of racial division, deepening the gulf between Creeks who, like Whites, conflated blood quantum with affinity to the tribe, and those whose fealty went beyond notions of racial purity. Speaking on behalf of the Unrestricted Indians of the Muskogee Creek Nation, Charley Ward's words serve as a forewarning that Collier's efforts might be for naught. Stripet's friend "alleged that the new federal laws, if enacted, would deprive thousands of Indians of their rights who were less than half-blood."[47]

There's a trove of subsequent correspondence cosigned by Charley and

Stripet housed in the National Archives that includes a number of resolutions and land claims, as well as entreaties directed to President Franklin D. Roosevelt.[48] The mass of documents deserves a separate focus. Here it's mentioned only to underscore my family's active role in shaping their legacy. The record shows why Washington Adams worked on behalf of his people. It chronicles why his disappointing trips to the capital with Charley Ward were worth a shot, as his ties to the tribe were precious.

Annie, Midwife for Okmulgee County

While Tom Adams oversaw the acquisition and expansion of the vast Adams's landholdings, the designation of homesteads, and the fealty of the Adams clan, Annie, the wife of his son Lewis Adams, would head the next generation of Adams.[49] As midwife for Muscogee County, her influence would rival and even surpass that of her sisters-in-law who were respected teachers at the public schools in Beggs.

Annie's origins are somewhat obscure. The daughter of Antwine Chamberlain and Sarah Hurse (who may have been part English or Dutch from southern Tennessee), her parents lived in Sparta, Illinois, and Annie was born in Randolph County. In an interview with her brother John Charles (Johnny), the seventy-four-year-old stated that he was born in Perry County, Illinois, on an Indian reservation and that his father was Shawnee, Delaware, and Spanish, while his mother was Cherokee. Among the many branches of Shawnee that wandered the region and mingled with other tribes along the Ohio, Missouri, and Mississippi Rivers, some are known to have lived in settlements in southern Illinois. In fact, Ohio and Missouri, along with Illinois, all have Perry Counties named after Commander Oliver Hazard Perry, who defeated the English during the War of 1812 in the Battle of Lake Erie— shortly before, many towns on these old Indian trails had been established by French, German, Irish, and Italian settlers. Although no Indian lands remain, Perry County lies just north of the Shawnee National Forest, where the tribe's legacy echoes still.

Some say Annie came down with the German or Dutch missionaries and that her family was christened in the Catholic faith. On the Creek Rolls, she is designated as "Non Citizen." Her name does not appear on any other roll of the Five Civilized Tribes. Some thought her a White woman, but despite her very fair skin and light eyes, she spoke the Muskogee language fluently and would disappear from time to time—neatly turned out with her silver hair trimly tucked into a bun under a clean kerchief and sporting a freshly starched apron—walking off or riding out alone to gatherings in the woods. Whatever religious practices she engaged in must have contained no evangelical mission as she shared no information about them with the rest of the family. Returning home from these ceremonies, she was silent about where she had been and what had transpired. However, her ties to the Creek Nation, already strong through her affiliation with the Adams clan, were cemented through the marriages of her sisters to prominent Muskogeean lineages, the Perrymans and the Derisaws, and later, through her son's marriage into the Harjo family.

Luckily, we have her own words, as dictated to a family member on January 13, 1938:[50]

> I was born in Illinois, December 10, 1871. I came to the Indian Territory with my folks, and lived with Mary Beaver at Sally and Foster's place west of Okmulgee, where we stayed two years, then moved to Chief Sam Checote's place. Our occupation was farming.
>
> When we first came to Okmulgee it had only three stores, Trent and Sever's owned a store together; Parkinson had his own store. Captain Belcher operated a Post Office and Silas Smith was owner of a hotel. Indians, Whites, and colored all ate together in the hotel.
>
> I went to school in the northeast corner of the old Council House, which at the present time has been turned into a museum. My teacher's name was Blanch Hereford.
>
> Indian Council's were held once a year, except on special occasions. The last Council that was held during any time was when Chief Pleasant Porter was acting as Chief.
>
> The nearest railroad was at Muskogee, and the mail transported between Okmulgee and Muskogee by mail hacks.

We also have the words of Annie's brother, John Charles Chamberlain, who, in a lengthy interview, recalls his times "with the Indians," giving some context for Annie's grit:[51]

> I was born in Perry County, Illinois on an Indian Reservation. The date

of my birth is not recorded only as I have given it previously in the county here, and that would make my age 74 now. I had rather think it 70 or 71 from the way I feel. My parents kept no records of our births. They probably told me, but I at the time didn't give it any serious thought, so now I do not know my exact age. I remember many things I actually saw and experienced in my life with the Indians, and some things told me by my parents and by others. My parents and we children loaded up the wagon for an extended trip. Our wagon had canvas covers. This was in 1880. I remember crossing the river at St. Louis and traveling through Missouri to Kansas, which was our first destination. There were six children in the family when we left Illinois but on the way to Kansas two of the children died and were buried. They didn't die at the same time, so were buried at different burial grounds. I was young and do not recall to mind when these children were buried however, I do know they were buried in regular Indian burial grounds in the vicinity where death overtook them.

My parents had twelve children in all. My father was Shawnee-Delaware and Spanish mixed. My mother was of the Cherokee tribe. We lived in Kansas two years and came into Indian Territory in 1882. I have lived here since and have grown up with the country. I have been associated with Indians all my life and have observed their customs and practices. One was the early custom of hunting and traveling. A few days previous to the day of departure a boy would be sent around among the Indians telling them of the intended trip and when and where they were going. This was in the Sac and Fox country on the Cimarron River. All would meet at the appointed place and travel on their ponies and take their guns or bows and arrows. I remember being on these trips where a lot of the Indians carried bows and arrows. I have hunted with the bow and arrow myself, and now have several at my home. These parties numbered from fifteen to twenty-five men. Each carried some groceries, and we killed game as we advanced. These Indians were guided by strange signs. One of these signs watched and religiously observed, was the snake sign. If a rattle snake was found stretched out, that was a sign to continue on the way, and that all was well, but if a rattle snake was seen coiled up ready to strike, that was an evil omen and a warning of danger ahead. So the party would return to their homes and make a new start later. This was fifty years ago and there were bunches of wild Indians roaming the plains, and sometimes trouble was had with them. Our Indians were peaceable and wanted to avoid any unnecessary trouble, so tried to miss these parties. Another custom was the fire. If smoke arose, that was a sign of fair and fine weather, but if the smoke settled near the ground that indicated the approach of a storm. If we were near home we returned. We were very careful to put out all fires before dark. One reason was to prevent other bands of Indians from locating us, and another of course was to prevent the spread of fire when we were asleep. Indians were prone to gamble for pretty high stakes, sometimes at cards and other times at shooting matches. There is a tale of two Indians of the Sac and Fox Reservation which was where Oklahoma City now stands, who had been out west of there on the Iowa Indian Reservation. This was west of the Sac and Fox Reservation. They had been out on a gambling spree and were returning when they met the "king." This occurred on Dry Creek and the "king" was concealed by bushes. However, the king spoke to them prophesy. He told them that Jesus Christ said that on a certain day a certain one of them would die. He also told them to return to their people and prepare to warn them of the exodus of their people. That their lands would be taken from them (Sac and Fox Indians) that they would be scattered, (this was in 1885) and for them to call together all the people at their stomping ground where they were to be told about the vision and warning. This removal was to occur four years from the date, and the Indians were to beat their drums continuously from that time on until removal. The man died on the day appointed and sure enough the Sac and Fox Indians were scattered in 1889–1890, some going to Iowa, some to Montana, but most of them staying in northern Iowa. Some are still in the Osage county.

I attended many of their dances during this four years. The Indians were great fishermen. I saw five thousands of them fed not scriptural five thousand, but great crowds. The way they secured this quantity of fish was by poisoning the streams. They gathered certain herbs and put them in sacks and beat them thoroughly. This was placed in the stream and left long enough to poison the water sufficiently to addle the fish or make them drunk. They were easily caught then, and a sufficient number would be obtained to feed great crowds.

The Indians were always ready to open their doors and share their food and home with travelers who passed through without charge. But traitor—better beware as they were treated badly.

Her brother makes clear the family's strong ties to traditional native ways. It was Annie's sister Sophie who married into the full-blood Creek Perryman clan. A lively woman, Sophie also appeared nearly White. The Perrymans were fair, but Sophie had a child by another Indian man who was quite dark. Out riding one day with her husband, Sophie spied her lover. Impetuously, she made to jump from the buggy into his arms. Instead she fell, splitting her spleen, and died. Sophie's death had far-reaching consequences for her daughters Frances and Martha. The young girls were quickly tagged as prime fodder for Indian boarding school and shipped off to Carlisle, Pennsylvania. Established in 1879, the objective of the Carlisle Indian Industrial School was assimilation. The focus was on learning English as a gateway to embracing White culture. Plagued with disease and homesick children, the school would serve over ten thousand students, but, during its thirty-nine-year run, many ill-prepared students stayed only a few weeks. Some were proud to have persevered for a year or two, yet only a small fraction would graduate after completing the full program of study.[52]

Despite the harsh environment and its assimilationist objectives, both Frances and Martha would later urge other family members to send their children to the school. It is paradoxical that the sisters, who had their mouths washed with lye soap when they spoke Creek, would associate attendance at the school with maintaining the integrity of their native heritage. But in principle, only Indians were admitted, and as the tribe's racial lines blurred, that particular badge of honor was clear.

Sophie's daughter Martha, a lively woman in her own right, added to the checkered family history. Married to a wealthy member of the Checote family, she found herself with a chauffeur-driven car but a drunken Indian spouse who, when not off on an extended binge, was abusive to her and their four children. In his more lucid moments, Martha's husband, an amateur historian, would while away the hours around the courthouse. Eventually, Martha ran off with Mr. Washington, a handsome Black man who was their gardener. The desultory Checote suddenly was all focus and action, tracking Martha down and committing her to an insane asylum. Tom Adams's daughter-in-law would be the one to find a lawyer to have her released, but Martha did not stay with her abuser. Instead, she finally left town with Mr. Washington. At that point the courts took over, taking first her full-blood sons and then her daughter under the protection of the

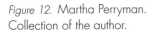

Figure 12. Martha Perryman. Collection of the author.

court. The very fair-skinned Martha would go on to marry her paramour and have five dark-skinned children.

It is interesting that Annie would note but make no comment on the fact that "Indians, Whites, and colored" would eat together at the hotel in Okmulgee. Whatever she may have thought of the different racial groups jockeying for position in the Territory, Annie actually exemplified the strong pioneering spirit that White settlers would be credited with in romanticized sagas of the movement west. She oversaw the farm and helped Lewis run the Adams General Store in Beggs, attended births, and cared for the children of women who succumbed during labor, or while their infants were still babes in arms. Raising many sets of orphaned children was part of her role as midwife, for who else would see to the small ones when the men of the family needed to tend to crops and livestock? Still, these tasks did not take her away from raising Jersey cows prized for their milk or ensuring that the smokehouse was stocked and the larder filled with enough provisions to last through each winter and on to the first harvests of spring.

The provisions would feed not only her family but those down on their luck. Small family groups knew they could come to Annie for food and shelter. She kept a big kettle of sofkee, a stew made from dried corn, simmering at the back of her cast-iron stove. The nourishing gruel was at the ready to ladle out for men, women, and children, who, once fed, would help with chores for a day or two and then move on. Even when times were lean, Annie and her sons "could make a way out of no way." When there was nothing in the pot, Annie would give the hungry a handful of dried corn and bacon rinds to tide them over.

A petite woman, Annie had the strength and determination to turn and deliver a breech birth calf all by herself, saving the lives of the mother cow and her newborn. It was Annie who oversaw the tending of the Adams orchards, the picking, drying, or canning of apples, apricots, sand plums, and peaches. Her daughter-in-law, Stripet's wife, Grace McIntosh, would win prizes for the farm's Elberta peaches at 4-H club festivals. Oversized jars were needed to can the peaches, which were too large to fit through the standard openings of mason jars. Annie took care of the grape arbor and the blackberry bushes, ensuring that dried possum grapes were always on hand for making dumplings.

Over time, Annie delivered hundreds of babies, hitching up her buckboard, loading her rifle on the seat beside her, and riding out, often into the night. Dr. Berry, the local physician, admired her aplomb and respected her abilities. They often worked side by side on difficult births to save the lives of both mother and child. Dr. Berry's admiration of Annie was evident in the conversations they had over strong coffee under the crepe myrtle that shaded the old front porch.

The highly capable Annie might rule the roost with an iron hand, but her steely will would be tested again and again. Her daughter Hepsa would die young while her daughter Ethel, or Tut, would marry a man named Theodore Sneed but also die before her time. Ethel, a pretty woman with long hair, was reputedly quite prim. She never wore her dresses higher than just above her ankles. In her early twenties, Ethel, always a touch melancholic, would grow disenchanted with a world she saw as being overtaken by evil. She succumbed to tuberculosis but not before seeing her beloved brother Crugee. At the end, with Dr. Dubois, trained at the Meharry Medical School, attending her, she rallied around one in the afternoon, saying, "I'll wait on my brother." Crugee was making the long journey from his Double A Ranch on horseback, walking from time to time to rest his horse. He arrived about three o'clock. Entering the sick room, he embraced his sister, said a few words, and she died.

Annie's eldest boy, Washington, was the one known as Stripet. He'd run a successful blacksmithing business in Beggs but fell deathly ill and had to undergo a painful and costly operation at the Mayo Clinic in Rochester, Minnesota. The surgery he had undergone took bone from his leg to shore up his spine, enabling him, after extensive therapy, to sit up without so much pain. In 1933, during his extended recovery, his wife, Grace, and their ten-year-old daughter, Marcelle, accompanied him on a long train journey for one of several visits to the clinic. Grace would sell most of the mineral rights to her Allotment land while Stripet mortgaged the 160 acres he owned south of Beggs to pay their bills. When Grace and Stripet lost their land, they moved to his mother's house in town. By then, Annie had moved to the country to care for Crugee's second set of children after their mother died.

Annie would mortgage her own land to pay for a handsome casket for her husband Lewis. Although she would outlive him by many years, undaunted, she continued to run the farm with the help of her sons, Leo, Stripet, and Andrew. In adolescence, Andrew would gain the name "Crugee," which some associated with "little turtle." Although her family took turns bringing in the harvests for the extended Adams clan, Annie was too proud to have her sons work for anyone outside her blood relatives. This stance would later prove pivotal when cash was tight.

Annie spoke a form of Muskogee (or "Creek") with her sons. After the hard labor of the week, they were fond of sitting in the yard and speaking Creek among themselves on a Saturday or Sunday afternoon. They would talk and smoke their corncob pipes, including Annie, who savored her tobacco.

As the seasons turned, other family gatherings brought together the extended clan. When it was time to fish, the family would gather on the riverbanks for a few days. Arriving in wagons that were covered at night to serve as sleeping quarters, the women organized meals while the men prepared the concoction that would coax the fish into submission. Sometimes the family—fifty or sixty strong—would come together in the fall to reap hay or to butcher three or four hogs for the coming winter. Similarly, holidays were a communal affair, carried out among the family wagons at a nearby campground.

Crugee Adams

Unlike his mother, my maternal grandfather, Crugee, openly took part in religious and community events, including traditional stomp dances. His daughter, my mother Mary, has fond memories of the turtle shell rattles her father strapped on for round dances. Little constrained his joie de vivre. Crugee was a handsome, trim man with jet black hair and skin the rich red color of rosewood. With his high forehead, his face beamed intelligence while his eyes were perpetually crinkled with humor. More than happy-go-lucky, Crugee was all focus when he wrestled steer, bucked broncos, and lassoed cattle for prize money in the rodeos that came to Beggs, Tulsa, or other neighboring towns. He rode alongside famous riders that traveled the rodeo circuit, demonstrating the bulldogging technique perfected by Bill Pickett (biting the lip of the steer to bring it under control). Stories about this charismatic man are legion. Lauded for his skill and beloved for his warmth and humor, tales of his prowess abound.

Crugee attended the Nuyuka Mission Indian School, where his grandfather, Tom Adams, had been a founding board member. He stayed until about sixth grade, when Annie decided he was needed at home.[53] Big-hearted and gregarious, Crugee mingled with everyone. He was therefore no stranger to the town's pool hall, and of course he was very handy with a cue stick. Wagering enlivened the play and Crugee's reputation was for winning. One story goes that Sam Stell, one of the usual crowd, was jealous of the charismatic Crugee. Determined to best him, one day Sam challenged Crugee again and again to yet another round of pool. Finally, losing got to the sorry player and he threatened to kill Crugee. Stell set off to get his gun and was on his way back when he encountered Monroe Brown, one of the pool hall regulars. On hearing the threat, Monroe had stepped away to Stripet's house where he knew that, like most places during that time, a loaded rifle stood at the ready behind a kitchen door.

The two gunmen met near Stripet's blacksmith shop. Monroe shot Sam Stell dead with a single bullet, dismayed that Stell had the nerve to threaten Crugee. When the sheriff arrived at the scene, he checked to see if the weapon that Monroe had used to bring Sam down actually belonged to Stripet and the rifle was placed back behind the kitchen door. Although the sheriff did arrest Monroe Brown, he was quickly released. In the eyes of the town,

Figure 13. Crugee Adams. Collection of the author.

Crugee's defender was not guilty of a crime and he was never charged, let alone tried or imprisoned.

Rich from mineral royalties, as well as handsome and charming, Crugee had the pick of the ladies. He married an attractive colored girl from Musk-ogee, a town dominated at the time by moneyed "Negroes" aspiring to set up profitable businesses beyond the taint of entrenched Southern racism. Cru-gee's wife, Connie, was an Allison, her mother a Dixon. The Dixons were one of several families drawn to the promise of greater opportunities that the growing town of Muskogee offered.[54] However, their time there was brief, as they soon moved away to pass for White, the last of them slipping off in the middle of the night.

During the height of Muskogee's golden days, times also were good among the Creeks, as many oil wells were pumping black gold. Those who attended Crugee and Connie's lavish celebration recalled that the couple received half a dozen new cars as wedding gifts. Like many wealthy Creeks, Crugee would be assigned a guardian to protect his interests. By some accounts, Crugee was worth a million dollars when he turned twenty-one. Sadly for the bright young couple, Connie Allison would die following the birth of their fourth child.

Figure 14. Connie Allison. Collection of the author.

Crugee's second marriage with Sallie Harjo, a full-blood Creek, would produce three children before Sallie died of a fever. Fueling tales of his virility, at sixty, Crugee would marry a Black woman of twenty-nine, Grace Miller, with whom he had three boys and three girls, making for a grand total of thirteen children spanning thirty years—an entire generation. With his rainbow of wives, Crugee would have children who spanned the entire spectrum of people of color. Some had hazel eyes, some were cinnamon-skinned, while others were pale or dusky. Their varied features carried no superfluous baggage. Crugee taught them that they were all sisters and brothers, all one family. This rainbow clan, all born on Allotment land, sprang from the melding populations sharing lives on the western frontier. The blood quanta that preoccupied federal bureaucrats were of no concern to them.[55]

As the children grew, the nearby town of Beggs shifted from a White town to one with a considerable African American presence (today nearly one in five inhabitants are African American, well above the national average of 13 percent).[56] More like the intersection of a main thoroughfare with a couple of lesser streets, the town's population mingled freely. My mother, Mary, recalls that racial divisions were absurd in the mind of the sheriff, who refused to enforce Jim Crow laws requiring separate drinking fountains and toilets. While these laws ossified race relations in the South, the sheriff was adamant: "This here is Beggs," he said. "We don't have that kind of thing here."[57]

One source of tension arose from pressure to send the Adams children to Indian boarding schools. The close-knit family agonized over the difficult choice of entrusting their young ones to the distant schools or keeping them close at hand. The choices were not good ones. The boarding schools punished students for speaking Creek and, high-minded as they might be, the conditions were crowded and often filthy. Students returning home at the holidays frequently were flea-bitten and riddled with lice, making shaved heads nearly synonymous with an Indian school education.[58]

As one of only a few towns on the Bee Line between Tulsa and the county seat at Okmulgee, the Beggs catchment area had a large enough student body to warrant two segregated schools. Indians were not admitted to the White school but could enroll in the Phillis Wheatley public school. Completion of a stoic attendance at the Indian schools was a badge of honor for those who had suffered separation from the family and endured the strictures of an assimilationist curriculum. Those who stayed behind in Beggs were drilled in the heroism of the colored school's namesake. At neither school were Indians, or their ways, truly valued.[59]

The families' decisions created rifts between its members that were reinforced by the different educations their children received. These conditions may have nudged many members of the Adams clan to further disassociate themselves from the tribe while attempting to maintain the family's stature in the growing community. Without the presence of their mother, the fate of Crugee's first set of children led to disputes between well-meaning relatives who sought to safeguard the family's integrity only to see it compromised as pride and fierce independence battled with the collective spirit of shared values that had held the Adams clan together.

The family's struggles would be exacerbated, both through loss of wealth and increasing debt. Misfortune had been no stranger to Crugee or his beloved Double A Ranch. His early wealth was such that the government had seen fit to appoint a financial guardian to oversee his accounts. Sadly, the guardian placed most of Crugee's holdings in his own wife's name then apparently "died" under suspicious circumstances, leaving the formerly wealthy Crugee in virtual poverty and the guardian's family set for life.

Meanwhile, Crugee worked hard to provide for his growing family but did not fail to have fun in the process. Despite his excellent marksmanship and skill at hunting, fishing, and generally carousing with the fellas, Crugee made the most of his time with his children. One version of an oft-told tale recounts that to teach them to swim, Crugee gathered his sons and daughters down at the pond below the vegetable garden. Through the dense brambles of the wild berry bushes, the pond was brown and murky. The hogs that sometimes found their way there were not put off by the long green snakes that sometimes skimmed its surface. Though it's possible that Crugee may have indulged in some early imbibing that summer afternoon, he might just have been amused and ready for a little fun. Whatever the reason, he took each child in turn out to the middle of the pond. On his muscular shoulders they might only have been taking a cool ride. But, once the water was deep enough to come to his chin, he let them go and, retreating to the bank, told them to learn to swim. His daughter Mary recalls that the boys made it to the bank just fine, while she struggled, both terrified and thrilled that her dad could be so daring.

The Bounteous Land

The Adams clan was proud to say that they were entirely self-sufficient. The only thing that had to be purchased was flour from the mill. All else was grown, raised, hunted, or bartered for within the family. If what is known about the Adams's religious practices forms a slender chapter in their history, their reputation as farmers was widespread. For a time, the plans Tom Adams realized for his spread ensured self-sufficiency for his family. The fruits from a mixture of fields, pastures, and orchards yielded a bounty of smoked meats, canned fruits and vegetables, beans and grains, plus sweet milk and butter. Dried apricots, English walnuts, pecans, and hickory nuts were carefully stored against the harsh winters, while fish from Adams Creek, quail, pheasant, squirrel, rabbit, and deer from the forests, supplied by Tom's sons, graced the table, each in its seasonal splendor.

Throughout their lives, the Adams family leased land for oil and gas rights continuously. As early as 1910, Thomas Jefferson Adams's wife, Mahala, was leasing land to prospectors. By 1914, both she and Thomas had passed away, leaving the land to their children who, in turn, leased it, mortgaged it for cash, and repaid loans for the release of the land.

The Adams family may have thought of itself as progressive. Unfettered by the old ways, they were proud of the productivity of their Allotment land, the fruits of their labor. Keeping their land within the proud family was a high priority. Just as Annie did not allow her boys to work for other families, the Adamses tried hard to keep their land among their kin. Records in the Okmulgee County Courthouse show that an Adams with the means to do so would loan money to another family member using that member's land as collateral. The land was then released on repayment. Again and again, the records show the mortgaging and remortgaging agreements among the Adams family, with those who were able coming to the rescue of those undergoing hard times. Still, even when times were good, some would come to sell their land.

Ole man Tom's daughter, Martha, was eighteen and in the early days of her marriage to Peter Boon when she put the land bordering Beggs up for sale. The sale followed her application to unrestrictedly alienate a part of her allotment for town site purposes. The Department of the Interior agreed and on November 17, 1905, it granted her application to sell the land at fifty dollars per acre, or two thousand dollars. Still, as that parcel passed out of her control, she amassed more. On August 5, 1907, Martha granted her husband power of attorney to select land for their deceased son, William Washington.[60] Hanging onto the land would become harder as restrictions tied to blood quantum affected every transaction.

"Energetic to Accomplish an Undertaking"

During the 1920s and 1930s cash was hard to come by as parcel by parcel of Allotment land was sold off or taken by the banks that were eager to extend loans to property-holding Indians and mixed-bloods.[61] A large chunk of Annie's land would go to pay for her son Stripet's operations. As the Adams's land diminished, the family would regroup on one of their other landholdings as grandparents went to live with their children or their adult grandchildren. Although Annie had a fine house in town, she moved to the country to help the widowed Crugee raise his children. At the time, Crugee, unable to sustain his own farm, was living on his sister Ethel's land. At the age of forty-four, for the first time, the once wealthy Crugee was forced to work for people other than his kin. The pay from his day job at a lumberyard did not go far.

The Adamses would borrow just enough money from the banks or neighbors to tide them over until the crops came in. Their vast hay meadow supplied many farms in the vicinity and folks knew they could be counted on to repay the loans. Yet one loan too many, one crop that failed, meant that part of the hay meadow was lost, then another parcel, and then most of it.

An image etched in the mind of Crugee's child Mary was of Annie, standing proud in her immaculately starched apron but with shoulders slumped, as she met the tax collector who came to the farm's gate to take possession, in lieu of the cash they did not have, of her most prized Jersey cow. Annie stood a long time after she'd closed the gate, watching the dust rise as the revenuer led the Jersey off down the road. To give up the source of so much pride, the font of her renowned milk, cream, and butter, made the always dignified women break down in tears.

Throughout adversity, the self-reliant family hung together. Unmindful of their relative poverty, Crugee's children remember living a charmed life of plenty, plenty from the fields and groves, and abundant love in the safety of the fold. Instead, of having store-bought toys, the children built corrals with sticks for the grasshoppers they used as cattle and the ants they collected to serve as horses. Under Annie's critical gaze they helped out with jobs like fanning flies from the apricots they dried on the tin roofs of the sheds, or dropping freshly churned butter into the cool depths of the well. My mother, Mary, fondly remembers baking days and seasonal canning, smoking meats, and gathering hickory nuts from beneath the stately trees that bordered the eastern paddocks.

In a reversal of sorts, when his second set of children began to head off to college, Crugee moved back to town so he could walk to work. His rambunctious days over, Crugee and his third wife, Grace, settled into a comfortable routine as they raised the last half-dozen of Crugee's brood. Their much-reduced circumstances did not diminish Crugee's regard within the community, his many jokes and tall tales, or his affable presence at Roosevelt's Beer Garden at the edge of town. Crugee's always jolly take on life would see him spry to the end, with only one or two strands of gray at the temples of his neatly combed head.

When he died, to accommodate the crowd, his funeral was held at the Baptist Church in Beggs. The ceremonies lasted two days, with services in Creek and English. The food came streaming forth from all segments of the community. Tables groaned with the abundance normally reserved for the traditional Busk, a Green Corn Ceremony, with every type of corn-based dish represented.[62] But unlike the celebration with corn that marked the end of the purifying fast required for a child's naming, Crugee's celebration marked the end of a time when pride and ability were tempered by humor and devotion to the clan. Crugee was proud of who he was, of his rainbow family. That legacy abides in each and every one of his progeny.

Making Do

The Davis/Bowlin and the Adams clans shared the experiences of acquiring and cultivating land in a manner consistent with the ideals embraced by founding fathers, such as Washington, Adams, Jefferson, and Madison, who as gentlemen farmers took a serious interest in botany.[63] In hindsight, expectations that the families within Indian Territory would settle into the same agricultural rhythms as their White counterparts seem absurd.

The algorithm that determined the nature and extent of acreage to be granted in relation to the strength of each individual's ties to the Cherokee or Creek Nation adds a singular dimension to their stories, a complex overlay to America's agrarian history. In securing their lands, the families' claims in regard to race, kinship, and tribal identity formed a subtext of manipulated truth. For the Bowlin/Davis and the Adams families, the truth was manipulated both by federal policies and individual ambition. For all these reasons, laying out these family histories made me long for a more honest assessment of the Allotment Era, but the process of claiming their race, even at this late date, seemed equally important.

Initially, correcting the record and, by extension, interrogating interpretations of America's historical accounts was very far from my intent. As I delved into land records and checked the backstory with my elders, I was drawn further down an investigative path that I could not resist. How these families were able to make do was at times heroic.

In 1930, pursuant to Section 4 of the act of Congress of May 10, 1928,[64] the land allotted to Martha (who'd remarried) was designated as tax exempt "as long as the title thereto remains in the said Martha Adams, now Powell, or in any Fullblood Indian heir or devisee of said lands" not to extend beyond April 26, 1956.[65]

The language contained in Martha's allotment papers speaks volumes about the mood in the old Territory on the eve of the Great Depression. It evokes the good intentions of those who would give Indians a fair start through tax exemptions, yet it raises all the still-unresolved issues surrounding the use of racial quantum that distinguishes the United States from many other nations in oversimplifying the pedigree of its mixed-race peoples. It also placed time limits on that fair start, ensuring that taxes would fall due, eventually. Meanwhile, members of the Adams family were becoming increasingly diverse as Indian Territory attracted all manner of settlers and additional policies designed to undermine tribal integrity took hold. It appears as though the Adams family embraced this particular period of multiculturalism as evidenced on a census card that lists a fellow marrying into the family as Hosey (a clear misspelling of the Hispanic "Jose").

By the time that tax collectors counted full-blood Creek allotees among their debtors, the federal government would be engaged in designing policies to end Washington's special trust relationship with Indian nations.[66] These policies sought to extinguish self-determination, pressing the idea that tribes had become remnants, that blood dilution had obscured distinct tribes and eroded their cultures to such a degree as to render them nonexistent. In the words of Angie Debo, it was "the road to disappearance," the only viable end point in the minds of those who oversaw Indian Territory at that time.[67]

Family elders describe the tactics that census takers employed to underestimate degrees of Indian blood. Some simply discounted any claims of Indian blood since phenotypes could be interpreted to suit the purpose of undermining land claims. As for language, speaking Creek was something done in private, among relatives or close friends, a cultural practice not often probed by White census takers. These pressures to assimilate, coupled with a push to take up farming, led many with higher ambitions to leave the land they'd tried to safeguard. Still others, beat down by unrelenting carpetbaggers, made their way to Arizona, Texas, or nearby Kansas.

Some determined to dig in their heels. For many years, the Adams family managed to carry on its proud traditions. A photo of Tom Adams that hung in the Council House in Okmulgee became a touchstone for the family's place in the region. Adams Creek ran through their land, while the Adams Cemetery guarded their pedigree.

The Adams Cemetery contains the remains of Tom Adams, his wife Mahala, and their sons and daughters. Tom's grave is marked by a large and handsome obelisk, heavily engraved; its pyramidal apex rises higher than the other stones despite the weighty dignity conveyed in the tombstone's heft.

As with the Bowlins' family burial ground, over the years, inclusion in the cemetery was based on the purity of bloodlines, although skin color might occasionally trump blood. Matriarchs or patriarchs conferred in private over who might find their final resting place in that hallowed ground. Though some might mutter complaints, all respected the authority of the Adams clan to recognize its own.

In the ensuing years, the Adams family continued to be proud of its history and origins. The men were strong, handsome, skillful, enterprising members of the community, while the women were capable and independent. In the face of adversity or calamity, they could be relied upon to offer a steady hand and a determination that commanded respect. In 1971, reflecting the new-found pride of the American Indian Movement (AIM), Willie Adams, a great-grandson of ole Tom, was among the vanguard of Indians who occupied the Island of Alcatraz—a clear indication of continued connections to native roots, if not the Muscogee Nation per se.

Ultimately adversity would wear on the family, leading them to make hard choices that would take them far from the land of their birth. Specific details, contained in the records of land transfers in the Okmulgee County Courthouse, help describe their fate.

The Land Dwindles

Like an open book, land gives a clue to the shifts that time had wrought on the Indian, mixed-blood, and freedmen allotees. In 2006, I combed the files of the Okmulgee County Courthouse to clarify a number of questions that I had about the Adams land that my family couldn't answer. Tracing land transfers from the Allotment period to the present made clear the legal ownership of the land where my mother and I were born, as well as the hardships of holding on.

In the brittle pages of the giant leather ledgers, I found that by the time ole man Tom Adams passed away, his entrepreneurial vision was already dimming as a series of setbacks compromised the Adams's properties. As early as May 1929, Adams land was sold to the county to cover expenses when bartering wouldn't do. In 1931, the county sheriff held a lien against Lewis and Annie's property, with the Pickering Lumber Sales Company listed among the plaintiffs. In the dead of winter, on a chill January morning, the property was sold at auction to J. C. Milner for four hundred dollars. The Adamses would borrow from Pickering Lumber again and again, repaying loans when the harvest or butchering went well and revising the conditions of loans when times were hard.

By 1944, both Annie and Crugee were widowed. Faced with more debt, they sold land to C. N. Gilbert, a White man working in the oil fields and living west of Beggs. At least in that exchange, the Gilberts and their daughter Betty Jean were friends of the family. In late summer and early fall, Annie and Mrs. Gilbert would frequently spend days together canning.

Occasionally, the sale of Adams land was dictated by the right-of-way of Oklahoma Natural Gas for the construction of pipeline. Initially, mineral rights were exempted from the land allotment restrictions, but blood quantum and a limited timeline also affected the implementation of this rule. By the 1930s, the Adamses were selling oil and gas plus mineral rights in one-year increments. Transfers of ownership also took place among the many adopted relations, half-brothers and -sisters, and the minors or guardians who formed the extended Adams family.

Crugee's children had been shocked to learn, on his death, that the land they thought of as their home belonged to his nephew Leo. Leo had acquired the land when times were hard for Crugee. Annie's son had never been able to buy back the property that was originally allotted to his beloved sister Ethel, the land where all of his sets of children where raised. Once he'd retired, Leo would sell part of that land to his brother Chester. In their retirement the two brothers returned there (Leo from California and Chester from Detroit), establishing homes in tract houses that were equipped with the regulation stove, refrigerator, and washer and dryer that the Bureau of Indian Affairs (BIA) provided in keeping with the brothers' tribal eligibility.[68] Each would live out the rest of their days on the land originally allotted to Ethel that lay south of Beggs. Leo grilled chicken to accompany his well-earned martinis, while Chester was a fixture at the Creek Nation Bingo Hall, never missing a meal for seniors.

In *Black, White, and Indian: Race and the Unmaking of an American Family*, Claudio Saunt profiled Chester and his views on race. The entry claims Black ancestry for my great-great-grandfather, the Creek chief justice, Thomas Jefferson Adams, and notes visibly African features in his children.[69] Yet, Chester asserts that some of the family passed for White while other members were considered Black. Growing up, he recalls, "when I went to the store with my black cousins . . . we sat in the segregated section. When I went with my white cousins, we sat in the white section." When Chester went alone, he sat wherever he wanted. In retirement, Chester had found Beggs more segregated after his many years in Detroit, but he chose to pass the autumn of his life on the land originally allotted to his kin.[70]

Eventually, the land would pass on to Leo's and Chester's progeny. Chester's only daughter, Paula, would sell her portion, leaving only about eight acres from the original five thousand reportedly held by the Adams clan to Leo's children who, just as their parents did, reside in California.

And so it went, with brother selling to brother or as the land passed from father to daughter, on down to the present, the Adams family holdings cover a period of more than a century. That legacy carries with it a reverence for the vision that Thomas Jefferson Adams had for the land. Buoyed forward by his descendants, themselves larger-than-life characters, his stature is enough to leave the present generation with the conviction that we form but an insipid shadow of our ancestors, but we are also part of an extraordinary lineage. It would take four generations before the Adamses produced another attorney (another Andrew) and the first of Tom's descendants to earn a doctoral degree (that would be me). Ironically, in 2005, an election campaign poster for "Pickering" (perhaps related to the family that alternately bailed out and indebted the Adams family over the years) hung prominently on the wooden fence near the gate to the last remaining parcel of Adams's land.

Leaving the Land

Following the Depression, the family's pride and poverty would feed disenchantment with the land, painting a bleak future for those who had placed their hopes on continuing Tom Adams's vision. Soon enough, World War II would give the young men a taste of more exotic shores, making it especially hard to "keep 'em down on the farm, after they'd seen Paree."

The young women also hoped for more than the grinding drudgery of farm life devoid of indoor plumbing and electricity. Only a generation before, the Adams spread had been considered the epitome of progress. The desire to rise above the mundane would continue its strain through the proud Adams family as its sons and daughters considered themselves "special." Tom's entrepreneurial spirit, Annie's calm determination, and Crugee's charisma would be matched in the next generation by Mary Louise Adams. Crugee's second daughter, the feisty girl whose long tumbling locks inspired her nickname, Jelly Red, is my mother.

With an impish charm, Jelly Red would win over her family and teachers. Her endless questions and boisterous nature would tax her older sister Ethel and her grandmother Annie, who would raise Crugee's children when his wife died shortly after the birth of their second son. But Annie would not stay mad at Jelly Red for long. The girl's outgoing ways conveyed a joyous warmth and an infectious energy that clearly amused her aging grandmother.

When Jelly Red married John Davis, they moved to Vinita and into the fold of the less demonstrative but no less capable Bowlin/Davis clan. Mary was impressed with the well-ordered household overseen by her mother-in-law, Henrietta. The big country kitchen was a focal point for the large family and there was always an elaborate meal in the making. In the poultry yard, fat chickens were killed, plucked, and prepped for diner. Handy with needle and thread, John's sisters gathered frequently to quilt, crochet, embroider, and tat but also to sew suits and dresses, or jackets and winter coats, in the latest styles and colors. The Davis larder brimmed with canned vegetables and preserved fruits, while the meticulously kept barn held gleaming tools and plenty of feed for the livestock.

Though life was full for John and Mary, they were soon tempted to join the Great Migration north. When a cousin returned home for the holidays driving a Cadillac and assuring John that he could earn more money on the auto assembly lines than working for the railroad, the young father headed to Detroit. He returned quickly to fetch Mary and their two young daughters. The bustling industrial city offered opportunities not found in rural Oklahoma. One by one, Jelly Red persuaded her brothers to move north. Andrew Jr., with two years at Langston University on the GI bill, had little

Figure 15. Mary Louise Adams (Jelly Red). Collection of the author.

Figure 16. The Davis family with Annie Adams. From the papers of Frances Wooten Lax. Courtesy of Beverle Lax.

hope of using his education in Beggs. Mary convinced him to take a chance on Detroit. He was soon working alongside John at Pontiac Motors. Amos, Crugee's youngest son and a veteran of the Korean War, would eventually bring his wife and son to the Motor City. Elder sister, Ethel (named for her father's sister), would take a more circuitous path, first following her husband to Missouri then trying to make a life in Los Angeles. By the late 1950s, her siblings enticed her to join them in Detroit. It wasn't like home, but they were together.

Others of Mary's generation found work just over the Oklahoma state line in Wichita, Kansas. As their respective families grew, memories of their childhood homes in Oklahoma would mist over, shrouding the difficulties of eking out a living on exhausted soil with too few hands, while the good ole days were tinged with a rosy glow.

Mary captured some of the nostalgia in a longhand remembrance:[71]

Growing up as the great grand daughter of a Native American Chief gave me a feeling of being a special person. My father and the rest of the family spoke of this man as a great leader of the tribe.

All families lived nearby. When it came to hunting, fishing, gathering the crops and any major jobs that had to be done, all the family around would come and give a hand until it was finished. The women got together to can food or to help each other finish their quilting. If anyone was sick or hurt they would go and cook for that family member or wash their clothes—just anything to help out. Get the kids off to school just about anything they could do to fill in and take care of one another.

After all the crops were in and they could relax and go fishing then all the families would meet at the river and they brought all their families in wagons. The men would go upstream and place the roots (the Devil's Shoe String) that had been gathered wrapped and tied in bundles in the river. Soon you could see the fish rise to the top. They came up to get air. All the men would take up their bow and arrows and shoot the fish—only what we needed, and after a while the fish would be alright, it only lasted a short time. As you know, they never took more than they needed or could use, the rest was dried for later use.

We had lots of fun. It was like a feast where we got together and saw new babies that had been born. The women visited with each other and you got to know your kinfolk. Some of the new born were delivered by my grandmother [Annie]. She would go with anyone that came to get her, sometimes staying all night until the baby was delivered. I would see her gather up twine, tallow (beef fat), in a bucket and other items that she would need and it was after I became a teenager that she would tell me where she was going and what she was doing.

She was a remarkable woman; doing all and anything she could to help the family. It would not be taken lightly if any time you denied or refused a family in any way [where] you could offer help. If they needed help, a place to stay, or food to eat, she would always give a helping hand.

She always talked things over with her sons on any issues that came up and they would take care of the business at hand, always check with her sons about anything. They never disagreed with her or talked back to her, they gave her the utmost respect and so did anybody else—all races. She was truly the matriarch and the ruler of the families and all of her descendants on both sides.

There were always meetings at the Council House, discussing what and how they would handle any problem that came about. My uncle, Washington Adams (Stripet), Charley Ward, Jim Allen, and Bill Lovall, they went to the White House and talked to the President about the treaty that was signed and was not honored. All they ever got were promises and delays or they were put off and given a later date and then that would be cancelled.

They continued to raise money to go to Washington, most times never getting to talk to anyone, but they were determined. They were treated unfairly and were very hurt and disappointed. Things were taken away from them as if they were nobody and they did not get any help or get anyone to pay attention to them.

All the while, they continued to farm and do what was necessary to keep what they had, to take care of their families. My uncle and father did carpenter work, building houses, going to the butcher's house and getting the meat ready to go to the grocery stores or the meat market. They were very skilled in what they called dressing out the beef or pork for market.

I cherish the time I spent with them. They were all wonderful and good people. They loved children and would put them first. We never felt that we were not loved.

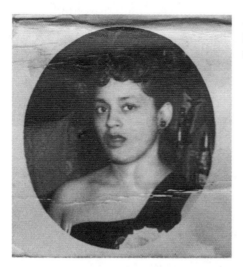

Figure 17. Mary Louise Adams, on a matchbook cover. Collection of the author.

As the Adams family spread across the nation, each member sought the economic stability that eluded them on their allotted lands. The identities they forged were as varied as their skin color, but each retained a pride in their Adams pedigree and the land where they were born. They were no less than the descendants of Thomas Jefferson Adams, member of the House of Warriors and chief of the Muscogee Creek; of Annie Adams, midwife for Okmulgee and Muscogee Counties; and of Crugee Adams, a man of equal parts charm, skill, and the authority that wisdom and a generous heart command.

Members of the conjoined Adams and Davis families would develop strong ties, maintaining a network to carry news as well as hickory nuts from Beggs, or pickled okra from Bowlin Spring, to their wandering kin. Leonard Bowlin's children were largely content with the bustling rhythms of running the country store, but some married and moved to larger towns near main highways like Vinita or Nowata where Joe Davis established his veterinary practice. Then there were those who were eager to claim the good life promised in sunny California.

For members of both families, the moves away from their land may have seemed a temporary measure, designed to generate enough money to return at a later date to the land they loved. As far as possible, they tried to live in close proximity to each other, returned home often, and always talked lovingly

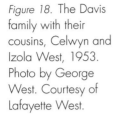

Figure 18. The Davis family with their cousins, Celwyn and Izola West, 1953. Photo by George West. Courtesy of Lafayette West.

of their elders. As Leo and Chester approached retirement they returned to Oklahoma more frequently. When they finally moved back to Beggs, neither one seemed to miss California or Michigan, where they'd made their careers. Unlike my mother's siblings, they had come full circle. Fortunately for them, they had Allotment land to return to.

In tracing the Adams's land transfers to the present—while tracking each family's move away from the Sooner State—at last, I had an inkling of why my family waxed nostalgic for "home" but couldn't find their way back. They wanted to return to more certain times, when their family names garnered respect, when their lands were bounteous, and when their color wasn't contested by Whites, Blacks, or Reds. Then, they had a sense of belonging and purpose that eluded them as they moved further away. But unlike Leo and Chester, it wasn't quite so easy to go home again. Tom Adams's once grand two-story house had caved in and the Adams cemetery was overgrown. Even though family members were settling in California, the Bowlin/Davis clan's enclave remained largely intact, if somewhat insular. Among the Adamses, only Leo and Chester, both passed on now, had managed to hold onto the last of the Adams allotment land. For my mother, her sister, and their brothers, the land that they'd called home was gone.

The answers I sought have led to more questions. In reclaiming the

Figure 19. Mary, Andrew Sr., Andrew Jr., and Chester Adams on the last of the Adams land. Photo by the author.

memories, identities, and values of my relations I wonder: Did an overreliance on the federal government doom the Adams family through unfounded optimism that they would share in a brighter future? Was the Bowlin family better able to parley their smaller holdings into a more stable prosperity through a greater self-reliance or a shrewder mistrust in the political climate in the spanking-new state of Oklahoma? Are Americans ready to hear about the Allotment policies that led to the loss of identity, land, language, family ties, and self-determination for so many mixed-bloods? Do they, or why should they, care? How can we move forward if we fail to honor all the parts of our past?

This is my heritage, the legacy for my generation: to have a deep sense of reverence for the land of my forefathers, pride in their accomplishments, frustration with the policies that shortchanged their worth, and the misfortunes that shortened their halcyon days. Those days may be gone but we forget them at our peril. We all have work to do.

4

Who We Are

And ye shall know the truth, and the truth shall make you free.

—KING JAMES BIBLE, JOHN 8:32

W hen I started this quest, I was looking to find concrete answers about the racial heritage of my family. As I delved into publicly available documents and rummaged among the skeletons in our ancestral closets, the weight of my reclamation project gathered momentum, pushing me beyond a simple family history. The story of our family unfolded to reveal a dual system of racial categorization that was arbitrary, contradictory, and riddled with inaccuracies. My attempts to pinpoint the truth produced evidence that ran counter to the contents of the neatly ordered census cards and carefully microfiched records of the Allotment Era housed in the nation's archives. Making things more interesting still was the fact that I am descended from both Cherokee Freedmen and Muscogee Creeks. I embody the contradictions. My racial identity is a complex mesh of contested claims.

Claiming Race

So here I am, born on allotted land among mixed-race peoples with tribal affiliations, contested racial claims, but a belief that the records can be corrected, that we can honor our mixed-race peoples by telling their stories. I have a stake in America's future. My stake has a moral foundation. I believe that truth brought to light will be valued. I'm convinced that our diversity is a strength, not a burden. Telling the truth about our past requires courage.

If that truth fuels even a slim desire to right the wrongs of the past it might just "widen the trail" for others seeking some measure of racial justice.[1]

The stories revealed here show all manner of prejudices. Blacks are castigated as "wannabes" for believing they have Indian blood. Indians are vilified for kicking "darkies" out of the tribe. And Whites are surprised to find these issues still in dispute, still unresolved.[2] Surely, we are only looking for acknowledgment of who we are, for the respect and dignity that are due.[3] Yet, getting some perspective on these views requires fortitude. It is not for the fainthearted.

My path to understanding the trove of knowledge that I gained in my quest has been long. When I began my search, I wanted financial help to defray the costs of a master's degree. The evidence I had to hand consisted of the roll numbers I found for my paternal Cherokee relations. Only later would I realize that my initial search focused on the low-hanging fruit. All I knew at the time was that I could not hold membership in more than one tribal nation, so I neglected to search my Creek lineage where, in the absence of readily accessible roll numbers, there appeared to be no easy leads. It would be years before I began researching the Creek side of my family, so initially I was left empty-handed in terms of concrete evidence of my Indian heritage. As to getting at the "truth," that task proved to be a larger challenge than I ever could have anticipated for both sides of the family.

Although my uncles' storytelling and jokes could keep everyone howling with laughter, it has been my mother, Mary, who has safeguarded the family history. She is the one who writes, noting significant occasions with poems or capturing thoughts that come in times of quiet moments of reflection. Her inspiration for composition comes almost unbidden but rarely exceeds two sides of an envelope. At one point, it occurred to me that as much as writing meant to her, she would never set down the story of our amazing family, of her charismatic and handsome father, her enigmatic uncle the medicine man, or her grandmother the steadfast midwife.

Though she always deferred to her father's considerable ability to spin colorful yarns, her stories were captivating. Throughout our childhood, she loved recalling the exploits of her dad and the accomplishments of her grandmother. Over the years, she has shared her stories and I have become the scribe. I have learned a great deal as she recalls and I record. One of her favorite stories was about my birth.

Large with her second child, she had gone down to help Grandma Annie bake and prepare for Christmas. I wasn't due until mid-January, so the ninety-mile trip from Vinita down to Beggs didn't seem like an imprudent undertaking. Always the keen hunter, Grandpa Crugee had taken my father out one evening to shoot possum. I imagine them in the light of the full moon, crunching snow as they whispered about other hunts on winters' nights like that one, stopping now and again to orient themselves, deciding whether to keep on into the night or to turn back and head for the warmth of home. Near first light, they appeared at the back door, loud, now that they had their brace of possum. Crugee would be calling for Annie to clean the kill, but the wiry little woman would have stopped their noise, must have said, "Shush now, we're having a baby in here," and sent them back outside.

I surprised everyone by coming early, a full week before Christmas. I came into the world about 7:30 in the morning: Sagittarius, sun, moon, and rising. After he had cleaned the kill and washed up, Crugee examined me and pronounced that I had weak eyes. He'd call me Mousy well before I started wearing glasses. But my real name, one he also gave me, was that of a favorite lady friend. Mom had decided to honor her mother by giving each of her children names beginning with the letter "C." Connie had come first, and I was to be Caroline. On that snowy morning, it was to be otherwise. Jelly Red could not resist her father's request to call me Darnella.

More about me than my eyesight was mousy. A sandy-colored and sandy-haired child, I had a shadowy cast that fit my shyness. This suited my aunt's frequent admonition that children were to be seen and not heard, a stance I later understood as echoing our Indian roots. Children were to learn by observing and keeping silent. Their silence might gain them access to conversations to which they would not otherwise have been privy. In my muffled state, it isn't surprising that I found great interest in books, preferring to read than to be outside playing in the sunshine. The world of books would lead me on a path of continuous learning, introducing me to exotic peoples, fascinating thoughts, and exciting ideas. To my mother's stories I can now add my own.

Her stories and the books I've cherished have not been the only stepping stones along this numinous path. My generation has witnessed quite a bit of history. Growing up in 1960s Detroit, I was swept up in the phenomenal changes brought about by the Civil Rights Movement. During that time, the influence of Martin Luther King Jr. on attitudes about race and pride

Figure 20. John and Mary with five of their six children, 1955. Photo by George West. Courtesy of Lafayette West.

in being Black created tremendous excitement. Many girls in our family abandoned efforts to make their hair appear straighter or longer through the use of synthetic "falls." Several members who could do so proudly grew Afros. I remember walking with my mother, sisters, and brother, down the middle of Woodward Avenue, Detroit's main thoroughfare, in a rally supporting Dr. King. For that day, and it seems all the days hence, Blacks could claim the big industrial city of Detroit as their own.

For the Adams family, the Black Power movement would bring tensions and further divisions because some family members were not Black *enough*. Some felt awkward claiming Blackness when the family was so clearly mixed. Some would also feel more than a little invisible in a society neatly divided between Black and White. The family recalls my brother being beaten up at school on a regular basis because students believed he was Arab, part of the large Middle Eastern community that was settling in Detroit and suburban Dearborn. Once, my mother went to see a teacher about a younger sister's grades. Without bothering to check for my sister's name on the class roster, the teacher informed my mother that she was in the wrong room because there were no White children in her class. Meanwhile, I was pulled along with the wave of affirmative action. Each morning I was bused to a majority White middle school in an attempt to racially balance Detroit Public School's student body.

While busing took me away from the familiarity of my neighborhood and the commuting drained my preteen self-reflection time, I benefitted from aggressive college recruiting at Cass Technical High School, a city-wide exam entry school where I'd studied fashion illustration in the art department. Parsons School of Design, Pratt Institute, Rhode Island School of Design, and even the California School of the Arts regularly sent recruiters with scholarships to our prestigious school. As a public school with a national reputation, Cass Tech offered a convenient concentration of talented minority students for colleges that were inclined to diversify their student bodies. I was overjoyed to find myself a scholarship student at Parsons in New York City.

The experience of New York for a young person like me would boost my confidence out in the wider world while whetting my appetite for travel and new adventures. It also taught me the value of my work ethic as I held my own among my talented classmates. With the allure of learning firmly established, I was more than ready for the lamp of knowledge to guide my path. After working and traveling for a while, going back to school to complete a master's degree in fine arts seemed a natural extension of my early interests. Years later, pursuing a doctorate in education policy enabled me to reflect on opportunities for minorities, a topic that had long preoccupied my thinking. Living in Washington, it made sense to learn about the nation's past through research on federal Indian education policies.[4] My background, education, experiences living in Senegal and Morocco, and traveling even more widely, seem to have taken me on a long but clear path that has led me back to the heart of my family, to uncovering these family histories and appreciating their dense cultural relevance to the racial discourse that is often called for but never seems to arrive. We speak of race but our conversation fails to capture widespread public attention. Rarely does it lead to collective action.

As my inquiry about my forebears progressed, I vowed to make a difference at the personal level. In 1995, our family enjoyed a tour of Indian Country, starting in Albuquerque, looping through the Pueblos, the Navajo

Reservation, along the Grand Canyon, to the Four Corners, and back down through Jicarilla, Taos, and Santa Fe. Pleased to be in a position to expose our children to parts of America still largely inhabited by native peoples, as far as possible we stayed in Indian-run hotels and tried to get off the beaten path.

A visit to the acclaimed Sky City of Acoma Pueblo represented a bit of a dilemma. Visits to the ancient town were strictly regulated with entry fees and timed tickets. We were told that buses would transport sightseers up the steep track leading to the village, depositing them on a plaza that turned out to be replete with gaudy souvenir shops. This scenario was designed to tempt tourists into buying trinkets rather than exploring the cramped confines of the adobe houses perched on the plateau and the narrow passageways running between them. This scheme held little appeal for us as we tend to avoid anything even vaguely touristy. But since Sky City was not to be missed, we agreed to climb the adobe stair rather than take the bus. But first we had to buy our entry tickets.

The two Acoma women behind the ticket counter seemed either bored or jaded, showing no sign of either enthusiasm or interest in their work or potential customers. Perhaps because I wanted to reach out in some way, to make a connection, or maybe because the cost of the tickets for a family of four came to more than we'd expected, I asked if there was a discount for Indians. Rarely has the expression "laughed in my face" been so apt. The women were nearly doubled over with hysterical giggles, so preoccupied with my "joke" as to be unable to respond to my question. Being hopeful, I optimistically took their irresponsiveness as a request for my tribal card, since they clearly didn't "see" me as Indian. Rummaging in my wallet, I pulled it out and handed it to one woman who seemed to be regaining her composure. She traced my "1/16th degree of Indian Blood" designation with her fingernail as she showed the card to her colleague. Now smirking and repressing more giggles, they informed me that there was indeed a reduced rate. We then produced the girls' tribal cards, leaving only my husband to pay full price. That humiliating exchange certainly underscored the parochial vision of Indians who imagine all other Indians as resembling themselves. The experience taught me a lesson about racial stereotyping and what it takes to debunk it. But that was after I'd gotten the tribal cards.

To understand how I got them, we need to go back to the National

Archives. After my failure to obtain a CDIB using my Cherokee links, I shifted gears. Equipped as I was, with only a few roll numbers for my mother's side of the family, my search for a Creek pedigree nonetheless went fairly quickly.[5] Establishing the bloodlines to my maternal grandfather was straightforward in contrast to my claims to Cherokee citizenship through ownership. Staff at the National Archives helped me find the census data, which registered the father, the mother, their ages when the census was taken, and where they lived—sometimes noted as a post office location, sometimes by a landmark such as a river. All this information was legibly listed on field cards that had been microfilmed and filed by drawer number. At that time, the number of drawers filed with Creek Nation census data was not large. The records go back only so far. Before Removal, in the East, all but a very few names are in Creek.

At the height of my research, there were three-hour limits on microfilm reading machines, so I juggled my requests for machines with hour-and-a-half waits for original manuscripts. Hours spent affirming the existence of one relation somehow balanced the sudden revelation of an as-yet-undiscovered or long-forgotten member of the clan. As I worked my way through the files, the available information seemed cryptic and I wanted to know more.

On my last day of research, I asked Jim Rushes up on the top floor—who by then knew me well—whether there was anything I hadn't covered. The Dawes Rolls and their applications, the Parsons and Abbott Rolls, the Guion/Miller Census, and the Wallace Rolls I'd checked and checked again. I'd looked at the Creek census cards, following the long-cold trail east to the non-Anglicized names where I could no longer find my way. I'd photocopied most of the proceedings surrounding the application and subsequent contestation of Georgeanna Thornton's Cherokee Freedmen status, all eighty-four items. So, Jim said, "That's it."

Next, I turned to the Smithsonian Photographic Archives, imagining that there would be many pictures of Creeks in council, all the principal chiefs and at least some of the minor ones. Instead, in less than an hour, I'd gone through every photo of a Creek in the oft-cited collection. Ninety-nine percent of which I'd already seen elsewhere.

The Oklahoma Historical Society was next. Over the phone, someone there had promised to help me with land allotment records.[6] I also contacted the Creek Nation's historian. At each juncture, my project seemed to become both clearer and at the same time larger in scope. Having also drafted a family survey, I realized that I would need to accompany it with a family tree. Query-ing immediate family members quickly led to gaps but also served to jog foggy memories as I tried to match archival and oral histories. Inevitably, there were contradictions. Wading through contemporary histories of Creek or Cherokee society often helped contextualize seemingly conflicting accounts.

By this time, I'd received a final determination from the Cherokee Nation that denied me a CDIB based on a lack of evidence of Indian blood. The fact that federal policy failed to record any degree of Indian blood among Chero-kee Freedmen wasn't taken into account.

As to my quest, once I had my Creek documentation in hand, my next move was to make my application for Muscogee Creek Nation citizenship. I now had the roll numbers and the requisite forms and birth certificates showing my blood lineage, leading back to a recognized member of the tribe—in my case, it was to my grandfather, Crugee. My mother had stub-bornly refused to establish formal ties with the Muscogee Nation, despite the fact that throughout her life she has received minuscule payments for min-eral rights or land settlements. She cited the tribe's indifference to her family when they endured hard times as a reason to shun them. Her resentment shed light on her chilly regard for the Creek officials and her strong loyalty to close family.

In 1991, I attended a conference where the internationally renowned Flathead Salish artist, Jaune Quick-to-See Smith, gave the keynote address.[7] Known for her activism on behalf of beleaguered natives, she has also championed wom-en's rights and focused her oeuvre on the importance of our indigenous cul-tures. In her keynote, Smith urged the attendees to write the history of America as we see it. She said that as minorities and as women our voices are, as yet, ignored. She admonished us to seek council from our elders and to learn to work as a team. Her remarks seemed tailor-made for me, designed to lift me up at a time when I was struggling to make progress. Such encouragement was rare back then and I am very grateful that her words spurred me onward.

Somewhere during this quest, confirmation of my tribal status arrived. The number on my Muscogee Creek tribal card is 43775. My degree of Muscogee Indian blood reads 1/16th, our daughters' cards read 1/32nd.

In an ironic twist, the girls received their cards before I did. After many frustrating inquiries and calls, it finally came to light that mine was the only application that mentioned the possible Delaware connection of my grandmother Annie.[8] In their attempt to research that connection, the Creek authorities had held up my application, even though they had granted citizenship to my daughters months before. In my last telephone conversation with a citizen board bureaucrat, I shed my final tears of exasperation and, with them, my reliance on anyone else to define me.

Any idea I might have entertained of contesting the degree of Muskogeean blood assigned to me, or establishing the bloodlines from my Cherokee forebears, lost its appeal long ago. I've no stomach for wrangling over unsound legalese. Any desire to set my records straight has evolved into a kind of serenity that springs from my knowing who I am, from having answered for myself the questions I posed to my mother, so long ago: Who are we? What part is Indian? Instead, I'm motivated to rectify other records, larger and loftier ones than my single claim.[9] The facts that I've uncovered now prompt me to broadcast the voices of my too-long silenced ancestors, unsung heroes of America's melting pot whose racial identity was forged during the Allotment Era. For them, and for the children who'll one day inhabit America, I want to have my say.

Longing for more telling details from my elders that might guide my search, I tried to read between the lines, alert to the fact that what we don't know is also information. When it comes to minorities, there is evidence and even intention in the gaps in our knowledge.[10] I counted myself extremely lucky to have Georgeanna Thornton's archived testimony, John Bowlin's obituary, records of the deeds of Thomas Jefferson Adams, the interviews of Annie and Charles Chamberlain, plus living relations who could confirm and elaborate many of the stories and facts. That I found myself in a position to bring the threads of these families' lives together was uncanny. Yet, I still found myself wondering about so many unanswered questions.

In the absence of diaries and with only a few letters, I wondered about the ideals of my forebears and the communities they built. How did they see the future? When Thomas Adams designated his boys as half-bloods and left the girls as full-bloods, did he imagine that they would all continue to be equally welcome within the Muscogee Nation? Did he see himself, a member of an Indian tribe in a dual role—a dual citizen, as a patriotic American? When John Bowlin learned that although others had achieved Cherokee citizenship through intermarriage (a policy widely sanctioned until 1877) while he did not, was he content with the nature of the kinships he could actually claim? Having thrived after witnessing the sale of his mother, did Bowlin imagine that there might be fewer opportunities for his children's children?

Revisiting History

My questions join an increasing chorus of other minority voices that are interrogating history and correcting the narrative. In the time since I began this quest, journalists, historians, and students of culture have begun to replace potted histories with more carefully researched stories about the varied experiences of people of color. As my family joined the civil rights marches, traditional historical narratives became a battlefield of contested knowledge. From the 1960s forward, historians sought to redress the neglect of people of color as well as the contributions of women.[11] Their work highlighted the limitations of a male-dominated, Eurocentric point of view and underscored the gaps to be filled in representing the full range of human experience. Traditional history was criticized for silencing ordinary voices in favor of lauding the elite, of celebrating success while skimming over failures and the problematic. Calls for equality demanded a new history that embraced complexity, one that shunned biased and overly simplistic renderings of social and political conflict.[12]

As a result, scholars have provided a more balanced account of the nation's history but also noted the dearth of archival materials that could render the record complete. Primary sources might have illuminated a richer understanding of our collective development had the views of women, minorities, and the poor not been discounted. "The new history has brought us different stories, new actors, fresh images. . . . If they are not all pleasing, they do reflect a recognition that life past and present is complex, a study in shades of grey, rarely black and white."[13] In fresh analyses of extant archival data, historians have realized the centrality of Native Americans and people of color in the American West.[14] Looking at how and why these groups resisted and adapted to the challenges posed by life on the frontier gives us a richer, grittier understanding of our shared experiences. We now recognize that rethinking the past may aid us in reimagining the future, even as we struggle to grasp its complexity.[15]

In 2004, I learned that the University of Kansas and Haskell Indian Nations University were launching a collaborative effort to change how scholars approach identity and culture. For two years, the Shifting Borders of Race and Identity: A Research and Teaching Project on the Native American and African American Experience supported a series of conferences, lectures, seminars, workshops, and exhibits that challenged academics to move beyond binary concepts of "race" and to rethink our notions about identity.

In addition to the vibrant discussions that welcomed independent scholars like me, the Shifting Borders conference produced a compendium of essays and made them available online. Among others contributing to the historical revisionism about the comingling of Reds, Whites, and Blacks, one focus has been to understand the evolution of "race thinking" among indigenous peoples.[16] Some scholars are tracing the shifts from colorblind tribal traditions that readily incorporated outsiders through adoption or intermarriage to the exclusionary policies that echo White supremacist views, even as they serve to safeguard tribal integrity today. Re-examining the interplay of tribal encounters with White traders and settlers is now being contextualized within the ideology and practice of chattel slavery among Indians originating in the Southeast. Revisiting formerly accepted analyses highlights the limitations of both the earlier accounts written from a colonial or settler point of view and the problematic categories used to describe evolving notions of race and racial mixtures. Traditional histories of the Allotment Era have tended to focus on acculturation or land cessions while brushing aside the larger impacts of racial categorizations.

In *African Americans and Native Americans in the Creek and Cherokee Nations*, Katja May brings together a wealth of data and a trove of neglected interviews in reconsidering the Creek and Cherokee Nations as they adapted to new lands in Indian Territory. She plumbs census data that highlight the two tribes' commonalities as well as their differences, especially as they confronted the realities of accepting their former slaves as fellow citizens. Her work raises many questions about conflicting ideologies surrounding race as the Cherokees enacted many laws to keep their race intact.

Foremost among the ideological culprits skewing historical perspectives is "blood." In *Mixed Blood Indians*, Theda Perdue traces the evolution of the term from the eighteenth to the early nineteenth centuries as designations of purity or mixture were used and abused in the pursuit of power and influence in the early South. Fay Yarbrough, in *Race and the Cherokee Nation*, targets the Cherokee Nation as the bellwether of tribal legislation among the Five Tribes. Her study sheds light on regulations governing intermarriage and the legal rights of citizens as they were enacted, practiced, and resisted. Those rights would be defined and redefined in a hierarchy of influence that shifted along with the demographics of the frontier and the need for greater centralization of governance as the authority of clans and traditional towns waned.[17] While Celia Naylor, in *African Cherokees in Indian Territory*, and Claudio Saunt, in *Black, White, and Indian*, revisit the neglected records of Blacks among the Cherokees and Creeks, respectively, in *Ties That Bind*, Tiya Miles exposes the hypocrisy of race-based policies invoked by the Cherokees in mirroring a White ethos. Naylor, Saunt, and Miles each shed light on the glaring mistreatment of many slaves and freedmen who lived, unequally, among these tribes.

Miles, for example, suggests that mixed-bloods might have gained some legitimacy as a distinctive group had their Indian and Black pedigree breached the tripartite Allotment eligibility regulations that admitted only "Indian," "intermarried White," and "freedmen." In the same vein, Krauthamer, writing about the Choctaw and Chickasaw in *Black Slaves, Indian Masters*, laments the lost histories that erased the racial complexity of individuals and families enrolled in the catchall category of "freedmen." She carefully mines the remnants of their archived chronicles to uncover the antecedents of Allotment during Reconstruction when claims to property and race fueled debates over who would command tribal lands. She describes the social and political forces that eventually shaped the allocation of land for most mixed-race tribes. Yet, without clearer explications of individuals' cultural grounding, in contrast to rights as tribal citizens, the conflation of racial purity and cultural integrity may continue to hamper the historiographical progress of triracial studies. In this respect, my family history presents an opportunity to reconsider acculturationist policies from the perspective of those whose progeny have survived. Our families' stories offer a mother lode from which to forge more appropriate terminology in referring to people of Red, White, and Black heritage.

My forebears provide a possible answer to each of these scholars who has stared into a void and decried the lost stories of nameless individuals whose fates go unsung. Undeterred, students of culture have engaged in disassembling the social construction of "race"; they tender theories that reframe the intersection of race, culture, politics, and gender. Reinvigorating the dialogue, they offer new perspectives on the interplay of Red, White, and Black lives in the social construction of identity. These scholars agree on the pivotal influence of Black Indians residing in Indian Territory—whether born into tribes, bought, adopted, or free—that distinguishes their experiences from those whose lives played out in the South.

In *The Color of the Land*, David Chang looks at the intersection of race and landownership among the Creeks, following the torturous trail of land loss prior to, during, and after Allotment. For Chang, the tragedy was in the conflation of race, blood, and culture that devalued people of color and undermined their ability to manage the land ceded to them. In his view, the shift of loyalties from clan and tribe to family and nation was realized through a change in regard for land that was commonly held by the tribe to the acceptance of individual ownership. Part of the shift bucked tradition because women had worked the fields and improved the land. With the push to adopt yeoman farming, men were expected to quit their former roles as hunters and pick up the plow.[18]

Chang describes how Allotment forced the settler practice of *having* land rather than *making* land. For most tribes, this kind of shift took 150 years, but within Indian Territory the change, along with the dismantling of matrilineal productivity, was seen in a mere 40 years.[19] In examining landownership and its relation to slavery, western expansion, Indian resistance, the creation of wealth, and—as Indian influence waned—the rapid shift to White supremacy, Chang views Oklahoma's borders as encapsulating American history in miniature. It was the land of the Red man, for a time fostered the Black Belt, and yet can still be called "White Man's Country."[20]

The legacy of the Allotment policies is discussed by Circe Sturm in *Blood Politics: Race, Culture, and Identity in the Cherokee Nation of Oklahoma*, a work on race and nation building among the Cherokees that broaches the topic of how far a blood connection can stretch and still warrant a tribal identity. Strum's ethnographic research among the Cherokees offers personal perspectives on the cultural versus the biological basis of the term *full-blood*. Such research is critical as the Cherokees include Whites with 1/1000th or even less of Indian blood among their members but rejected those whose forebears might be three-quarters Cherokee but displayed some "African" feature that placed them among the freedmen. Methodologically, she acknowledges the risks and benefits in the heterologic nature of her approach, which is as much about the self as about the meaningful interaction of the self and "other."[21] She also notes an absence of ethnographic research in Cherokee communities that, at one juncture, stretched from 1972 to 1995.[22]

Each of these scholars has taken a close look at a specific tribe, segment of time, geopolitical location, or racial construction. They are asking more interesting questions about notions of race, which, over time, evolved among the continent's indigenous peoples. Each has a piece of the puzzle that lends greater authenticity to the story we will pass on to future generations. Their work underscores the value in my family's extraordinary ability to resurrect the voices of our forebears in relaying the richness of our story to our children's children. That value lies at the nexus of historical writing and personal voice. I have felt the tensions surrounding standards of objectivity and the emotional involvement of recounting lived experiences, the limitations of cold facts and the liabilities inherent in symbolic truth. I have learned that this family story even has a label: "Presentism, the exercise of connecting the past to the present."[23] Rather than a mark against students of history, presentism is broadening the road. Similarly, for those working to make the past relevant, there should be no shame in stressing experience over theory. Slowly scholars are reaping the fruits of positing alternative interpretations and different, even personal, points of view that may counter those previously tendered as "omniscient, neutral objectivity."[24]

During National American Indian Heritage Month, November 2009, the Smithsonian Institution's National Museum of the American Indian initiated a dialogue about family and race in its exhibit, *IndiVisible: African-Native American Lives in the Americas*.[25] Under the auspices of the National Museum of African American History and Culture and the Smithsonian Institution Traveling Exhibition Service, the collection has crisscrossed the nation, ideally engaging people of all backgrounds in examining their thoughts about "Black Indians" and their descendants.[26]

There are many threads in the "unsettled issues of conquest" that color our national narrative.[27] As more information becomes available to a wider audience, we may be increasingly ready to move past stereotypes for a more nuanced recounting of the rich and varied experiences of African Americans with mixed bloodlines. Increasingly, fair-skinned peoples of mixed racial heritage no longer need fear that they will be discovered as passing for White (as did Anatole Broyard, the *New York Times* literary critic whose African American heritage was revealed only on his death). In a memorable commencement address, the writer Anna Quindlen suggested that graduates may do "better" than their parents if, among other things, they are the first generation to "see race and ethnicity as attributes, not stereotypes."[28] That would be progress indeed at a time when not every American citizen is treated like one.

One enticing possibility is that the science of DNA will spark both interest in and discussion of our collective origins and their myriad variations. Apart from the dilemma of parsing race and ethnicity from our unique biological genomes, for the moment, a crucial limitation exists in the relatively small representation of minorities in most databases.[29] When I submitted my first cheek swab, I expected my DNA search to reveal roughly equal parts Red, White, and Black. The European part was 35 percent (combining the somewhat arbitrary categories of northern European and Mediterranean), while the African portion came to 48 percent. Oddly, my pure strain of Native American bloodlines amounted to just 5 percent, but I was deemed 9 percent southwest Asian. This oddity, in the admittedly tentative data, might be explained by a focus on more recent versus more ancient native ancestry. After all, the initial database I used identifies Native American strands in central Siberia and Mongolia, which seems to put the cart before the horse.

A second database provided similar results but offered somewhat different groupings with more concise geographical mapping. For example, the Asian component designates that I am 1 percent Pacific Islander. The overlap is close:

DNA Results

I.	II.	
48%	51%	African
35%	37%	European
5%	5%	Native American
9%	7%	Asian

Adding my brother's Y chromosome to my initial mitochondrial data analysis replicated my results. Our one difference was that his yielded the "fact" that our ancestors appeared among the first groups to leave Africa heading north and east. Our ancient ancestors seem to have gotten as far into western Asia as present-day Kazakhstan before turning north and eventually west into northern Europe. Sketchy as these data appear, the only "pure" blood I have is that 5 percent Native American and 3 percent South African (like the Khoisan peoples whose languages feature "click" sounds).[30] For the database in question, all other groups are mixtures.

The few tribes using DNA to validate blood ties to existing citizens are necessarily proprietary about their data. Still, comparing notes may enhance our general education on the uses and abuses of this new tool. When a number of Cherokee Freedmen submitted DNA for analysis to shore up their claims of blood ties, they learned that tests of Y chromosome and mitochondrial DNA are hardly foolproof and quite limited in scope, but the genome-wide test is more comprehensive.[31] Using the genome-wide test gave the sample of Freedmen an average of just 6 percent of Indian blood, almost identical to the percentage found among East Coast African American populations. The test developer they worked with has generated software specifically designed to tease out differences among African American groups. He explained that although the percentage of Native American blood among the Freedmen was low, as a group they displayed higher levels of European ancestry than their East Coast counterparts (an average of 18 percent). It is this aspect that, ironically, may link them genetically to the Five Tribes.[32] Apparently, close proximity to White colonists beginning in the seventeenth century makes for a high percentage of European blood among the tribes that eventually moved from the Southeast to Indian Territory.

Though race is a construct, racial categorization has been a very big political issue in terms of social benefits. Eager to have their slice of the American pie, minorities have been torn between ensuring that their numbers, and therefore their portion of benefits, are maximized.[33] Less focus has been given to the hard work of forming coalitions with other minority groups vying for equal representation. Given our population's trajectories, demographers are struggling with creating appropriate census categories for determining benefits based on racial groups. We might all wonder how allowing citizens to check "mixed race" or more than one racial or ethnic grouping is playing out in terms of dollars allocated. As noted before, following the quincentennial of European contact, the numbers of natives soared, along with their demands for the privileges "enjoyed" by their fellow tribal members, such as health services, reduced college costs, and even those infrequent payments for the use or appropriation of tribal land.

For American Indians, we can hope that their self-determination stands on a sturdier foundation than doubtful claims to racial purity compromised by a failure to acknowledge their own cultural practices of adoption and intermarriage.[34] It would be interesting to see what the litigants would make of the use of DNA analysis in comparing the "blood quantum" of Cherokee blood citizens with their Freedmen counterparts.

If they are to retain their proud history, tribes cannot distort the facts or hide behind dubious records or antiquated notions of "purity." Nor can they remain oblivious to the fact that the practice of defining tribal citizenship in terms of blood quantum will, given current demographic trends, eventually lead to the very termination that indigenous people most fear.[35] In contrast, if tribal citizenship takes into account the maintenance of culture, such as through the fluent use of an indigenous language (as is the case in Mexico), the tribes' integrity might garner more respect.[36] Sadly, in the United States, race ideology had admitted few intermediate realities.[37]

As historical revisionists toil away, what is clear is that many explicit termination policies sought to marginalize native peoples. Depending on the year or the shifting policies, there were costs or benefits in narrowing racial slots. The ulterior motive was to isolate or prevent Indians from forming any coalitions that might have strengthened their numbers. In truth, policies, social predilections (such as linking physical characteristics with behavioral ones), and serendipity were all at work in shifting the identity of Indian peoples during the Allotment period. At that time, "the executive branch had embraced mixed-bloods for the purpose of ceding land, but now denied them allotments once it divided the remainder."[38]

Doubtless, the American public has scant interest in reviving the kind of racial categorizing that relied on designations of quadroons and octoroons.[39] But our current notions about race need an overhaul. Acknowledging that racial mixing existed well before the liberal 1960s would be a start. Many scholarly works now underscore the value of my family's ability to assert their racial identities in contrast to those conferred on them by nineteenth-century federal policies. The path to shedding outmoded racial classifications will surely broaden as we commit to reformulating, accepting, or resisting designations that were never apt. The stories of the Thorntons and the Bowlin/ Davis and Adams families point the way. My peoples' lives illustrate just how and why mixing occurs. They bridge important gaps in our nation's understanding of the mixed-race peoples among us.[40] In revisiting history, they prompt us to ask ourselves questions like: Am I still employing the one drop rule and, if so, why?

Terms and Trends

Any first-year anthropology student knows that "race" is a social construct with no biological basis.[41] Still, the United States has a well-documented history of manipulating racial categories. Using "blood" literally or metaphorically, it has played the race card to confer or deny ownership, access to the franchise and public services, and, in the case of its indigenous peoples, rights relative to blood quantum. We've seen its double standards and still await a cogent rationale for continuing the use of outmoded racial terms, no matter whose sovereignty holds sway. But, we too, schooled and unschooled, are challenged to let go of the grip of outdated terms and the racial frameworks that still cloud our perceptions.

In the 1960s, when the term *multicultural* emerged, references to US demographics shifted from talk of a melting pot to a tossed salad, where various racial and ethnic groups exist as distinct elements, retaining their unique cultural identities against domination by Anglo-centric views. In the last decade of the twentieth century, scholars began to refer to the partial assimilation of distinct cultural groups as an "ethnic stew."[42] These terms have been used and abused in larger social, political, and academic dialogues focusing on the public and private role of "diversity" at the state and national levels.[43]

Historians, demographers, social scientists, and human geographers have unpacked the concept of the melting pot as initially limited to White males from largely European countries. These "founding fathers" composed a new society fused from a mixture of "races" migrating from the old world. That old world was narrowly defined, excluding people of color and even swarthy folk from the southern or far eastern regions of the European continent. The idea of the "tossed salad" signaled the reluctance of racial and ethnic groups to relinquish their cultural characteristics. While the ethnic stew recognized a combination of both concepts (melting pot and tossed salad), it marked a turning point. No longer was the felicitous integration of minorities a publicly held ideal. That ideal devolved, marking a melding of private predilections amid various degrees of tolerance.

In hindsight, if the Allotment period reflected an assimilationist mood, the Civil Rights Era signaled a popular movement toward valuing diversity. Yet, after mid-century prosperity peaked, minorities and immigrants began to see an erosion of public programs that previously supported diversity, such as bilingual education or multicultural curricula.[44] Meanwhile, those minorities whose actions fell outside the paradigm of participatory democracy were labeled unpatriotic.[45] Some now argue for a "new exceptionalism" in which governments have the right to exclude nonassimilating individuals from the full exercise of their citizenship.[46] But this smacks of old prejudices dressed up to disguise the fact that we are blaming the victim. Incredibly, our old prejudices seem to be fueling current policies that are making it harder for underrepresented voters to exercise their franchise. The ideological divides seen in recent election cycles further highlight the conflict between those who believe that the founding fathers wrote the definitive word on democracy when they penned the Constitution and those who see room for growth and change within that document. That is why the Allotment period forms such a fascinating precedent. It was a time that saw the racial mixing inherent in a nation of multiethnic equals but, in hindsight, explained it away as an aberration. How near did we come to having the colored state of Sequoyah instead of combining the Indian and Oklahoma Territories in what became a majority White state overnight?[47] John Bowlin and Tom, Annie, and Crugee Adams all embraced the melding of races but, like the call for the state of Sequoyah, their voices have been muffled and their stories untold. Are we surprised that few have studied this lost chapter of multiculturalism?

Embracing Complexity

Perhaps it is time to replace the categories of "Red," "White," and "Black," to retire their use, just as we rid ourselves of the ethnically offensive names of sports teams and mascots.[48] Is it time to shrug off our adolescent trappings and embrace an adult complexity in our discussions of race? Might the United States learn a thing or two from other countries? At least two nations parallel US history in terms of White occupation of indigenous lands. Both have spawned large populations of mixed-race peoples. Each provides an opportunity to reflect on how different things might have been and what we might learn from others' growing pains.[49] Each offers a different lexicon of terms for understanding and interpreting how we conceive of race. At a time when some Americans are questioning the patriotism of disenchanted minorities, few interpret such stances as the defensive reactions of threatened Whites. The gradual browning of America is not a topic widely celebrated on the common ground tendered by evening newscasts.

Complexity Is the Essence of the Samba

A fusion of intricate rhythms, sensuous cadences, and expressive phrasing, the samba challenges the notion that native sounds are somehow primitive or simple. Like the development of jazz, the story of the technically demanding yet earthy samba is rich with the infusion of many diverse cultures. As the new histories suggest, it is complex. In myriad ways, Brazil embraces and celebrates this complexity, the fusion of African, European, Asian, and indigenous influences.[50] Although US history has acknowledged the presence of many races and ethnicities among its citizenry, the contributions of this rich stew of peoples has been overshadowed by popular myths that make caricatures of former leaders of color and relegate their many distinguished contributors to footnotes in forgotten chapters of the forming republic's history. In the face of a more complex reality, rather than embrace equalitarian pluralism, the United States reverts over and over to the Pilgrim myth of Europeans of humble means but high moral fiber who suffer but eventually attain supremacy over the simple heathens in the woods, choosing their tough persistence in this "new land" as the way to remember our nation's beginnings.[51]

In contrast, Brazilians are well-schooled in their multicultural history, giving greater attention to racial and ethnic distinctions. With as many as three hundred distinct categories, Brazilians may be as susceptible to prejudices as US citizens, but they are keenly aware of racial nuances, noting the many ways that connections to the mother land of Africa permeate their society and are ongoing.[52] Slavery was not abolished in Brazil until 1888 and newly arrived Africans often retained their native languages. The West African Yoruba language is still widely used in the spiritual rituals of Candomblé and most Brazilians know the major African deities that form that religion's pantheon.

Thousands of Brazilians celebrate Iemanja, the Yoruba orisha (goddess) of the ocean, maternal protector of fishermen and children. The many festivals in her honor cluster around the Christmas holidays and vary by region. In Rio de Janeiro, millions of white-clad hopefuls line the beaches on New Year's Eve, floating flowers or tiny candlelit offerings to the deity on the waters of Guanabara Bay. The crowds swell as serious worshipers, midnight revelers, and tourists jostle at the shoreline to launch their fragile hopes for blessings from the African goddess in the year to come.

There's a saying in Brazil: "Tudo mundo tem um pé a cozhinha" (Everyone has one foot in the kitchen). In other words, everyone acknowledges some genetic connection to that country's huge population of African slaves. What can such acknowledgment teach us? The answer may be found in the idea that an inadequate and narrow vocabulary about race has stymied our national dialogue. Embedded in the concepts of "ethnic stew" and "the new exceptionalism" is the legacy of a nation resistant to valuing all of its people, of continuing to see some citizens as more American and therefore more worthy than others. Is it possible then to invent or borrow images and terms that do not carry the negative connotations associated with our stale jargon? Can we expand our stories beyond the sharecropper "Negro," the "savage" Indian, the Hispanic "wetback," and the "Chinaman" railroad worker? Are we ready to ask why we are still wedded to our one drop rule, a rule that vastly oversimplifies the heritage of mixed-race families like my own?

In Salvador de Bahia, a colorful mural runs along a wall fronting the beach north of Rio Vermelho. In the upper left-hand corner, Portuguese ships float on stylized waves, and below is a richly lush green land where indigenous peoples emerge from towering bushes. As the narrative moves to the right, White, Red, and Black peoples mingle. On the far right, their encounter is captured on computer monitors depicted on each desk of a class full of rainbow-colored students. I cannot imagine such a "teaching" mural in the United States, nor one that carries the crystal-clear message that our racial future is a function of our mixed-race past.

Brazilian music is enjoyed throughout the world, arguably as popular as music from the United States. Many popular Brazilian tunes laud the exploits of Black leaders who resisted the bonds of slavery. Few realize that the songs that drive each samba school's highly competitive bid for first place at Carnival are often composed of historical references to the power and endurance of African culture as a source of Brazilian pride. Fewer still may know that samba can be roughly translated as "prayer." Engaging with samba is considered a connection with the spiritual, just as gospel music is practiced in the United States. Traditionally, samba and capoeira, its martial arts equivalent, take place in, and honor, the circle (*Samba de Roda*), where everyone is equal and positive energy flows.

Anyone spending more than a week or so in the country can see that Brazil's legacy of African culture is not only openly acknowledged but celebrated widely by the general population. While their gated communities may keep out the "riffraff" and the poor, there is no denying the muddled bloodlines or the popular allure of the *morena*, the ideal, luscious, brown-skinned woman endowed with the ability to shimmy her generous hips. Foreigners are surprised that well-known celebrities, such as Caetano Veloso, who in the United States might pass as White, proudly acknowledge their African blood. It's no secret that the African-inspired samba beat that drives Carnival is universally embraced by Brazilians of every class and hue. Brazil is no Eden. Today's Brazilians are far from free of the prejudices that place a premium on lighter complexions or longer, straighter, blonder hair. Grinding poverty and rampant violence also can be counted among Brazil's many challenges, but embracing its racial heritage has enriched the lives of all of its citizens.

South Africa

South Africa is a different story. There, to a casual observer, the hierarchy of peoples resembles a layer cake with (oversimplifying somewhat) Blacks at the bottom doing menial jobs if they are lucky enough to work for pay, the coloreds having the blue-collar jobs, while the East Indians appear to manage things for the Whites, who seem to own everything. Beyond appearances, the country reportedly has the most democratic constitution in terms of equitable treatment among its citizens. The Rights of Man figure prominently in many of the country's public monuments. Suffice it to say that it molded two of the twentieth century's luminaries. It is the birthplace of Nelson Mandela and the country where, as a young lawyer, Mahatma Gandhi advocated for civil rights.

As a society, South Africa must place great faith in the hope that government policies and procedures, such as the Truth and Reconciliation Commission hearings, will eventually lead to a brighter future. Such hopes are embodied in Johannesburg's Apartheid Museum. The rough stones and horizontal lines of the complex of modern buildings beautifully mirror South African terrain. Once inside, however, the visitor is immediately sorted by race. Whites follow one path, while coloreds follow another. Ultimately the two groups are joined in spaces that showcase the difficult struggles that led to the emancipation of Mandela and the end of Apartheid. Only a handful of institutions, such as the Holocaust Museum in Washington, DC, and the Kigali Genocide Memorial Center in Rwanda, provide the visitor with such challenging experiences. These places form an ideal opportunity to re-examine our perceptions of peoples we think we have understood.

South Africans acknowledge that they currently fall short of the equality laid out in their constitution. Nonetheless, having witnessed the evolution of US ideals, the authors of the South African doctrine have set the bar high, encouraging a respect for human dignity and a hope that people may attain true equality someday. By addressing the truth of the past, they have paved the way to looking forward. Former president Obama might well have been speaking of just such challenges to American race relations during a May 2011 speech on the Middle East when he noted: "That is the choice . . . between hate and hope; between the shackles of the past, and the promise of the future. It's a choice that must be made by leaders and by people."[53]

Clan Ross

One people who seem ready to embrace the truth of the past in a society of equals are the Scots in general and the clan Ross in particular. Scotland presents an interesting study in contrasts. It reveres its ancient past, preserving pagan sites and customs such as large gatherings honoring the solstices. With an eye to the future, it is open-minded as host to the world's largest international festival, fringe festival, and—made famous by Monty Python—the Beyond the Fringe Festival, which attract visitors from around the globe.

As noted above, adversity forced many to leave Scotland seeking better fortunes not just in the Americas but in virtually every place on earth.[54] Not surprisingly, Scotland draws a steady stream of folk searching for their roots.

The descendants of the clan of Ross are no exception. As I've traveled in the Highlands, despite my lack of Picktish or Celtic features, I'm frequently asked if I am researching my ancestry. I've wandered into tiny hamlets on walks around the Black Isle and, while chatting about the Ross connection in my family tree, been told, "Well, welcome here. We're also Ross, so you are family."

The seat of the Ross clan is in the Royal Burgh of Tain. Established in 1066, it is the oldest of the royal burghs and home to the shrine of Saint Duthac, an early Christian pilgrimage site. There, the Tain Museum houses the Ross Project, which documents the descendants of the clan. Staff gladly recorded our 2014 visit with a photo of me and my mother that was posted on their website and made part of the official archive. Scotland respectfully acknowledges its sons and daughters, even if the Cherokee descendants of John Ross do not.

For a country that considers itself a world leader, we have far too few opportunities here in the United States to make peace with our genocidal policies toward indigenous peoples or our long practice of slavery. In *Slavery by Another Name*, Douglas Blackmon has done an admirable job in his research on the murky period following Reconstruction. He does us all a service in showing that African Americans were virtually re-enslaved by Jim Crow policies and that their forced labor supported the nascent mining, steel, and other industries that continue to contribute to the nation's prosperity. His research provides a missing link for those who do not see how our present condition has any connection to the exploitation of former slaves. Like South Africans, Blackmon finds hope in bringing the wrongs of the past to the fore.

Brazilians and South Africans suffer no illusions about the violent and bloody treatment of slaves and indigenous peoples at the hands of their White settlers. In unvarnished narratives, the two countries challenge the United States to relinquish its sugarcoated history in favor of a more credible acknowledgment of what constitutes an authentic America.[55] It is telling that Australia considers itself a "settler nation" acknowledging its displacement of the indigenous population and, since 1998, commemorating that fact each May 26 in National Sorry Day. Perhaps what we can learn from these experiences is not to celebrate eminent Blacks during the month of February and native peoples in November but to acknowledge and appreciate our collective Black and indigenous heritage on a daily basis.

Story and Voice

For too long, we assumed that there was little more to learn about the experiences of our nation's minorities, that their records had been thoroughly plumbed, that they lacked the education or the dispassionate analytical skills to tell their own stories well. But here are the descendants of Allotees speaking for themselves, offering fresh perspectives on the multicultural nature of past policies and social movements. Their account differs from the tales of cowboys and Indians that too often describe the limits of our knowledge of the frontier.

In the citizenship debate among the Cherokees and Cherokee Freedmen, many admit to not knowing anything about the nineteenth-century treaties and tribal traditions that underpin their current disagreements, but I was curious. What I found provides a chance to inform that debate, to see the motives behind the choices that were made, the rationale—defensible or not—for our racial designations. Here is a guide for anyone wanting to begin to analyze the repercussions of the domination of one culture over another. It is an entreaty to sidestep the convenience of the popular media sound bite in favor of asking our own questions in our own voices, of uncovering—and listening to—authentic voices from the past that can still speak to us. In all seriousness, I ask, what's in *your* closet?

Our National Archives hold a wealth of information about our bloodlines, now made immeasurably more accessible via the internet. They are an open book available to any comers. In this land we are told again and again that success is not guaranteed but we all have access to opportunity. We hear that the key to a participatory democracy is participation. When we are confronted with gaps in the records and misrepresented or oversimplified histories, we are duty-bound to question, to speak up. Our stories and our voices cannot be heard if we do not speak.

In recovering and restoring our past, "who tells the story" matters a great deal. Our attitudes and beliefs are shaped by the voices from the past, whether the tale is told by George Washington or Geronimo. Whose story is heard matters. It matters now and it will matter in the future. Ideally, those whose access to the public square has been historically constrained will find their voices. Voices can extend beyond mere personal expression. Films such as *Belle*, *The Butler*, or *12 Years a Slave* can bring little known true-life narratives to the attention of millions of Americans. Anytime a stereotype is dismantled we gain authenticity. As the venerated twentieth-century Supreme Court justice and social activist Louis D. Brandeis wrote: "If the broad light of day could be let in upon men's actions, it would purify then as the sun disinfects."[56] That perspective is especially precious for those who see a different truth. For too long, minorities heard others make caricatures of their people, bending often violent truths into harmless yarns. The historian Michael Kammen spent his life examining American identity. He bemoaned the fact that we revere yet misunderstand our history. He believed that we "have taken too much pride and proportionately too little interest in" the ideals contained in our Constitution.[57] We can do better.

Barbarism and Civilization

The United States has styled itself as a beacon of democracy. Its form of government is admired for endowing its citizenry with a level of freedom that others envy. Its resources are vast, its influence mighty. Some see life in the United States as the pinnacle of civilization. The promise is that anyone here can flourish.[58] We can all become our best selves.

The reality is that over the last thirty years we've seen increasing inequality, placing the fulfillment of our best selves beyond the reach of those cowed down by poverty and hunger. History tells us that such inequality can be socially and politically destabilizing, ultimately influencing every aspect of our lives. From mighty states that have fallen we should know that enemies from within can be as potent as those who would breach our borders. In this respect, we might worry less about illusive weapons of mass destruction or vying with other countries for supremacy than with battling our own internal, domestic demons.

Counter to the concept of civilization is barbarism. Here, US power should not be confused with civilization. Yes, we are powerful, but how civilized are we? Do we understand that "barbarism is not a lack of power—it is unbridled, unprincipled power; power in the absence of reason, virtue and taste." If we follow that line of thinking, we can see where a powerful nation such as the United States can be defeated from within by barbarism or decadence where "barbarism is strength without sensitivity; decadence is sensitivity without strength."[59]

It is not a stretch to see the past treatment of Reds, Blacks, and mixed-bloods in the United States as barbaric, as insensitive and, at times, weak. We can see the power of the Allotment strategy as insensitive to the dignity of native peoples. Although the Bowlin and Adams families enjoyed a period of relative prosperity, their descendants are haunted by half-truths about their place in this country's history. Their peoples' treatment has been insensitive and reparation efforts have been weak. Today's freedmen controversy shows that the prospects for achieving justice for past mistreatment through tribal authorities or the federal government are still mired in ugly accusations that focus on the minutia of legal precedent but miss the big picture. *E pluribus Unum*, really? To achieve a more authentic America, perhaps we need to take a more philosophical view.

Not so very long ago, Indians were popularly regarded as savages, but there are countless examples of what Americans have learned from their indigenous brothers.[60] One morally laudable stance taken toward the well-being of the collective community can be seen in the Creek tradition of holding an annual ceremony for purging misdeeds. After fasting and cleansing in the clear waters of a river or brook, an entire community lets go of any wrongs committed, any disputes or grudges, worries or sorrows that could constrain their ability to treat one another nobly. The sole exception is murder, an act that, despite material restitution to the bereft family, is never excused. The Creeks understood the value of acknowledging wrongs, dealing with them, and then moving on. The Australians have accepted their mistreatment of indigenous people in their national Sorry Day.

A healthy acknowledgment of wrongs was not at the forefront during the Allotment Era. We may never know if Georgeanna Thornton was in a position to voice the true source of her feelings during her application for recognition as a Cherokee Freedman. Maybe it was better to hold her tongue as she applied for Cherokee citizenship, not to tell the full truth about running away from the tribe, but maybe we can hear that truth now. Maybe we can recognize the depth, range, and constraints on her authenticity.

Sadly, the land allotments that initially seemed to hold such promise ultimately corrupted. They corrupted the identities of our forebears by devaluing or erasing bloodlines. In one short generation, they corrupted efforts to forge stable communities out of the people who had already endured the terrible displacement to the West on the Trail of Tears. No serious effort was made to stem the tide of settlers eager to take land from the Indians—and that land was their lifeblood.

All politics is local. You start where you are. As the anthropologist Margaret Mead is credited with saying, "Never doubt that a small group of thoughtful, committed, citizens can change the world. Indeed it is the only thing that ever has." As a trained researcher and a temperamentally inclined seeker, it has been natural for me to dig deep in answering the question "Who are we?" I have found that I'm not alone in probing our past to better understand why our current racial discourse is stymied. My attempt at shedding light on the causes and conditions that shape our dialogues about race in American comes from a sense of duty. Illuminating these painful issues is not welcome in some parts. Yet, in following this bent, I join a small group of citizens revisiting the historical record in hopes of preparing the way for a more authentic future. By exposing the roots of our mixed-race past we may yet realize that illusive postracial society that, so far, we only glimpse. A fresh American paradigm is long overdue. An African proverb suggests that if you want to go fast, go alone; if you want to go far, go together. Can we gather in our diversity to meet the challenges of the future? Will the United States offer civilization, enabling its citizens to flourish, or will it stop short in simply amassing power?

Pluralism, Patriotism, and Democracy

What will it take to enable every American citizen of any color to stand shoulder to shoulder as equals, to be proud rather than ashamed of their connections? Who will model the democratic ideals that we can all endorse? Obama offers an example of what constitutes the whole package. Whatever our political persuasions, we recognize that he is accomplished, smart, and dedicated. He wholeheartedly believes in the democratic process. He is gratified when citizens actively participate in public discourse. He would like us all to flourish. Not surprisingly, that stance threatens the status quo. The "haves" question the worthiness of the "have-nots." Those with power see no reason to share it. Gated communities spring up where a few generations ago folk more readily opened their homes to those who were not like themselves.

As we mark a thirty-year trend in increasing inequality, political polarization and ideological divisions embolden many factions to sneer at any hint of compromise with their adversaries. Is this how we remain proud of who we are? On the walls of the National Museum of the American Indian are traces of a middle ground, an opportunity to frame a vision for a common future. Before construction began, founding members were invited to have their names permanently inscribed on the museum's walls. Following current conventions, I sent in my check along with my name and tribal affiliation, which were well within the restricted number of characters. Sadly, my tribal affiliation was dropped. Apparently including "Muscogee Creek" after my name was too impolitic for that institution. It seems that no one wanted to offend future donors by flaunting tribal membership among the initial supporters. So, another expression of pride was stilled.

Is America in decline? Is it sowing the seeds of discord, feeding inequalities and ideologies that will lead to an implosion? At this juncture, shouldn't we know and acknowledge who we are as a people? Can't we express the source of our feelings in public without rancor, consider divergent views rather than trend toward polarization over bipartisanship? Or is our civilization dépassé? If we can no longer walk a mile in another's shoes, there will be no healing, no true movement forward. As I have grown and deepened as a result of this searching, I have been healing. I have been healing from a lost identity. Now I know who I am. I know who we are. I claim my race: I am of mixed heritage with a formal tribal affiliation to the Muscogee Nation. My ancestors were Red, White, and Black. Their blood was blended during the Allotment Era, on the land where I was born and where my forebears are buried.

I could say that it doesn't matter if others see what I see in my murky features, but I know that America has not yet owned its racial story and that it is the poorer for it. For America to journey back to its roots, it cannot remain mute about its cruel policies, overlooking the continued inequities inherent in a former slave-holding society, one that sought the demise of its indigenous inhabitants and rationalized White supremacy. My forebears embraced a belief in an American work ethic that could earn dignity and respect for all. How far short we have fallen from those ideals could be heard in Obama's plea, honoring the victims of the 2011 Tucson shootings, that we live up to the expectations of the nine-year-old girl born on September 11, 2001, and shot while waiting to meet her congresswoman.[61] Like that young girl, the Bowlins and Adams families hoped that our democracy would be as good as they imagined. Although Stripet's visits to Washington were sometimes futile, our families continue to take their franchise seriously. We are stunned at those who do not vote and appalled at the idea that we do not or cannot make a difference. Why, then, do we feel like second-class citizens in the land where we were born?

Whatever its intentions, in its day, Allotment was a dehumanizing experience. Equating the degree of racial purity with a proportionate provision of acreage invited corruption and subterfuge. Although the policy of linking blood quantum to tighter constraints was imposed in well-meaning efforts to protect the innocent, many more provisions eroded those lofty goals.

In the end, the overt effort to civilize the Indians barely hid the covert desire to dilute tribal cohesion. Throw everyone into the pot and let them all melt. That would make it harder for them to claim allegiance to a tribe or culture. Divide and conquer is a very old trick. "Dilute and Stir" would leave many Indians adrift in a hazy no-man's-land of blended culture, ashamed of being Indian, often opting to play White or Black if there was an advantage in it.[62] Those who resisted the "Dilute and Stir" campaign tried to hold fast to the old ways, laying low and waiting out the onslaught of anti-Indian policies that for so long pervaded intergovernment relations. Some of these self-destructed as vulnerabilities to alcoholism and obesity eroded their quality of life. Drunk or sober, diabetic or suffering from cirrhosis of the liver, they held fast to the dubious CDIBs dispensed by the government, girding themselves against the next assault. For them there was no question of who belongs, for they have paid their dues. I know, for these are also my uncles, cousins, and nieces, my kin by blood.

There is little wonder that, in her Cherokee Freedmen crusade to reinstate the inclusive spirit of tribal communities, Marilyn Vann met with such stiff resistance.[63] Yet she is equally determined to achieve justice for her forebears and will not be denied the truth of her lineage. She too is about the business of claiming race.

A Witness to History

I come from a highly accomplished family whose members were leaders of the community. They were educated, owned land, ran businesses, wore suits as well as tortoise-shell rattles, won prizes, owned cars, china, oriental rugs, cared for the sick, and donated goods and services to the poor. Through our biased historical accounts these upstanding people became neglected, overlooked, mute, and ultimately invisible. Shouldn't the accomplishments of John Bowlin's descendants be acknowledged? Shouldn't their Indian roots be recognized? Doesn't Thomas Jefferson Adams deserve to remain in the Oklahoma textbooks just as much as his White counterparts? Aren't Annie's efforts as a respected midwife and her fierce determination to safeguard her clan (a clan whose fealty may have been more influenced by its Scottish forebears than its Indian blood) worthy of being placed in print?[64]

Hoisted on the shoulders of these giants, is there any wonder that I want to live life fully? That I don't want to miss a thing? I want to grow in depth through facing the truth and expressing my values. Why shouldn't I be a witness to history? Why shouldn't I resurrect the voices of all of my forebears? I ask, why not me, just as I am, not easily defined or suppressed.

Today, I wonder who values these histories and these people. Just as the freedom riders of the Civil Rights Movement shared a vision of a less barbaric time, who now envisions an America where we can all just get along, a land where Red, Black, White, Brown, and Yellow see themselves as enriched by each other? Is it enough for me to gain knowledge, claim race for myself and my forebears, sending our voices out across the land? If I believe in a participatory democracy, I must play my part. I must contribute the voice of my best self. As a person of color, I must respond to calls for enriching the canon by claiming my voice, by speaking, by sharing what I have learned, and interpreting what I know. It is not enough for me to share my families' histories placing them not in the context of Oklahoma's history or the debate over Black Indians but in the broader context of the nation we aspired and continue to aspire to flourish in, a nation that lives up to its own expectations, recognizing that its huddled masses form a dynamic mix of races that strengthens rather than diminishes us all.

In my family, it all comes together. In them, our stories of origin, democratic ideals, land ties and ownership, slavery, cultural transitions, racial melding, and White supremacy are interwoven. Our joys and struggles converge here by the grace of a couple of colorful and contrasting threads that span more than 130 years. Would that my forebears could see us now. For, just as mixed-bloods and Blacks sought a brighter future through their Indian ties (arguably most closely realized among the Creeks), we all seek the comfort of a community where we have a hope of flourishing as well as a sense of belonging.

One Hundred Years On

Annie Adams remarked that in the town of Okmulgee, White, Indian, and colored all ate together in the hotel. For that brief moment, in that small place, America achieved a degree of racial harmony that has turned out to be rare. Our people flourished, and they have not forgotten. Today, more than one hundred years after our family's saga with Allotment land began, we seem poised once again to explore opportunities for being all together. The government policies that denied the truth about our racial identities in favor of a master plan for Indians did much to squelch the nuances, the subtleties, of interracial relations. Do the stories of the Thorntons, Bowlins, Davises, and Adamses tell us that the federal government succeeded in transforming a communal culture into one that is solely occupied with individual wealth and nothing more? In one hundred years, has a community once proud and totally self-reliant completely disappeared?

Perhaps the truth is that John Bowlin flourished despite the shackles of his origins in slavery, that Thomas Jefferson Adams thrived at a moment in time when Indians and mixed-bloods held respected positions in nascent multi-cultural communities. If the greatest struggle for an oppressed group in a racist society is the struggle to reclaim collective memory and identity, then the memories and identities collected here serve not just the oppressed group.[65] They serve notice to the oppressor that people of color are not prepared to be something they are not. The Bowlins are part Cherokee by blood, regardless of their missing CDIBs. The Adamses are Creek by virtue of their continued contributions to the tribe, their cultural traditions, and a collective reverence for the land of their birth. The family members who left in the middle of the night to pass for White also form a part of our collective past. In embracing the full history and culture of these two families, in all their complexity, we begin to uproot the prejudices that stilled their voices.

Sadly, this tale of my forebears as mixed-race Allotees is coming to a close. The town of Beggs is almost ghostly; the Phillis Wheatley School is a ruin, the latest matriarchs of the Bowlin family passed away as this work was completed. For years, the Adams cemetery was overgrown and neglected. The tombstones of the Davis family are weathered and broken. As part of their upbringing, our sons and daughters know their roots, the places where we were born, but there are few who will return to visit that land. Those trips home may endure only in the minds of the seventh generation and in the memories recalled here.

This work places a clearer picture of the value of my ancestors' lives in the hands of their descendants. For others, it offers a different, an alternative, view of an American family and the American promise of democracy, a glimpse of the future of our mixed-race and multiethnic society in a crisper image of the past. That crisper image moves away from a sweeping vision where all people of color share the same origins in southern slavery, where differences in skin color are explained in terms of proximity to the master's fields or parlor. It distances itself from the comforting belief that racial mixing in the United States is limited and aberrant versus widespread and increasingly prevalent since the elimination of laws prohibiting miscegenation. It asks more concisely "who we are," as distinct from "who we think we are" or who tells us "who we are." It begs us to consider if that promissory note that Dr. King spoke of, in 1963, gives people of color equal access to the rights of life, liberty, and the pursuit of happiness, and if not now, then why not and when?

We are a young nation, one perhaps still incapable of appreciating the deep complexities of the human condition. We tend to want a quick fix, easy answers, someone to tell us what to think and to do. For nearly twenty years, I too had wanted someone to tell me what part of me is Indian. What part of me is African American? What part of me is of European descent? Finding my own answers has taken a tenacity that I never knew I had. Hopefully, in searching for my own answers, a larger healing will ensue, perhaps within my family, for our community, within the tribe, among races, and maybe even for our nation.

To know where to go often means understanding where you have come from. We want to teach our children about their roots and wings. I am privileged to possess so many strands that reveal my family's roots; strands that bind us to the deep fabric of a half-forgotten time but join us here in the present. My task of untangling the Red, White, and Black heritage of my elders has enabled me to refashion my wings. Honoring them, we rise. *Mvto.*

APPENDIX A

*The Thornton/Bowlin Cherokee Application Transcripts,
National Archives, Washington, DC, Department of the
Interior, Commission to the Five Civilized Tribes*[1]

Transcript I. Elizabeth Bowlin
Chelsea, I.T., May 31, 1901
RG 75, M 1301, Roll 0296, Case 1444

Transcript II. Georgeanna Thornton
Chelsea, I.T., May 31, 1901
RG 75, M 1301, Roll 0296, Case 1443

Transcript III. John L. Bowlin et al.
Vinita, I.T., October 7, 1901
Supl. C. F. D. #445

Transcript IV. Georgeanna Thornton
Vinita, I.T., October 24, 1901
Supl. C. F. D. #445

Transcript V. Elizabeth Bowlin et al., and Georgeanna Thornton
Muskogee, I.T., June 18–19, 1904
Cherokee Freedman D 444 & 445

Transcript VI. Elizabeth Bowlin
Cooweescoowee, C.N., July 22, 1889
RG 75, M 1301

Transcript VII. Henrietta Bowlin
Cherokee Land Office, May 30, 1906
Roll 296, Case 1444, SCF

Transcript VIII. Helen F. Bowlin
Muskogee, Oklahoma, June 29, 1908
Roll 296, Case 1444, SCF

■

Transcript I. Elizabeth Bowlin
Department of the Interior,
Commission to the Five Civilized Tribes,
Chelsea, I.T., May 31, 1901

In the matter of the application of Elizabeth Bowlin for the enrollment of
herself and seven children as Cherokee Freedmen, and for the enrollment of
her husband, Jon L. Bowlin, as a Cherokee Freedman by intermarriage; said
Bowlin being sworn and examined by Commissioner C. R. Breckinridge,
testified as follows:

Q. Give us your full name.
A. Elizabeth Bowlin.
Q. How old are you?
A. I was born in 1862.
Q. You are about 38?
A. Yes sir.
Q. What is your postoffice?
A. Chelsea.
Q. In what district do you live?
A. Cooweescoowee.
Q. Do you want to be enrolled as a Cherokee Freedman?
A. Yes sir.
Q. Do you want to apply for anybody besides yourself?
A. Yes sir.
Q. Do you want to apply? Have you a husband?

A. I have a husband.

Q. Do you want to apply for him?

A. Yes sir.

Q. How many children have you?

A. I have six living and one dead; I mean seven living and one dead maked eight.

Q. Are these seven children all under 21 years of age?

A. Yes sir.

Q. Are they all unmarried?

A. Yes sir.

Q. You can apply for the whole seven then?

A. Yes sir.

Q. How long have you lived in the Cherokee Nation?

A. I have lived there ever since '83; no '82.

Q. Give me the name of your father.

A. Amos Thornton.

Q. Is he alive?

A. No sir.

Q. How long have has he been dead?

A. I don't know how long.

Q. Was he a Cherokee Freedman?

A. He was a Cherokee Indian.

Q. Give me the name of you mother.

A. Georgianna Thornton.

Q. Is she alive?

A. Yes sir.

Q. Where is she living now?

A. She lives with me.

Georgianna Thornton, being sworn and examined by Commissioner Breckinridge, testified as follows:

Q. Give me your name.

A. Georgianna Thornton.

Q. How old are you?

A. I can't tell you that. (Hands paper to Commissioner.)

Q. This paper says that you were born in 1845?

A. Yes sir, that is right.

Q. Then you are about 55 or '6 years old?

A. Yes sir.

Q. How long have you lived in the Cherokee Nation?

A. I always lived in the Cherokee Nation; I was born in the Cherokee Nation.

Q. Were you a slave in the Cherokee Nation when the war broke out?

A. Yes sir.

Q. Who was it you belonged to?

A. Amos Thornton.

Q. Was he a recognized Cherokee citizen?

A. Yes sir.

Q. Is this woman your daughter?

A. Yes sir.

Commission of Applicant: Give me the name of your husband?

A. John L. Bowlin.

Q. How old is your husband?

A. 51 years old.

Q. Is that your husband sitting over there?

A. Yes sir.

Q. How long has he lived in the Cherokee Nation?

A. Ever since I have; since '82.

■

2

John L. Bowlin, being sworn and examined by Commissioner Breckinridge, testified as follows:

Q. Give me your full name.

A. John L. Bowlin.

Q. You are 51 years of age?

A. Yes sir.

Q. What is your postoffice?

A. Chelsea.

Q. Are you a Cherokee Freedman?

A. No sir.

Q. What are you?

A. Intermarried.

Q. You are an intermarried Freedman?

A. Yes sir.

Commissioner of Applicant: Your husband is a state man?

A. Yes sir.

Q. And only claims as an intermarried Freedman?

A. Yes sir, that is all.

Commissioner of John L. Bowlin: Have you your marriage license and certificate?

A. Yes sir. (Presents certificate)

The applicant presents an official copy of the records of Cooweescoowee District showing that on the 7th of August, 1885, she and her husband were united in marriage under a Cherokee license and in accordance with Cherokee Law. This is filed herewith.

Q. Have you and your wife lived together ever since you were married?

A. Yes sir.

Q. And all the time in the Cherokee Nation?

A. Yes sir, not all the time in the Cherokee Nation; we were married in Kansas first.

Q. But you have lived in the Cherokee Nation ever since you were married under this Cherokee license?

A. Yes sir.

Q. You had before that been married under United States law?

A. Yes sir.

Q. When were you and she married under United States law?

A. In 1880.

Commissioner of Applicant: Were you ever admitted to citizenship by the Cherokee Commission or Council?

A. Not by Council; I was enrolled on two rolls.

Q. But before you were enrolled, were you ever admitted to citizenship by any Court?

A. No sir.

Q. You never applied to be admitted to citizenship?

A. No sir.

Q. You say you have been in the Cherokee Nation since '82?

A. Yes sir.

Q. Where were you before that?

A. I was in Parsons, Kansas.

Q. Were you born in Kansas?

A. No sir.

Q. Where were you born?

A. Fort Gibson, Cherokee Nation.

Q. And they carried you out during the war?

A. I don't remember anything about the war.

Q. You first remember Kansas?

A. The first I remember of Kansas was in '76.

Q. Do you remember any place before you remember Kansas?

A. I remember Fort Gibson.

Commission of Applicant's husband: Were you ever married before you married this wife?

A. No sir.

Commissioner of Applicant: Were you ever married before you married this husband?

A. No sir.

Commissioner of Applicant's mother: Where was your daughter born?

A. At Fort Gibson, right in my master's house before the war.

Q. Well hardly before the war, the war had been going on a year or two if she is 38?

A. It was before the war.

■

3

Q. She is a little older than that?

A. It was before the war got in the Cherokee Nation.

Q. Were you carried up to Kansas during the war?

A. No sir, I was freed right here at my master's house.

Q. You didn't go out of the Cherokee Nation during the war?

A. No sir.

Q. What was this girl doing up in Kansas?

A. That was way up after the war I sent her to school.

Q. Where did you send her to school in Kansas?

A. Manhattan.

Q. How old was she then?

A. I don't know.

Q. A little thing?

A. Yes sir.

Q. How long did you keep her up there?

A. One year. I sent her in the fall and in the spring I went after her.

Q. And then what?

A. And then brought her back and stopped at Parsons three months and worked.

Q. And then what?

A. And then brought her to Fort Gibson home.

Q. But that was some time before she married?

A. Yes sir.

Q. But then she married in Kansas?

A. I had taken her back.

Q. How long after that was it you took her back from this time you brought her down?

A. I don't know how long it was.

Q. What did you take her back for?

A. To get married.

Q. You didn't take her back until she went up there to get married?

A. No.

Q. She was engaged to be married, was she?

A. Yes sir.

Q. What place was she married in Kansas?

A. Parsons.

Q. You weren't living at Parsons at the time?

A. No sir.

Q. Well, how long did she stay up there after she got married?

A. I don't know how long it was; she stayed a winter and then moved down in the spring is all I can tell you.

Q. Was she never in Kansas except when you sent her up there as a little thing to school and the time you took her there to marry?

A. No sir; she never was in Kansas.

Q. Just those two times?

A. Yes sir. I sent her with General Davidson.

Q. Who was General Davidson?

A. He was in the Army. He was the commanding officer.

Commissioner of Applicant: Well now, you said you had lived here since '82?

A. I have been here ever since '82.

Q. Where were you before that?

A. In Parsons.

Q. How long did you stay there?

A. I stayed there until '82, I guess.

Q. When did you begin staying there—how old were you?

A. I don't know. I don't know my age.

Q. How big were you when you went to Parsons, were you a little thing?

A. I was considered a young lady when I went back in '80.

Q. You told me just now that you lived in Parsons down to 1882, and you said you were born in Fort Gibson, I believe, did you say that?

A. Yes sir, I said I was born in Fort Gibson.

Q. How long had you been living in Parsons before you left there in 1882? How long had you been there?

A. That is all I know, I went there in 1880 and I moved here on Pryor Creek in 1882.

Q. Where were you before 1880?

A. I was at Gibson all the time, working around there at Fort Gibson with my mother.

Q. Then you lived at Gibson down to 1880, did you?

A. Yes sir, at Gibson until 1880, except when she sent me to school.

Q. Then you lived in Kansas about two years after you were married?

A. Yes sir, until 1882.

Q. Your mother was speaking about your coming back in two months?

A. She don't know no dates and I don't either; we didn't then.

Q. You think the way you state now is about right, do you?

A. Yes sir.

■

4

Q. Now, give me the names of your children?

A. (Hands paper to Commissioner.)

Q. Then the oldest child for whom you apply is Henrietta, it is?

A. Yes sir.

Q. She is about 18 now?

A. Yes sir.

Q. And your next child is William B?

A. Yes sir, William Henry.

Q. He is about 15?

A. Yes sir.

Q. Then the next child is Eunice C?

A. Yes sir, Eunice Cornelius.

Q. He Is 12 years old?

A. Yes sir.

Q. Then the next child is Helen F.

A. Yes sir.

Q. She is about ten years old, is that right?

A. Yes sir.

Q. The next child is Doda C?

A. Yes sir.

Q. She is eight years old?

A. Yes sir.

Q. And then Leonard E?

A. Leonard Elmer, yes sir.

Q. He is three years old?

A. Yes sir.

Q. And then Sophia A?

A. Yes sir.

Q. She was born the last of last March?

A. Yes sir.

Q. Are these children all living now?

A. Yes sir.

The 1880 authenticated roll of the Freedmen of the Cherokee Nation examined and the names of the applicants not found thereon; nor the names of the applicant's father or mother.

The 1896 census roll examined and the names of the applicants not found thereon.

Q. Did you draw strip money?

A. Yes sir.

The Kerns Clifton Roll examined and the name of the applicant is found on page 103, No. 2578, Elizabeth Bowlen, Cooweescoowee District.

Q. Did you draw for these children?

A. Yes sir.

The Kerns Clifton Roll examined and the names of the applicant's children are found thereon as follows:

Page 103, No. 2574, Henrietta Bowlen, Cooweescoowee District.

Page 103, No. 2576, Will Bowlen, Cooweescoowee District.

Page 103, No. 2577, Eunice Bowlen, Cooweescoowee District.

Q. Did you draw for Helen?

A. No sir.

Q. You only drew for these three?

A. I drew for all of them, except Helen. I drawed for Doda, but not for Helen.

The Kerns Clifton Roll examined and the name of Doda Bowlin in found on page 178, No. 4364, Doda Bowlin, District not given.

Q. Didn't you give in the name of this child, Helen?

A. Yes sir.

Q. Do you know how it happened to be left off the roll?

A. I don't know.

■

5

Applicant's husband- Mr. Kerns claimed it was a clerical error.

The name of Helen Bowlin does not appear on the Kerns Clifton Roll.

The Wallace Roll examined and the names of the applicants and her older child are identified thereon as follows:

Page 157, No. 8, Elizabeth Bolyn, Cooweescoowee District.

Page 157, No. 10, Henrietta Bolyn, Cooweescoowee District.

Note: No evidence that they are the children of Cherokee Freedman, and no evidence that Henrietta was born before March 3, 1883. They are on the questioned list.

Commissioner of Applicant's husband: You have never been on any roll at all?

A. No, sir. (He is not identified on any roll.)

W. W. Hastings of Applicant: With whom did you live while you were going to school in Kansas?

A. I lived with General Davidson.

Q. How long did you live with him?

A. I don't know how long I lived with him; I couldn't tell the years then.

Q. Your best judgment?

A. I lived with him about one year, I guess, until my mother came after me.

Q. Your best judgment is that you lived with him about a year?

A. Yes sir.

Q. How long was that before you married?

A. I don't know; I married in 1880.

Q. How long before that was it when you lived up in Kansas with General Davidson?

A. I told you one year.

Q. You stated that you lived with him one year?

A. Yes sir.

Q. Was that the year immediately before you married—was that the year '79?

A. I don't know.

Q. How long before you married was it that you lived with General Davidson?

A. All I know, I married in '80.

Q. When did you live with Davidson?

A. I don't know the year; I went there to school, but I don't remember the year.

Q. Did you go to school?

A. I went to school a while.

Q. How long?

A. About two or three weeks.

Q. Who to?

A. Some woman by the name of Miss Cunningham.

Q. That was all the school you went to in Kansas?

A. I had to work and she give me schooling.

Q. Where did you meet your husband?

A. In Parsons.

Q. The first time?

A. Yes sir.

Q. How long before you married him?

A. I met him there in—I don't know, some where along in the '70s, '76 or '79, or somewhere along there.

Q. Had you been in Kansas a number of years before you married?

A. No sir, it wasn't a number of years. I would come home and then go back.

Q. You were living with other people beside General Davidson?

A. No other people that I know of.

Q. How old were you when you went up to Kansas?

A. I don't know.

Q. Do you think you were as much as eight years of age?

A. I don't know.

Applicant's mother: She was about that high.

(Indicated.)

Applicant further testifies:

Q. You went there about the close of the war?

A. I don't know.

■

6

Q. You don't remember when you went?

A. It was some time in '70, I don't know.

Q. You were too young you don't remember the facts?

A. Well, I don't know that I was too young; I don't remember. I know I went with General Davidson.

Q. Do you remember the trip?

A. I wasn't too young to know that I went with him; I don't know what year it was.

W. W. Hastings of Applicant's mother: About how old was this girl when she went up to Kansas after the war?

A. Oh, Lord, I can't tell you now.

Q. About how tall was she?

A. She was about that high. (Indicated)

Q. You think she was about as much as five or six years of age when she went up there?

A. I can't tell you about that.

Q. Do you think she was older or younger than that?

A. I guess she was five or six.

Applicant: I guess I was older than that.

Applicant testifies further:

Q. How did you go to Kansas in a wagon or on the train or how?

A. I went with General Davidson on the train.

Q. Where did you take the train?

A. We took it right here in the Cherokee Nation.

Q. What point?

A. I guess it was Cherokee Nation, at Muskogee.

Q. Did you take it at Muskogee?

A. Yes sir.

Q. Was that the first time you went to Kansas?

A. Yes sir, that was the first time in my life.

Q. Who else went with you?

A. General Davidson.

Q. Did he have a wife?

A. General Davidson and his family.

Q. You took the train in Muskogee?

A. Yes sir.

Q. Where did you go to, to what point?

A. I went to a town called Manhattan.

Q. You made your home with General Davidson up until '80?

A. No, I made my home in the Cherokee Nation; that is where I lived, only during the time I went to school a little bit.

Q. You only went to school about two or three weeks?

A. And worked the rest of it.

Q. What did you do the rest of the time?

A. I worked I said.

Q. For General Davidson?

A. I stayed with General Davidson a year.

Q. Who else did you work for?

A. I come back home.

Q. You say you only stayed one year?

A. Yes, with General Davidson.

Q. You stayed with someone else, did you?

A. In a year, my mother came after me; I never stayed with no one else.

Q. I would like for you to tell about how old you were when you went to Kansas?

A. I couldn't tell; I don't know.

Q. Do you swear positively that all the time you stayed in Kansas that you stayed with General Davidson up until the time you married—you worked for no one else and stayed with no one else?

A. I didn't. I did swear positively that I only stayed one year with General Davidson.

Q. You came back in '80?

A. I came back with my mother in the Cherokee Nation.

Q. When?

A. I don't know.

Q. How long was it before you married?

A. Three years, I guess.

Q. Were you living here when you married?

A. I told you I was married in Kansas.

Q. How long had you been up there that time when you married?

A. I went back there in '80 and I guess I had been there about five or six months.

Q. Five or six months when you married?

A. I guess, I don't know.

Q. Had you seen your husband before?

A. I met him there in '76 or '79.

Q. You don't know which?

A. It was one of them.

Q. Was your mother up there at the time you married?

A. She came after me and brought me back there, and I went back. Yes, she was with me.

■

7

Q. How long had she been up there at that time?

A. She was there three or four months.

Q. Was she up there any time before then?

A. No sir, only when she come after me at that time.

Q. Do you know she came after you?

A. Yes, I know that.

Q. How did she come after you?

A. She came on the train.

Q. Do you remember living any at all at Fort Gibson before you went to Kansas?

A. Yes, I know we stayed at Gibson.

Q. Who did you live with?

A. With my relation and all around there.

Q. Who were some of your relation?

A. Patsy Dennis on Four Mile Branch.

Q. Did you live with her?

A. Yes sir.

Q. Who did you mother live with before she went up?

A. With her relation, her father.

Q. What was her father's name?

A. John Fields, or John Fox Fields.

Q. Who was her mother?

A. I don't know.

Q. Did you live in town?

A. Part of the time in town and part of the time in the country.

Q. Did she have a home in the town?

A. Yes sir, in Fort Gibson.

Q. Who was your neighbors?

A. Chief Bushyhead. We lived close to him, right on the bank of the river; all around in there in town.

Q. How far from that old business part of town down in there to the river?

A. I don't know how far the river is from the business part.

Q. How far did you live from the old business part?

A. I lived with my mother all the time.

Q. You lived near Chief Bushyhead's place?

A. We stayed there a while.

Q. Did your mother own a home there?

A. That is her home.

Q. Did she own a house?

A. She didn't own any house; she was a widow.

Q. When did you father die?

A. I don't know when.

Q. Since the war?

A. I guess he did.

Q. Do you remember him?

A. Amos Thornton? I don't remember when he died.

Q. You came back here in '82?

A. Yes sir, in '82.

Q. Did you get married according to Cherokee law directly after you came back? Pretty soon after you came back?

A. I had to be here six months before I could do that.

Q. As soon as that time expired you married?

A. Yes sir.

Q. Where is your home now?

A. On Pryor Creek.

Q. South of here?

A. North.

Q. How far north?

A. They call it six miles from Chelsea.

Q. Is that the place you came to when you first returned?

A. From my home I did.

Q. From Kansas after you married?

A. Yes sir.

Q. And you lived there ever since?

A. Yes sir.

The applicant applies for the enrollment of herself, her husband and seven children. The applicant is 38 years of age. She is identified on the Wallace Roll and the Kerns Clifton Roll, up upon the questioned list of the Wallace Roll. Attention is called to the note given in the testimony in connection with her enrollment at that time and that of her child Henrietta. Neither the applicant's mother or father, the former of whom is still living, and who has given testimony in this case, is identified on the roll of 1880. The applicant's change of name by marriage is established by the marriage license and certificate filed here

■

8

with. Since the foregoing part of this decision was rendered, attention is called to the fact that the names of the applicant and a deceased child, but not the child, Henrietta who is applied for now, are found upon another division of the Wallace Roll, which appears to be a division of persons who were accepted at that time and whose names were transferred from the questioned list. Careful attention is called to the applicant's testimony in regard to her residence in Kansas, and to that of her mother, who has not yet applied for herself, but who has given testimony in this case. For the further consideration of the case, under the conditions stated, the applicant will now be listed for enrollment as a Cherokee Freedman on a doubtful card, and the final decision of the Commission will be made known to her at her postoffice address. Her husband is a colored man, but is of the States, and he applies only as an intermarriage freedman. He is shown by the license and certificate filed herewith to have been married to his wife under a Cherokee license and in accordance with Cherokee law on the 7th day of August, 1885; they had previously been married under United States law in Kansas in 1880; neither of them was married prior to this marriage, and they lived together in the Cherokee Nation ever since 1882. He will now be listed for enrollment on a doubtful card as a Cherokee Freedman by intermarriage, and the final decision of the Commission will be made known to him at his postoffice address. As for the seven children named in the testimony, they are all minors and are said to be now living. The child, Henrietta, is identified on the Kerns Clifton Roll and on the questioned list of the Wallace Roll. The children, William H., Eunice C., and Doda C., are identified on the Kerns Clifton Roll. These children will now be listed for enrollment as Cherokee Freedmen on a doubtful card with their mother and father. The child, Helen F., it appears should be on the Clifton Roll, but its omission appears to be due to a clerical error. The children, Leonard E. and Sophia A., are too young to be upon any roll. The applicant is desired to supply the Commission with certificates of births of the three last named children and they will be listed for enrollment as Cherokee Freedmen on a doubtful card with their father and mother, and the final decision of the Commission in regard to these children also will be communicated to the applicant at her postoffice address.

The under signed, being duly sworn, states that as stenographer to the Commission to the Five Civilized Tribes, he correctly recorded the testimony and proceedings in this case, and that the foregoing is a full, true and correct transcript of his stenographic notes thereof.

(Signed) E. G. Rothenberger.

Subscribed and sworn to before me this 1st day of June 1901.

(Signed) T. B. Needles
Commissioner.

Maggie Kennedy, being first duly sworn states that as stenographer to the Commission to the Five Civilized Tribes, she made

■

9

the above and foregoing copy that the same is a true and correct copy of the original transcript.

//Maggie Kennedy//

Subscribed and sworn to before me this the 15th day of December 1904.

//Charles H Sawyer//
Notary Public.

■

Transcript II. Georgeanna Thornton
Department of the Interior,
Commission of the Five Civilized Tribes,
Chelsea, I.T., May 31, 1901

In the matter of the application of Georgeanna Thornton, for enrollment as a Cherokee Freedman; she being sworn by Commissioner C. R. Breckinridge, testified as follows:

Q. What is your name?
A. Georgeanna Thornton.

Q. What is your age?

A. I can't think of it.

Q. About how old are you?

A. I can't even guess.

Q. About 70 [or so] years along there?

A. Yes sir I guess that is it.

Q. What is your post office?

A. Chelsea.

Q. Do you live in Cooweescoowee district?

A. Yes sir.

Q. Do you want to be enrolled as a Cherokee Freedman?

A. Yes sir.

Q. Do you want to enroll anybody besides yourself?

A. Just myself.

Q. How long have you lived in the Cherokee Nation?

A. I has always lived with the Cherokee Nation.

Q. Give me the name of your father?

A. John Fields.

Q. Is he dead?

A. Yes sir.

Q. How long has he been dead?

A. He died after the Wallace Roll.

Q. Give me the name of your mother?

A. I don't know my mother, she was sold when I was little.

Q. Were you a slave in the Cherokee Nation when the war broke out?

A. Yes sir.

Q. To whom did you belong?

A. Amos Thornton.

Q. Was he a well known Cherokee citizen?

A. Yes sir.

Q. Where were you during the war?

A. Fort Gibson.

Q. Were you there all during the war?

A. Yes sir.

Q. Didn't go out at all during the war?

A. Yes they took me out to Springfield, Missouri, and we spent a winter
   there and then come back, in the spring.

Q. Was the war going on when you were in Springfield?

A. Yes sir.

Q. You have been married have you?

A. No sir I is not married.

Q. You have been married though?

A. Yes sir.

Q. How many times?

A. Once.

Q. To whom were you married?

A. A State raised man.

Q. Give me his name?

A. Toney Wright.

Q. Where did you marry him?

A. On the Virdigris river.

Q. When did you marry him?

A. I can't tell you the year.

Q. Was it after the war?

A. Yes sir.

Q. How long after the war?

A. Long time after the war, can't tell you the year.

Q. You have a daughter who just applied?

A. Yes sir that was my daughter.

Q. What is her name now?

A. Elizabeth Bowlen.

Q. Give me the name of her father?

A. Amos Thornton, that was my master.

Q. There was never a marriage between you and this woman's father?

A. No sir.

Q. How long after the war was it when you married Toney Wright?

A. 5 or 6 years.

Q. Is Toney Wright dead?

A. He is out in Oklahoma somewhere, he run away from me.

Q. How long did you and he live together?

A. A year.

Q. And you have never married since then?

A. No sir.

Q. Do you remember what year they brought you back from Kansas?

A. Never went to Kansas.

Q. Well Springfield then—in Missouri?

A. No sir I don't remember the year.

Q. Where have you lived since they brought you back?

A. At Fort Gibson.

Q. All the time?

A. Yes sir, working in and out of there.

Q. Where did you work out of Fort Gibson?

A. At Fort Sill.

■

2

Q. Then where?

A. Then back to Fort Gibson.

Q. Where else.

A. No where else.

Q. Ever work in Parsons?

A. Yes sir worked up there two or three months, once.

Q. Anywhere else except these places you have mentioned?

A. Yes sir at Tahlequah.

Q. I mean outside of the Cherokee Nation?

A. That is all.

Q. Have you always gone by the name of Thornton?

A. Yes sir.

Applicant not found on the authenticated roll of 1880.

Applicant not found on the census roll of 1896.

Q. Did you draw strip money?

A. Yes sir.

The Kerne-Clifton Roll of the Cherokee Nation examined and the name of the applicant found thereon as follows:

Page 103, No. 3573, Georgeann Thornton, Cooweescoowee District.

Wallace Roll of the Cherokee Nation examined and the name of the applicant identified thereon as follows:

Page 142, No. 2965, Georgianna Thornton, Cooweescoowee District.

Q. Have you ever applied for admission to the United State Court, or the
    Cherokee Council or Commission, or anything of that sort?
A. I don't understand you.
Q. Have you ever applied to be recognized as a Citizen of the Cherokee
    Nation except on the Wallace and Kerne-Clifton Roll?
A. Yes sir.
Q. Where?
A. Fort Gibson.
Q. To what did you apply there?
A. When the payment was.
Q. How comes it that you are not on the 1880 roll?
A. I don't know, I ought to be down there.
Q. Did you ever get a paper from any court of any body of men, saying that
    you were readmitted or admitted to citizenship, or recognized as a
    Cherokee Freedman?
A. No sir.
Q. Have you ever applied to be enrolled by any other tribe or nation as a
    freedman?
A. No sir.
Q. Didn't you take your daughter who just applied, to Kansas to get married?
A. Yes sir.
Q. Did you stay there until she got married?
A. Yes sir.
Q. Did you come back when she came back?
A. Before she did.
Q. Did you ever go up there any time other than that to visit your daughter?
A. Yes sir.
Q. Where to?
A. Parsons.

Q. How many times did you go up there?

A. Just once.

Q. How long was that before your daughter was married?

A. I went there after she was married.

Q. Did you ever go up there to visit her before she was married?

A. No sir.

By W. W. Hastins, Cherokee attorney:

Q. Who did you live with at Fort Gibson just after the war?

A. I lived with the officers in the garrison and worked and then would go home.

Q. Where was your home?

A. Right where Florian Nash has his store, my master had his home there.

Q. And you lived with him?

A. Yes sir.

Q. How long did you live with him after the war?

A. 3 or 4 years.

Q. Did Amos Thornton have any family?

A. Yes sir.

Q. What is his wife called?

A. Minerva Vann now, she is Conan Vann's wife now, and she had a son named Lewis.

■

3

Q. He know of your staying down there does he?

A. Yes sir.

Q. Mrs. Conan Vann and Lewis Thornton would know all about you just after the war and would know of you ever since wouldn't they?

A. Yes sir.

Q. When did you go to Fort Sill?

A. I can't tell you the year.

Q. Who did you go with?

A. With the officers, Major Forsythe, that was in the [infantry] then.

Q. Was your daughter Eliza Bowlin with you?

A. Yes sir.

Q. You staid there 6 or 7 years didn't you?

A. 3 or 4 years, I can't count in years or days; I would just go and come when it got good and I never kept no count when I would come or go.

Q. Did you ever have a home at Fort Gibson of your own?

A. Yes sir, right in sight of where Mr. Bushyhead used to live.

Q. Did you live there when Mr. Bushyhead used to live there?

A. Yes sir, I waited on his wife when she died.

Q. Did you ever live in Kansas?

A. No sir I never did live there.

Q. Where have you been living during the last ten years—after you left Fort Gibson where have you lived—where are you living now?

A. On Pryor Creek.

Q. How long have you been living there?

A. Ever since my daughter has been living there.

Q. Are you living with her?

A. Yes sir.

By Com'r Breckenridge,

The applicant states that she has lived in the Cherokee Nation all her life except a brief period of absence during the Civil war; her further testimony indicated that she has spent some years at Fort Sill; she is identified on the Wallace and Kerne-Clifton Rolls, but not upon the 1880 roll or the census roll of 1896; for the further consideration of her case, she will now be listed for enrollment as a Cherokee Freedman on a doubtful card, and when the final decision of the Commission is reached she will be notified thereof at her post office address.

■

Chas. [Von Keiss], being sworn states that as stenographer to the Commission to the Five Civilized Tribes he reported in full all the proceedings in the above [course] and that the foregoing is a full, true and correct transcript of his stenographic notes therein.

[signature]

Subscribed and sworn to before me this the 3rd day of June, 1901 at Chelsea, I. T.

[signature]

Commissioner.

■

Transcript III. John L. Bowlin et al.
Department of the Interior,
Commission to the Five Civilized Tribes,
Vinita, I.T. October 7th, 1901

SUPPLEMENTAL TESTIMONY in the matter of the enrollment of GEORGEANNA THORNTON as a Cherokee Freedman, introduced on part of applicant:

Appearances:

L. T. Brown, agent for applicant.
W. W. Hastings, of counsel for Cherokee Nation.

Mr. Hastings of Mr. Brown: What do you expect to prove?
Mr. Brown: Ownership and return.

Mr. Hastings: Come now the representatives of the Cherokee Nation and protest against the taking of this testimony for the reason that testimony was taken in this case upon these points vis: Ownership and return, on the 31st day of May, 1901, at Chelsea, and that opportunity for the taking of additional testimony was given during all the month of June and month of September, 1901, and that none was offered until after the Cherokee Nation offered testimony on the 2d day of October 1901, and that these points upon which testimony is desired now to be introduced is not rebuttal testimony, but is testimony upon the original points at issue.

PATSY JOHNSON, being duly sworn by Commissioner Needles, testified as follows on part of applicant:

MR. BROWN: State your name?

A. Patsy Johnson.

Q. What is your age?

A. I expect I am about 52.

Q. Post office address?

A. Fort Gibson.

Q. Are you a recognized citizen of the Cherokee Nation?

A. Yes, sir.

Q. Is your name on the 1880 roll?

A. Yes, sir.

Q. Do you know Georgeanna Thornton?

A. Yes, sir.

Q. How long have you known her?

A. Ever since the war.

Q. Do you know where she was at the close of the war?

A. In Fort Gibson.

Q. How long did she continue to remain in Fort Gibson after the close of the war?

A. I don't just remember how long; she was working in the garrison, I don't know how long.

Q. Do you know where she was in the year 1866?

A. In Fort Gibson.

MR. HASTINGS: What year is this?

A. 1891.

Q. 1891?

A. Yes, sir.

Q. What year did we have that last Cherokee payment?

A. I don't remember.

Q. What year did Mr. Wallace make the payment?

A. I don't know.

Q. What year were you born?

A. I don't know.

Q. What year were you married?

A. I don't know that.

Q. What year was your first child born?

A. No, sir.

Q. You don't know a year in the world?

A. Yes, sir.

Q. '66?

A. Yes, sir; I do know that my first child was born in '68 on the bayou; that's one thing I always remember.

Q. What kin is this woman to you?

A. She is my first cousin.

Q. You never testified for her before did you?

A. No, sir; wasn't called on.

Q. Where did you live?

A. I live on Four Mile Branch, not exactly on Four Mile Branch, on the other side.

Q. How far from Fort Gibson?

A. Four miles.

Q. How old are you now?

A. 52.

Q. What was your father's name?

A. Peter Sanders.

Q. Where were you living the first year the war closed?

A. Fort Gibson.

■

2

Q. In the town?

A. Yes, sir.

Q. With whom was she living?

A. Aunt Nancy Thornton.

Q. She is dead is she?

A. I think she is.

Q. How long did she live with Aunt Nancy?

A. I could not say, she never lived any one place long.

Q. Was she ever up at Springfield, Missouri?

A. Yes, sir, there is where she come from when she come to Gibson, come with the soldiers.

Q. The soldiers remained there for about 20 years after the war?

A. Yes, sir, I think so.

Q. Did you ever see this woman up in Parsons?

A. No, sir.

Q. Did you know whether she ever worked up there or not?

A. Yes, sir, I think she said she did; when she was at my house I don't know how long that has been claimed she had a girl going to school.

Q. Do you know Lewis Thornton?

A. Yes, sir.

Q. What kin is Lewis Thornton to her master?

A. Is her master's son.

Q. Where was Lewis Thornton living in 1865 and '67?

A. He was living in Fort Gibson, I think he was butchering for Mr. West.

Q. Well, Lewis Thornton would know where this woman was, wouldn't he?

A. I don't know whether he would or not, sometimes she would visit us when she would not visit Lewis Thornton.

Q. It was a small town wasn't it?

A. Yes, sir.

Q. How long did this woman ever live about Fort Gibson?

A. I could not tell you the date just exactly.

Q. Live there as much as a year?

A. Oh, longer than that.

Q. Well, your best judgment?

A. I could not say just exactly, she was there up until she went with the officers to Fort Sill I think.

Q. Well, when was that?

A. That must have been about '68 I think, it was the year before my girl Fanny was born.

Q. '67 then? You said your girl was born in 1868?

A. Yes, sir, that is right.

Q. She left there in 1867?

A. No, sir, I think she was living there by the river I think.

Q. I thought you said she left the year before your child was born?

A. Yes, sir, she would go and would come and go, but she was in here at Fort Gibson.

Q. Where is she living now?

A. I don't know.

Q. How long has it been since she lived at Fort Gibson?

A. I don't know really how long it has been.

Q. Well, has it been 30 years since she left there?

A. No, sir.

Q. 20?

A. No, sir.

Q. How long then?

A. It has not been that long; you have got me kinda thinking; I told you when she come to my house and stayed a while.

Q. How long did she stay at your house?

A. She stayed there two or three months.

Q. Have any children then?

A. No, sir, she only had one.

Q. Where was it born?

A. Born right here in Fort Gibson.

ALECK NIVENS, being duly sworn by Commissioner Needles, testified as follows on behalf of applicant:

MR. BROWN: State your name?

A. Aleck Nivens.

Q. Your age?

A. About 60.

Q. What is your post office?

A. Fort Gibson.

Q. Are you a recognized citizen of the Cherokee Nation?

A. Yes, sir.

Q. Does your name appear upon the authenticated roll of 1880?

A. My name appears upon every roll that you can find.

Q. Do you know Georgeanna Thornton?

A. Yes, sir.

Q. To whom did she belong at the beginning of the war?

A. Amos Thornton.

Q. Was Amos Thornton a citizen of the Cherokee Nation by blood?

A. Well, I don't know; he claimed to be a citizen of the Cherokee Nation.

■

3

Q. Do you know whether or not Georgeanna Thornton went out of the Cherokee Nation during the war?

A. Yes, sir.

Q. Where did she go?

A. She went up to Cane Hill.

Q. With whom did she return?

A. She come back with the regiment. That is the Command, the whole Command.

Q. Were you along?

A. Yes, sir.

Q. Do you know where she was in the year 1866?

A. She was at Gibson.

Q. In the Cherokee Nation?

A. Yes, sir.

MR. HASTINGS: How old are you?

A. I am about 60.

Q. What year did Wallace make that payment?

A. I don't know exactly what year it was, knowed too but I forget, I can't keep remembrances or nothing.

Q. Is Georgeanna Thornton any kin to you?

A. No, sir.

Q. Do you know Lewis Thornton?

A. Yes, sir.

Q. What kin was he to Amos Thornton?

A. Amos Thornton's son.

Q. Where was Lewis Thornton in 1865 and '6?

A. He was there at Gibson.

Q. What in the town?

A. Yes, sir.

Q. How big a town was Fort Gibson then?

A. It was not such a big town, I could not tell the miles distance or yards.

Q. Any bigger than it is now?

A. Might have been a little bigger.

Q. Well, it is five or six hundred now?

A. I don't know, I never counted the houses.

Q. Well, what is your best judgment?

A. I could not tell exactly.

Q. Did you say you wasn't any kin to this woman?

A. No, sir.

Q. Did you testify for her five years ago?

A. No, sir.

Q. Didn't testify for her down to Fort Gibson the other day?

A. No, sir, never was called up for her before.

Q. Did Lewis Thornton have any position with the soldiers there in 1866?

A. If he had any I don't know; some of them says he did but if he did I don't know.

Q. Soldiers up there in the garrison?

A. Yes, sir, they were up there in the Garrison.

Q. Now, where was this woman, what was she doing?

A. Well, when I lived there Georgia was just staying in a little log hut on the bank of the river.

Q. By herself?

A. No, her and an old lady by the name of old Aunt Mollie Rankins' daughter.

Q. What time did you leave there?

A. I went away from there along, I think it was in '67 when I went off.

Q. What time did you see them there first?

A. I saw them there in '63 and '66 and '67.

Q. Saw her there in '64?

A. Yes, she was there in '64.

Q. '63?

A. Yes, sir, we brought her here, we brought her down there in the Nation in '63.

Q. And she continued to live there until after you left there?

A. Yes, sir.

Q. What time did you leave there?

A. I left there along about '67.

Q. Do you know what time of the year?

A. No, sir, I don't.

Q. Know whether it was in the spring or fall?

A. It was kinda in the fall.

Q. How long after the war was over?

A. I don't know.

Q. What was you doing in those two years?

A. Well, I went down in the bottom and farmed a little.

Q. Who for?

A. Myself.

Q. Did you own a farm down there?

A. No, sir, I was working on a little patch the Creeks left there during the war, they used to farm and I was working on it.

Q. You saw Lewis Thornton there at the same time?

A. Yes, sir, saw him there all the time.

■

4

L. D. DANIELS, being duly sworn by Commissioner Needles, testified as follows, on part of applicant:

MR. BROWN: State your name?

A. L. D. Daniels.

Q. Your age?

A. 56.

Q. Post office?

A. Lenepah.

Q. Are you a recognized citizen of the Cherokee Nation?

A. Yes, sir.

Q. Is your name upon the authenticated roll of 1880?

A. Yes, sir.

Q. Do you know Georgeanna Thornton?

A. Yes, sir.

Q. To whom did she belong at the beginning of the war?

A. Amos Thornton.

Q. Was Amos Thornton a citizen of the Cherokee Nation by blood?

A. Yes, sir.

Q. Did Georgeanna Thornton go out of the Cherokee Nation during the war?

A. If she did I don't know it.

Q. Do you know where she was in the year 1866?

A. Yes, sir.

Q. Where?

A. Fort Gibson.

Q. In the Cherokee Nation?

A. In the Cherokee Nation.

MR. HASTINGS: You testified in the Andrew T. Watie case D. #502?

A. Yes, sir, I did.

Q. You said you saw him here in the Cherokee Nation in 1866?

A. Yes, sir.

Q. He came back to the Cherokee Nation with General Stand Watie?

A. I didn't say who he came back with.

Q. That was in 1866?

A. Yes, sir, in the fall of 1866.

Q. Where did you see him?

A. At the ranch, at the Porum Gap.

Q. About the Tom Starr place?

A. Probably four or five miles, probably further than that.

Q. I will ask you who he was with when you saw him?

A. I didn't know the men, one or two Cherokee fellows had a bunch of hogs there.

Q. Well, did you testify for this Joe Lynch, the one known as little Joe?

A. Not as I know of, there is so many of them, I don't know what I am talking about.

Q. With whom was Georgeanna Thornton living when you knew her after the war in Fort Gibson?

A. Well, sir, she was right with the army; Second Regiment camped at Fort Gibson, Cherokee Nation, sir.

Q. Up there in the Garrison?

A. No, just below the garrison on that little draw.

Q. Did they remain there?

A. Part of the time.

Q. How long?

A. I found them there in February, '66.

Q. Was Georgeanna Thornton with them?

A. Yes, sir, she were there, and then we moved down to the Salt Lick about
20 miles from there and Dan Pinder's wife and I hauled her in my
wagon Bob Ross' baggage was in.

Q. That was in '67?

A. That was in the fall of '63.

Q. I am trying to get after the war; where was she right after the war?

A. Right in Fort Gibson.

Q. After the war?

A. Right there with the soldiers.

Q. With whom was she living at that time?

A. She was staying with Nancy Thornton.

Q. Now, in what part of town was Nancy Thornton living?

A. Nancy Thornton lived about a 150 yards probably from where Mrs. Davis
lives in this direction.

Q. Well, north, east or south from the Garrison?

A. No, from the old garrison used to be where the railroad runs, at that time
that was the town.

Q. Well, how long did you see her living there?

A. I left there I believe; let's see, the 10th cavalry come there in '67 and she was
doing the laundry work for them up in the garrison and if I mistake not
she was there in the spring of '68, for they left two companies there.

■

5

Q. Well, then where did she go?

A. I think she married a man that belonged to the army and I think she went
to Kansas, I don't know where she went, wherever the soldiers went.

Q. Did you see her after that date?

A. Yes, sir.

Q. When?

A. I seen her when Jess Buskyhead was going to run was Chief.

Q. Was that the first time you had seen her?

A. I seen her before that.

Q. When was that?

A. Let's see I moved from there in 1875 and I got a school in the '78, well I met her there in Gibson in '78.

Q. That was the next time you had seen her?

A. Yes, sir.

Q. Now, from the time she left in 1868 you never saw her until 1878?

A. I say that I moved from there in 1875 and I seen her twice after I moved from there, and I seen her the third time in '78.

Q. Now, she lived there in '68 with the soldiers?

A. Yes, sir.

Q. When did you see her next?

A. I seen her about, it must have been '70 something before I moved from there, might have been '72 or 3.

Q. Well, do you mean that this is when you moved or saw her?

A. I seen her after she first left Fort Gibson and went with the soldiers she come back there.

Q. When was that?

A. That was in '72 or '3.

Q. How long did she stay there?

A. I don't know.

Q. How long did you see her there?

A. I saw her there once or twice, I was living five miles from Fort Gibson.

Q. When did you move out five miles from Gibson?

A. I moved the 5th day of July, 1867.

Q. And did you continue to live out there until you left Fort Gibson?

A. I continued so, but I was in Fort Gibson more so than I was out home.

Q. But you never saw this woman from 1868 until this time, '72 or '3?

A. No, sir.

Q. Now, after you seen her in '72 or '3 when was the next time you seen her?

A. I think it was in '78 or '9.

Q. Where did you see her then?

A. Right at the picnic ground, I think it was in '79 I met her there at the fair ground, I met her there with Joe.

Mr. Brown: I would like to have this testimony made part of the record in the case of Elizabeth Boland, D. #444.

J. O. Rosson, being first duly sworn, states that as stenographer to the Commission to the Five Civilized Tribes he correctly recorded the testimony and proceedings in this case, and that the foregoing is a true and complete transcript of his stenographic notes thereof.

(Signed) J. O. Rosson

Subscribed and sworn to before me this October 11, 1901.

(Signed) T. B. Needles,
Commissioner,

Arthur B. Croninger, being duly sworn, states that as stenographer to the Commission to the Five Civilized Tribes he made the foregoing copy, and that the same is a true and complete copy of the original transcript.

Subscribed and sworn to before me this 5th day of December, 1901.

Notary Public

■

Transcript IV. Georgeanna Thornton
Department of the Interior,
Commission to the Five Civilized Tribes,
Vinita, I.T., October 24, 1901

SUPPLEMENTAL TESTIMONY in the matter of the enrollment of Georgeanna THORNTON as a Cherokee Freedman, introduced on the part of the Cherokee Nation:

Appearances:

Mr. J. S. Davenport for Cherokee Nation.

There is filed in the case of notice of the taking of testimony beginning at eight o'clock this day and endorsement shows that the notice was served on applicant on the 30th of September by John Parks, Marshall of the Cherokee Nation.

LEWIS R. THORNTON, being duly sworn by Commissioner Breckinridge, testified as follows:

MR. DAVENPORT: Give your full name please?
A. L. E. Thornton.
Q. How old are you, Mr. Thornton?
A. I am 64 years old, I was born in '37.
Q. What is your post office?
A. Fort Gibson.
Q. How long have you lived in the Cherokee Nation?
A. I was born in the Cherokee Nation.
Q. Have you lived here all your life?
A. Yes, sir.
Q. What was your father's name?
A. Amos.
Q. Where did he live at the breaking out of the war?
A. Illinois district.
Q. Well, after the close of the war, was your father living at the close of the war?
A. Yes, sir.
Q. Where did he live then?
A. At Fort Gibson.
Q. Did your father own a slave at the breaking out of the war by the name of Georgeanna?
A. Yes, sir.
Q. Did she leave the Cherokee Nation, or go away from your father's place during the war?

A. She left him in '64; no '65 when out with the Command and came back as well as I remember in 1864. She was living with us and her father come and got her sometime in 1864 and took her away and I never saw her any more.

Q. Well at the close of the war [was] she around your father's place, there at Fort Gibson?

A. Not that I know of.

Q. What were you doing yourself after the close of the war, if you were engaged in any mind of business?

A. For a while I stayed in the Commissary Department and a while I was in the Butcher business.

Q. Selling meats to the people around Fort Gibson?

A. Making contracts with the Government.

Q. How long were you engaged in the butchering business, and contracting with the government around Fort Gibson after the close of the war?

A. I don't know how long I butchered, I moved out of Fort Gibson in '67, in February.

Q. Well, from the time the war closed up to the time you moved out on the bayou in 1867, had Georgeanna Thornton, who was the former slave of your father, returned to Fort Gibson and lived near where Florine Nash's store is now?

A. No, sir.

Q. Well, are you able to state whether or not Georgeanna ever returned after the war and lived with your father at either Fort Gibson or near Fort Gibson?

A. She never did come and live there.

Q. Now, about how many years after the war before you saw or heard of Georgeanna being back in the country?

A. I could not tell you; about five or six years after I moved out on the bayou.

Q. It was five or six years after you moved out on the bayou and what year was it you moved out there?

A. I moved in '67, February.

Q. And you know that she didn't return and live with your father since the war where Mr. Nash's store is?

A. No, sir, my father lived with me.

■

2

Q. Had you any sisters?

A. One.

Q. What was her name now?

A. Mrs. Elisabeth Thompson.

Q. Mrs. Conong Vann was she your sister?

A. Step-mother.

Q. And your father lived there with you and she didn't come back there and live with you?

A. No, sir.

Q. Were you grown when the war broke out?

A. Yes, sir, I was 24 years old, I enlisted when I was 24 years old.

Q. Did you know whether or not that Georgeanna Thornton ever had a home at Fort Gibson after the war?

A. No, sir, I don't think she ever had any.

Q. Do you know of her residing there at any time?

A. I don't know.

Q. You have resided at Fort Gibson and near there ever since the war haven't you, Mr. Thornton?

A. Yes, sir, I have lived there off and on.

COM'R BRECKINRIDGE: Where were you at the close of the war?

A. I was at Fort Gibson, I mustered out.

Q. What year was that in?

A. '65, May.

Q. Where were you the next five or six years after that?

A. I was right there at Gibson, more of less all the time.

Q. Well, where were you making your home after you were mustered out?

A. I moved as I said in '67 on the bayou and before I moved I was living at Fort Gibson.

Q. How far is that?

A. About two miles and a half, called it three miles.

Q. That was in February, 1867?

A. Yes, sir.

Q. Were you living with your father in Gibson before that?

A. My father lived with me.

Q. You and your father lived together?

A. Yes sir, me and my wife.

Q. That is from the time you were mustered out until February 1867, when you moved out on the bayou, and then you only lived two miles and a half?

A. Yes, sir.

Q. When do you first remember seeing this woman, Georgeanna Thornton, after the war closed?

A. Well, I don't know exactly, I could not give it, five or six years though after she come out there where I had lived and she had just come back from somewhere.

Q. Come out to the bayou?

A. Yes, sir.

Q. And she never lived with you or your father after the war closed?

A. No, sir, but she lived with us a while during the war.

Q. That was after she went off with you father in 1864?

A. Yes, sir.

Q. How long had you been living out there on the bayou before she came?

A. I don't know, five or six years, maybe more.

Q. Now, she left you all in '64 did she, while the war was going on?

A. Yes, sir, father took her off.

Q. And you didn't see her and know anything about her until you saw her out on the bayou some five or six years?

A. Yes, sir.

Com'r Breckinridge: This will be filed as supplemental testimony in the case of Georgeanna Thornton, Cherokee Freeman doubtful card #445.

J. O. Rosson, being first duly sworn, states that as stenographer to the Commission to the Five Civilized Tribes he correctly recorded the testimony and proceedings in this case, and that the foregoing is a true and complete transcript of his stenographic notes thereof.

Subscribed and sworn to before me this October 8th, 1901

Commissioner.

■

Transcript V. Elizabeth Bowlin et al., and Georgeanna Thornton
Department of the Interior,
Commission to the Five Civilized Tribes,
Muskogee, I.T., June 18, 1904

SUPPLEMENTAL PROCEEDINGS HAD in the matter of the application
for the enrollment of ELIZABETH BOWLIN, ET. A., and GEORGEANNA
THORNTON as Cherokee Freedmen.

It appears that on May 13, 1904, the applicants, their agent, and the
attorney for the Cherokee Nation were notified by letter that an opportunity
would be given each of them to appear before the Commission at its offices
in Muskogee, Indian Territory, on June 16, 1904, and introduce further
testimony touching the points mentioned in said letter. Upon motion of
the attorney for the Cherokee Nation this case was continued until June 18,
1904, when the following testimony was introduced:

Appearances:

Applicants represented by John L. Bowlin, husband of Elizabeth Bowlin.
Cherokee Nation by the attorneys W. F. Hastings and L. B. Bell.
ARCH Carter, being first duly sworn, testified as follows:

By the Commission:

Q. What is your name?
A. Arch Carter.
Q. How old are you?
A. 58, 59 the 10th of this coming October.
Q. What is your post office address?
A. Fort Gibson.
Q. Do you claim to be a Cherokee Freedman?
A. Yes, sir.
Q. Do you know the applicants in this case, Elizabeth Bowlin and
    Georgeanna Thornton?

A. Yes, sir, Georgeanna, I do.

Q. You don't know Elizabeth?

A. Yes, sir, I do.

Q. How old are they now?

A. I couldn't tell you.

Q. Do you know how old Georgeanna is?

A. No, sir.

Q. Was either of these persons the slave of a Cherokee citizen before the war?

A. Yes, sir, Georgeanna was.

Q. How long have you known her?

A. Since 1862.

Q. Do you know whom she belonged to before the war?

A. Yes, sir.

Q. Who?

A. Amos Thornton, first cousin of the people that owned us.

Q. Did she go out of the Cherokee Nation during the war?

A. She followed the Army out.

Q. Do you know where she went to?

A. Yes, sir, she went to Neoche and back to Bantonville and then to Fort Gibson.

Q. Do you know when Georgeanna first returned to the Cherokee Nation after the war?

A. She was already here when peace was declared.

Q. She was here when the war closed?

A. Yes, sir.

Q. At what point in the Cherokee Nation was she living?

A. Right here at Fort Gibson.

Q. Do you know where she has lived since that time?

A. No, sir, not all the places; she left Fort Gibson in 69 and she went to Fort [Smith Sill].

Q. Did she live in Fort Gibson from the time peace was declared until 1867?

A. Yes, sir, she died right there.

Q. Was this child Georgeanna [means Elizabeth] born at that time?

A. Born before; claimed to be that old Amos Thornton was the father; that is what hurt Mrs. Vann and old man Thornton.

Q. Was this child born before the war?

A. Just about the breaking out of the war, a small little thing when she followed the Army around. I was a teamster.

■

2

Q. Was the child with its mother there in the Cherokee Nation from the time peace was declared until 1869?

A. Yes, sir, right with its mother.

Q. How long did she stay out at Fort Sill when she went there in 1869?

A. I don't know.

Q. When was the next time after that that you saw her in the Cherokee Nation?

A. I couldn't say; I never paid any attention.

Q. What is the best of your recollection?

A. I couldn't say, she was in and out, backwards and forwards; I don't know where she went; once in a while she would come back to the old lady that raised her, old aunt Nancy Thornton.

Q. Where is Georgeanna Thornton living now?

A. Out west.

Q. Who is her son-in-law, John L. Bowlin?

A. Yes, sir.

Q. Living there with her daughter Elizabeth and son-in-law?

A. Yes, sir.

Q. How low have they been living there?

A. I don't know.

Q. How long have they been living in the Cherokee Nation this last time?

A. I don't know sir.

Q. Don't know anything about that?

A. No, sir, all I know is she was here all during the war up to 1869.

By Mr. Hastings:

Q. Who did she come back here with during the war or in 1869?

A. She come back in 1863 with Col. Phillips.

Q. How long did she stay then?

A. Until 1869.

Q. Why do you remember it was in 1869?

A. Because I know it; I drove a team there with the same Company she cooked for Robert Ross.

Q. This same Robert Ross that was here to-day?

A. Yes, sir.

Q. Up until 1869?

A. Up until peace was made.

Q. I mean now just after peace, 1865 and '6 what did she do?

A. I don't know.

Q. Who was she working for?

A. I don't know.

Q. Who did she live with?

A. John Thornton.

Q. He a colored man?

A. Yes, sir, and right with Minerva Vann, old lady is dead and gone now.

Q. What kin was Lewis Thornton to Amos Thornton?

A. It was Amos Thornton's son.

Q. This woman belonged to Lewis Thornton's father?

A. Yes, sir.

Q. Lewis Thornton was the young master of this woman?

A. Yes sir.

Q. How old is Georgeanna Thornton?

A. I couldn't tell you.

Q. Was this woman grown when the war came up?

A. She must have been she had this child.

Q. When did she have this child?

A. I couldn't tell you the date.

Q. You know, you say, when she left positively, now this is important circumstance, when she had this child?

A. I was bred and born in Tahlequah and they lived at Gibson.

Q. Why do you know, if you know when she left there, why don't you know when this child was born?

A. That was something else, and I don't know.

Q. Was the child born before the war?

A. Yes, about the breaking out of the war.

Q. You say this woman did go out of the Cherokee Nation during the war?

A. Yes, sir, she followed the Army out.

Q. Where was her young master, Lewis Thornton, living at the close of the war, in 1865 and '67?

A. He was a butcher there for the government.

Q. You claim that this woman was right there in town at the same time?

A. Yes, sir.

Q. Can you read and write?

A. No, sir, but I have got pretty good mother wit.

Q. Her young master, Lewis Thornton, was right there?

A. Yes, sir.

Q. Was he there in '69?

A. Yes, sir, he was living on the bayou.

■

3

Q. How far from Fort Gibson?

A. Three miles.

Q. When did you move to Fort Gibson?

A. Been there always.

Q. Did you live at Tahlequah?

A. I was raised a mile and a half from Tahlequah.

Q. When did you move to Fort Gibson?

A. In 1863.

Q. During the war?

A. Yes, sir.

Q. You don't know who this woman worked for from 1865 to 1869?

A. No, sir.

Q. Who did she live with?

A. That old lady that raised her.

Q. Who?

A. Nancy Thornton.

Q. And she is dead?

A. Yes, sir, and worked for her old mistress.

Q. How long has she been away from Fort Gibson now?

A. I don't know.

Q. Has she lived there since 1869?

A. I don't know.

Q. Not to your knowledge has she?

A. No, sir.

Q. You don't know where she lived since that time?

A. No, sir.

Q. What year did Mr. Wallace made a roll of citizens of the Cherokee
    Nation?

A. I don't know.

Q. What year did Kern-Clifton make a roll of the citizens of the Cherokee
    Nation?

A. I don't know.

Q. What year was that payment made by Mr. Dickson?

A. I don't keep no record.

Q. You haven't kept any records about dates have you?

A. No, sir.

Q. What year were you married in?

A. 1865.

Q. What year was you first child born?

A. In '66.

By the Commission:

Q. You stated that this woman, Georgeanna, was at Fort Gibson when peace
    was declared and lived there until 1869?

A. Yes, sir.

Q. How do you place these dates so exactly?

A. I worked for the quartermaster and it was in '69, they said, when the
    soldiers went to Fort Sill.

Q. You were working for the quartermaster there in Fort Gibson?

A. Yes, sir.

Q. And this woman was living there all the time?

A. Yes, sir.

Q. What did she do there?

A. She was cooking and washing.

Q. For whom?

A. This Mrs. Vann, as I said, one of the women she belonged to.

Q. She was working for her after the war?

A. Yes, sir, after the war.

(Continued until June 19, 1904.)

June 28, 1904, the applicants appearing by John L. Bowlin, husband of Eliza-beth Bowlin, and the Cherokee Nation by its representative, J. S. Davenport, the following testimony was introduced:

EMILY THOMPSON, being first fully sworn, testified as follows:

By the Commission:

Q. What is your name?

A. Emily Thompson.

Q. How old are you?

A. 55.

Q. What is your post office address?

A. Fort Gibson, Cherokee Nation.

Q. You claim to be a Cherokee Freedman.

A. Yes, sir.

Q. Do you know Georgeanna Thornton and her daughter, Elizabeth Bow-lin?

A. Yes, sir.

Q. How long have you known them?

A. All my life.

Q. Where was Georgeanna Thornton living when you first knew her?

A. Fort Gibson.

Q. About how old is she now?

A. About 69 or 70.

Q. How old is her daughter, Elizabeth Bowlin?

A. She was born just the year before the war.

Q. Was she born there in Fort Gibson?

A. Yes, sir, when the war come in Gibson she was a year old.

■

4

Q. Did Elizabeth and her mother belong to a Cherokee citizen before the war?

A. Yes, sir, to Amos Thornton.

Q. He was a recognized citizen of the Cherokee Nation?

A. Yes, sir.

Q. Did Georgeanna and her daughter, Elizabeth, go out of the Cherokee Nation during the war?

A. No, sir.

Q. They didn't go out until after the war?

A. No, sir.

Q. How long after the war before they first left the Nation?

A. It was six or seven years, for Lizzie was a big girl.

Q. I believe you stated in your testimony given to-day in your own case that you lived at Fort Gibson up until the year 1879 or 1880?

A. Yes, sir.

Q. And this Georgeanna and her daughter lived there until six or seven years after the war?

A. Yes, sir.

Q. Then where did they go?

A. Georgeanna went to Fort Sill to work.

Q. Fort Sill, Oklahoma?

A. Fort Sill, Arbuckle, out west, they call it Fort Sill.

Q. How long did she stay?

A. The first time she went she stayed a year and then come back; she didn't take the child when she first went. She left her with Aunt Margaret Irons.

Q. Well she left the child in Fort Gibson, did she?

A. Out on 14 Mile Creek, she took it up there.

Q. Near Fort Gibson?

A. Yes, sir.

Q. She stayed out a year and come back and stayed how long?

A. Five or six months; she would go out and come back again.

Q. Did she make several trips like that?

A. Yes, sir.

Q. When did she finally come back to the Cherokee Nation to live?

A. I couldn't tell you that, when she come back to live, I don't know what year it was in; she came back and went to housekeeping and then she broke up and went out to Fort Sill again; I don't know what year that was in.

Q. Where is Georgeanna Thornton living now, if you know?

A. She is living with her son-in-law, up above me somewhere in the Cherokee Nation.

Q. Do you know how long she stayed out in the Fort Sill country all together?

A. No, sir.

Q. You have no idea?

A. No, sir, I don't know how long she stayed.

Q. During the time she was out there, do you know whether or not she retained any household effects or owned any farm or improvements on the public domain of the Cherokee Nation?

A. She didn't have nothing but herself and that child.

Q. She has no house or furniture?

A. Yes, sir, she rented a house and furnished it up and her and the child kept house and was keeping house in Gibson when I went out.

Q. That was in 1879?

A. Yes, sir, she was keeping house in Fort Gibson when I left.

Q. Then you were out of the Nation, yourself, most of the time from 1879 until 1896 and don't know anything about the whereabouts of Georgeanna during that time?

A. I was out until 1896.

Q. And you can't state positively where Georgeanna was during that time?

A. No, sir, when I come back home and first saw her I saw her at Vinita.

Q. You have said in your own case that you made several trips between 1879 and 1895 back to Fort Gibson?

A. Yes, sir.

Q. Did you ever see Georgeanna or her daughter around there then?

A. I saw her daughter, but I didn't see her.

By Mr. Davenport:

Q. Where was Georgeanna living when the war broke out, Emily?

A. In Fort Gibson.

Q. With whom?

A. Amos Thornton.

Q. Where was she living when the war closed?

A. Fort Gibson.

Q. With whom?

A. Nancy Thornton.

■

5

Q. Who was Nancy Thornton?

A. Slave of Amos Thornton.

Q. How far was she living from Amos Thornton?

A. About as far as from here to the Depot. It was about a quarter of a mile.

Q. You know Lewis R. Thornton?

A. Yes, sir.

Q. Who was his father?

A. Amos Thornton.

Q. Then Lewis R. Thornton's father who was the owner of Georgeanna
   Thornton?

A. Yes, sir.

Q. Now do you remember that Amos Thornton took Georgeanna Thornton
   away from the Cherokee Nation in 1864?

A. No, he didn't; he took her sister, Cynthia.

Q. How old was Lewis Thornton at that time?

A. He was a good big man.

Q. Nearly grown?

A. Yes, sir.

Q. Old enough to have remembered if his father had taken anyone away
    from there, their home?

A. Yes, sir.

Q. His father and he were living there together at that time?

A. Yes, sir.

Q. About the time the war closed and a short while after what business were
    they engaged in Fort Gibson?

A. Amos Thornton, was always judge and clerk of the court.

Q. Was Lewis Thornton interested in or working any business there about
    the time the war closed?

A. None as I know of.

Q. Isn't it a fact that Lewis R. Thornton, who was the son of Amos Thornton,
    worked for nearly two years after the close of the war in a butcher
    shop in the town of Fort Gibson, Indian Territory?

A. Not as I know of.

Q. If he had would you have known it?

A. Yes, sir.

Q. Do you know where Lewis Thornton moved to when he left Fort Gibson?

A. Yes, sir.

Q. Where?

A. Out on the bayou.

Q. What year?

A. I couldn't tell you.

Q. After the close of the war?

A. Yes sir.

Q. He has been living there on the bayou near the town of Fort Gibson
    nearly ever since?

A. Yes, sir, he has been living right there.

Q. When did Georgeanna Bowlin, who was then known as Georgeanna
    Thornton, return to Fort Gibson after she went out in Kansas and
    worked for General Davidson?

A. I don't know, sir.

Q. She did go out in Kansas and live with General Davidson sometime after
    the war?

A. It wasn't in Kansas.

Q. Where was it?

A. Out west here.

Q. In Fort Sill?

A. Yes, sir.

Q. She did go to Kansas, didn't she?

A. She might have after I left home.

Q. Didn't she go there before she was a grown girl?

A. No, sir, for she is older than me.

Q. Who was that went there and went to school?

A. That was her daughter.

Q. What was her name?

A. Lizzie.

Q. This is the first time that you ever testified in this case, isn't it?

A. Yes sir.

Q. You don't know where Georgeanna was living from the time the war closed until 1867, do you?

A. No, sir, she come backwards and forwards to Gibson is all I can tell you; she worked at Fort Sill and come backwards and forwards to Gibson.

Q. General Davidson wasn't living at Fort Gibson after the close of the war, was he?

A. I don't know who General Davidson is, she went with some general.

Q. She went with an officer of the United States Army just before the troops were mustered out at Fort Gibson?

A. No, sir.

Q. How long did she remain in Fort Gibson before she went away with this United States officer after the troops were mustered out?

A. Some seven or eight years, because she lived with Lewis Thornton a while.

■

6

Q. Lewis R. Thornton?

A. Yes, sir, in Mr. Kay's old store house.

Q. That was the Lewis R. Thornton that was the son of Amos Thornton, her former owner?

A. Yes, sir, and she took care of the baby.

Q. When was it born?

A. Just before the war.

Q. I will ask you if it isn't a fact that Lewis Thornton lived in the old store building after the surrender?

A. He lived there.

Q. Didn't he live there in 1864, in that old store building?

A. Yes, sir, and after that, too, because he had Georgeanna's baby and we all lived there.

Q. How long did he continue to live in the Keys store building?

A. After the surrender he lived there for about two years, until he got ready to move into the country.

Q. He moved to the country, according to his testimony, in February, 1867, he lived there until about two years before that?

A. Yes, sir, he did.

Q. That would have made it in the early part of 1865 that he lived in the store building, is that right?

A. He lived there from the time of the surrender until about two years before he moved out to the county.

Q. He moved to the country to what they call the bayou in the Spring of 1867, didn't he?

A. I don't know what year, but it was in the spring.

Q. And he had moved from the store building about two years before he moved to the bayou?

A. Yes, sir, because he moved across the street.

By the Commission:

Q. You say you were living in Fort Gibson about the beginning of the war and lived there until 1879 or 1880 all the time?

A. Yes, sir, we didn't live right in Gibson.

Q. In that neighborhood?

A. Yes sir.

Q. And did you know Georgeanna Thornton about that time?

A. Yes, sir, she was raised with us.

Q. And do you say she was in that neighborhood all the time until some seven or eight years after the war?

A. Yes, sir.

Q. You know that to be a fact?

A. Yes, sir, I do, because that if she wasn't with us she was—

Q. Do you know what year the cholera broke out in Fort Gibson?

A. No, sir. I was a kid and couldn't remember.

Q. About how many years after the war did the cholera break out?

A. I couldn't tell that.

Q. Three or four or one or two?

A. It was more than one or two.

By Mr. Davenport:

Q. Lewis R. Thornton would know exactly the years that Georgeanna and
   her child lived with him in Fort Gibson, wouldn't he?

A. Yes, sir, he has got learning enough to know.

JOHN L. BOWLIN, being first duly sworn, testified as follows:

By the Commission:

Q. What is your name?

A. John L. Bowlin.

Q. How old are you?

A. 54.

Q. What is your postoffice address?

A. Chelsea.

Q. You are the husband of Elizabeth Bowlin, who is the daughter of
   Georgeanna Thornton?

A. Yes, sir.

Q. Are you a Cherokee Freedman?

A. No, sir.

Q. When were you married to Elizabeth the first time?

A. In 1880.

Q. Under what law were you married?

A. Kansas.

Q. Then were you ever remarried under the Cherokee law?

A. Yes, sir.

Q. Did you procure a license?

A. Yes, sir.

Q. That license has been filed in this case?

A. Yes, sir, a copy of it.

Q. Do you claim a right to enrollment as a Cherokee Freedman by intermarriage?

A. Yes, sir.

■

7

Q. Does your name appear on any of the Cherokee tribal rolls?

A. No, sir, none at all.

Q. Were you ever recognized by the tribal authorities?

A. I have always voted since I was married.

Mr. Davenport: Objected to as incompetent and immaterial and not sufficient to show citizenship.

Commission: Objection noted.

Q. Did you ever draw any money at any of the payments?

A. No, sir, I never have.

Q. Did you ever hold any office in the tribal government?

A. No, sir.

Q. Were you ever recognized in any manner other than being permitted to vote as a citizen of the Cherokee Nation?

A. No, sir, I don't think I have.

Q. But you have voted at every election?

A. Every election.

Q. Were you ever tried for any offenses in any of the tribal courts?

A. Never was.

Q. Did you ever sit on a jury at any of the tribal courts?

A. No, sir.

Q. Did you ever get out permits to employ non-citizens?

A. Yes, sir.

Mr. Davenport: The representatives of the Cherokee Nation object upon the further ground that they are not evidence; that no clerk has power or authority to admit to citizenship by issuing permits to anyone.

By Commission: Objection noted.

Q. Did you ever present yourself before the tribal authorities for enrollment?

A. No, sir, never did.

Q. Did you ever have a suit in any of the tribal courts against anyone or were you ever sued?

A. We had a suit in our court.

By Mr. Davenport: Objected to as incompetent and immaterial. The record is better evidence.

By the Commission: Objection noted.

Q. State what the nature of the suit was?

A. It was a claim; there is a record of it.

Q. In what district?

A. Cooweescoowee.

Q. When was it instituted?

A. I think in 1889, '88 or '89, somewheres along there.

Q. You say it was a claim, what kind of a claim?

A. I was trying to protect my rights of my claim from old man Hunt intruding upon me. It was during the administration of R. L. Owen.

Q. That was a suit before the United States Indian Agent?

A. It went to court from him.

Q. The tribal court?

A. Yes, sir, it went to the Supreme Court at Telahquah; Judge Keys was judge, I think. It was during George [Bange's] administration.

Q. Can you furnish the Commission with a copy of that record?

A. Yes, sir, George Bange could do that.

Q. Will you see that the Commission is furnished with that record?

A. Yes, sir, I will do that.

■

8

By Mr. Davenport:

Q. You say you had a suit with old man Hunt?
A. Yes, sir.
Q. Who brought the suit, you or he?
A. I brought the suit.
Q. What was done with it in the circuit court?
A. I think they throwed it out.
Q. You know they threw it out on the ground of your not being a citizen, don't you?
A. I think that was it.
Q. And you know they threw it out of the Supreme Court on the same grounds, didn't they?
A. I expect; they threw it out; they never informed me; I don't know what grounds.
Q. Your attorney advised you that they did it on those grounds, didn't he?
A. He got my money and shut his mouth.
Q. How did you get the information that you speak of?
A. Through the newspapers.
Q. Well, you were interested enough to find out?
A. Yes, sir, I found it out.
Q. When were you and your wife married?
A. We was married according to the laws of Kansas in 1860 [sic].
Q. Where did you first meet her?
A. At Kansas.
Q. At what point?
A. In Parsons; she was going to school there.
Q. Where was her mother at that time?
A. Fort Gibson.
Q. How long did Lizzie go to school at Parsons?
A. One term.
Q. Where did you next meet her?
A. In Muskogee here.
Q. When you married where was she?

A. She came back to Parsons.

By the Commission:

Q. Do you know anything about the residence of your wife's mother in
    Oklahoma?
A. No, sir, she never had no residence there.
Q. Never lived there after you knew her?
A. No, sir.

By Mr. Davenport:

Q. Where did you get acquainted with her?
A. The first time I saw her was in 1880.
Q. 1880?
A. Yes, sir.

(Continued by agreement until nine o'clock A. M. July 15, 1904.)

July 15, 1904. The applicants appearing by John L. Bowlin, husband of Elizabeth Bowlin, and by attorney, R. W. Blue, and the Cherokee Nation appearing by its representative, James S. Davenport, the following testimony was introduced on behalf of the Cherokee Nation:

ELLEN S. THORNTON, being first duly sworn, testified as follows:

By the Commission:

Q. What is your name?
A. Ellen S. Thornton.
Q. How old are you?
A. 68 the 7th day of July.
Q. What is your postoffice address?
A. Fort Gibson.
Q. You are a citizen by blood of the Cherokee Nation, are you?
A. Yes, sir.

Q. Do you know the applicants in this case, Elizabeth Bowlin and
    Georgeanna Thornton?
A. Yes, sir.

By Mr. Davenport:

Q. How long have you known Georgeanna Thornton?
A. I have been knowing her ever since she was a child.
Q. What was your husband's name?
A. L. R. Thornton.
Q. Is he living?
A. No, he died the 18th of last June, a year ago.
Q. Where was Georgeanna Thornton living when you first knew her?
A. Living with her owner, Mr. Thornton, my husband's father.
Q. What was his name?
A. Amos Thornton.
Q. Where was Amos Thornton living at that time?
A. Right there were Mr. Hurt lives in Gibson.
Q. Fort Gibson, Indian Territory?
A. Yes, sir.

■

9

Q. How long was that before the war of the rebellion, about how long?
A. When I first got acquainted with the family it was about '55 but me and
    my husband was married in '[6]o, and then I was with them all the
    time; we was married in the year '50.
Q. Do you know whether or not Georgeanna Thornton went away from the
    Cherokee Nation during the war?
A. She never went only after my husband left and his father, her and all the
    colored people followed; went north and they went north.
Q. Did Georgeanna go with the colored people?
A. Yes, sir, and in ['62] they returned when the Army came back they all
    returned to Gibson.
Q. Do you know who claimed to be Georgeanna Thornton's father?

A. John Fields.

By Mr. Blue: Objected to as incompetent, immaterial and irrelevant.
Commission: Objection noted.

Q. After Georgeanna Thornton returned to the Cherokee Nation in '62,
   when the soldiers returned, did she continue to live there near Fort
   Gibson in the Cherokee Nation from that time on to the present time?
A. She was living there in Gibson in '64 with me and my husband, and in '64
   her father came and took her, took her off somewhere in the country.
Q. Then when did she next come back to Fort Gibson?
A. I don't know; we left Gibson.
Q. How long after '64 did you and your husband continue to live at Fort
   Gibson?
A. In '67 we moved out of Gibson.
Q. You lived in Fort Gibson continuously from 1864 to 1867?
A. Yes, sir.
Q. When you moved where did you move to?
A. Out on the bayou where we live now.
Q. How far from Fort Gibson?
A. Three miles.
Q. When first did you see Georgeanna Thornton after she left your place in
   1864?
A. I couldn't tell the first time I saw her; I never come to town myself.
Q. Did you see her from 1864 to 1867? The time you moved out on the
   bayou?
A. No, sir.
Q. You lived in Fort Gibson?
A. Yes, sir.
Q. What business was your husband engaged in?
A. Butcher until the time we moved.
Q. How long had you been living on the bayou when you saw Georgeanna
   after she had gone away in 1864?
A. I can't tell you how long.
Q. About how long?
A. Must have been about six or seven years, maybe longer, as well as I can
   remember; I can't recollect about how long it was; I never went to town.

Q. When Georgeanna came back did she say where she had been?

A. She had been in Kansas, I don't know.

Q. Did she say anything about it?

A. Never said anything to me about it; they all say she had been to Kansas.

Q. Where is she living now with reference to where you live?

A. I don't know where she lives now; I haven't seen her in a long while.

Q. She don't live in the same neighborhood with you?

A. No, sir, she lived with me and my husband about six months and her father came and took her; my recollection is awful bad; along in February or March he took her away from our house and carried her there somewhere in the country, I don't know where, and after that I reckon she came back to Gibson; I never saw her any more, but she lived with Mr. Thornton. She never did live with the old man Thornton, because he stayed with us.

■

10

By Mr. Blue:

Q. Mrs. Thornton, you say you resided at Fort Gibson before the commencement of the war?

A. Yes, sir.

Q. Where was Georgeanna Thornton then?

A. She belonged to Mr. Amos Thornton.

Q. That was your husband's father?

A. Yes, sir.

Q. How long after that did you continue to reside at Fort Gibson?

A. I left there in '67, me and my husband.

Q. You continued to reside at Fort Gibson until sometime in 1867?

A. Yes, sir, we left there in 1867.

Q. When you left there where did you go?

A. Out on the bayou, about three miles east of Gibson.

Q. What Nation were you living in on the bayou?

A. Cherokee Nation.

Q. While living there was it a village or a farm?

A. A farm.

Q. What time in '67 did you move?

A. In March.

Q. Where was Georgeanna Thornton at that time?

A. I don't know; I couldn't tell.

Q. Where had she been living before you moved out to the bayou?

A. I hadn't seen her after her father come and took her.

Q. Who was her father?

A. John Fields.

Q. Was he a Cherokee Indian?

A. Yes, sir, he was a Cherokee colored person.

Q. Do you know whether he is on the rolls or not?

A. I reckon he is; I don't know.

Q. His name is John Fields?

A. Yes, sir.

Q. Was he a slave of a Cherokee?

A. Yes, sir.

Q. Who was his owner?

A. That is what I don't know, what his name is either.

Q. What was your husband's name?

A. Lewis R. Thornton.

Q. And you and he resided there together at Fort Gibson from the outbreak
   of the war in '61 until March, 1867 and then you moved to the bayou?

A. Yes, sir.

Q. Have you ever lived at any other places in the Cherokee Nation?

A. No, sir.

Q. Now you say you don't know anything about where Georgeanna was
   from 1861 until 1867?

A. She was at home in '61, there in Gibson, and in '62, in September they all
   went north.

Q. Who all went north?

A. My husband, his father and my husband's brother and the colored people
   followed them.

Q. What colored people do you mean?

A. I mean what belonged to them.

Q. You mean their slaves?

A. Yes, sir.

Q. Do you know where they went?

A. To Fort Scott, I reckon.

Q. You don't know anything about that only hearsay?

A. No, sir.

Q. You were never in Kansas, yourself?

A. No, sir.

Q. When they went north, did you go with them?

A. No, sir, I stayed in Gibson.

Q. How long were your father and husband gone north?

A. From September until April.

Q. Of what year?

A. '62.

Q. Until April of what year?

A. '62.

Q. Did they come back then?

A. They all came back.

Q. You mean by that that those who had belonged to them came back then?

A. Yes, sir.

Q. Did Georgeanna Thornton go with them north?

A. Yes, sir.

Q. When was it, you say that her father came and got her?

A. '64.

Q. What month in '64?

A. I don't remember whether it was February or March.

Q. After that, you say, you don't know anything about her?

A. No, sir, not until several years after that.

Q. Where did her father reside at that time?

A. I don't know, somewhere around.

■

11

Q. You said a moment ago that he came and took her away in the country?

A. I did, but I don't know what portion.

Q. Did he live in the Cherokee Nation?

A. Yes, sir.

Q. He didn't live far from Gibson did he?

A. I don't know where he lived, out in the country somewhere; I never saw
 Georgeanna any more until—

Q. Mrs. Thornton, while you lived in Fort Gibson during that time did you
 visit about any?

A. No, sir.

Q. How much of a town was it then?

A. Just a little place.

Q. Was it a garrison for the soldiers?

A. Yes, sir, when the soldiers came back.

Q. I mean after Georgeanna came back there, wasn't it a military camp?

A. Yes, sir.

Q. You didn't go about much yourself?

A. No, sir, I stayed right at home.

Q. Are you positive that you didn't see Georgeanna along during these
 times?

A. No, sir, I didn't see her from the time her father took her from our house;
 I didn't see her any more.

Q. Until when?

A. Until about, I couldn't tell you how long that had been, we had been living on the bayou several years; I don't know where she had been.

Q. You don't know where she went with her father?

A. No, sir, I don't know where she was.

Q. I don't understand that you claim to know anything about her whereabouts after her father came and got her until after you moved out on
 the bayou?

A. No, sir, I never visited anywhere and after we moved on the bayou I never
 saw any of the people from town only as they came out where I lived.

Q. I asked you if you pretended to know anything about where she was after
 her father took her away?

A. No, sir.

Q. And you are not attempting to swear to where she was during that time?

A. No, sir, I don't know; nobody told me, and I don't know; just know that I
 never saw her for several years after we moved.

Q. Did you know Georgeanna's daughter, who is now Mrs. Bowlin?

A. Yes, sir.

Q. How long have you known her?

A. Ever since she was born; the last time I saw her she was just about this high (indicating).

Q. When was that?

A. In '64, she was about two years old, I reckon, my recollection is not good.

Q. You say she was about two years old in '64?

A. She must have been born in '61.

Q. Do you remember what time in '61 Georgeanna's daughter was born, now Mrs. Bowlin?

A. No, sir, I don't.

Q. Was she born before or after the war began?

A. After the war began.

Q. In 1861?

A. The war commenced in March of '64, I believe it began before that.

Q. Was she with Georgeanna Thornton when Georgeanna's father came and got her?

A. Yes, sir.

Q. He took her along?

A. He took Georgeanna and the child.

Q. What was her name?

A. Lizzie.

Q. Elizabeth?

A. Yes, sir.

Q. Now Elizabeth Bowlin?

A. Yes, sir.

Q. Had you seen her before, shortly before Georgeanna's father came after her and took her away?

A. Yes, she was staying with me.

Q. Was Elizabeth taken away at the same time?

A. Yes, sir, I have never seen her since.

Q. Never have seen Elizabeth since?

A. No, sir, not since then.

Q. How old did you say you were?

A. I was 68 the 7th of July.

Q. Of this year?

A. Yes, sir.

Q. Your health isn't very good is it?

A. No, sir, I am sick all the time.

Q. Is your memory good now?

A. No, sir, I [am] old and have had so much sickness, just an invalid for years now; I have better recollections about the war times than anything.

■

12

Q. You just tell these things as you remember them?

A. Just as I know.

By Mr. Davenport:

Q. I want to ask you if Georgeanna Thornton came back to Fort Gibson after the war and lived with Amos Thornton, your father-in-law, on the spot of ground where Florian Nash's store stands?

A. No, sir, she never lived with Mr. Thornton after the war broke out. She was his slave when the war broke out and they left, Lewis and his father, and they went.

Q. Did Georgeanna live with either Lewis or Amos Thornton after the close of the war, in Fort Gibson, three or four years?

A. No, sir, she lived with me and Lewis about six months.

Q. After the close of the war?

A. No, sir, in '64.

Q. I am speaking in regard to her living either with Lewis Thornton, your husband—?

A. Mr. Thornton never left house after he came back after the war.

Q. Georgeanna says in her testimony that she came back and lived with Amos Thornton on the site where Florian Nash's store stands for three or four years after the war, is that true?

By Mr. Blue: Objected to as incompetent and immaterial and not proper cross-examination and is in the nature of leading and suggesting.

Commission: Objection noted; witness may answer.

A. She is mistaken about that. She lived with me about six months, and my husband, and then her father came and took her.

Q. Did Georgeanna Thornton live with you and your husband six months after or before the close of the war?

A. Before the close of the war.

By Mr. Blue:

Q. Where was she living with you and your husband during that six months?

A. Right there in Gibson.

Q. In Fort Gibson?

A. Yes, sir.

Q. Was that six months continuous?

A. Yes, sir.

Q. Would she live with you part of the time and go off and return?

A. No, sir, she lived with me until her father came after her.

Q. She was living with you and your husband at the time her father came and got her?

A. Yes, sir.

Q. At what place in Fort Gibson did you then live?

A. There where Mr. Hurt lives now; it belonged to Mr. Thornton.

Q. Is that known as the Thornton place?

A. Yes, sir.

Q. Which Thornton?

A. Amos Thornton.

Q. Your husband's father?

A. Yes sir.

Q. Then it was the old Thornton home?

A. Yes, sir.

Q. Did Mr. Amos Thornton live with you and your husband at that time?

A. Yes, sir.

Q. Where did he continue to live after you moved out of Fort Gibson?

A. He move down below to Greenleaf.

Q. How long did he reside at Greenleaf?

A. Until he died.

Q. When did he die, if you know?

A. I can't tell; I don't recollect.

Q. About when do you think he died?

A. Must have been about; I don't remember the date.

Q. About how long has he been dead?

A. He has been dead about 20 years, I reckon, 22 years, I expect; I don't know.

Q. Mrs. Thornton, did Mr. Amos Thornton move off to Greenleaf at the same time you moved to the bayou?

A. No, sir, he moved away before we moved.

Q. How long before?

A. About a year before.

Q. And he continued to reside at Greenleaf until his death?

A. Yes, sir.

■

13

Q. After you moved to the bayou did you visit around any in the neighbor hood?

By Mr. Davenport: Objected to as incompetent and immaterial.
Commission: Objection noted, witness may answer.

A. Only to Mrs. Thompson's, right there.

Q. Then you don't know very much about what occurred and who were about in the neighborhood where you lived?

A. No, sir, I didn't know anything about Gibson after I left.

Q. Did you know Minerva Vann?

A. Yes, sir.

Q. How long did you know her?

A. I knew the Thornton's about in '57 or '9.

Q. Did you know anything about Georgeanna Thornton living with her?

A. She was Mr. Thornton's wife, Mrs. Vann was.

Q. Afterwards did she cease to be his wife?

A. Yes sir, they parted.

Q. After they parted do you know anything about Georgeanna Thornton living with her.

By Mr. Davenport: Objected to, because it isn't cross-examination of anything brought in the original testimony.

Commission: Objection noted; witness may answer.

A. I don't know anything about her living with Mrs. Vann after she was freed, because she was, after I left town Mrs. Vann lived in Gibson; I don't know whether Georgeanna lived with her or not.

Q. Then you don't undertake to say that Georgeanna wasn't in Fort Gibson after you moved to the bayou?

A. No, I don't know anything about that.

Q. At the time Mr. Amos Thornton was living with you and your husband had he and Mrs. Thornton, afterwards Mrs. Vann, separated?

A. They separated just after they came back from the north.

Q. Did she go north?

A. No, sir, she stayed in Gibson.

Q. You don't know anything about Georgeanna Thornton living with Mrs. Thornton after the separation of her and her husband?

A. No, sir.

Q. She could have and you not know it?

A. I don't know anything about Fort Gibson after I left there and moved to the bayou.

By Mr. Davenport:

Q. Mrs. Thornton, how far did you live from Mrs. Canon Vann, who was Mr. Amos Thornton's wife, during the time you lived in Fort Gibson from 1864 to 1867?

A. Right near.

Q. About how many hundred yards?

A. I reckon it was about a quarter as near as I can tell you.

Q. If Georgeanna had been living with Mrs. Vann at that time would you have known it?

A. Yes, sir.

By Mr. Blue: Object to asking witness' opinion upon statements of fact.
Commission: Objections noted; witness will answer.

Q. Was she living there from 1864 to 1867 with Mrs. Vann who was formerly
    Amos Thornton's wife?
A. No, sir, I reckon she was living in the country, because I went to Vann's
    and paid her a visit just before we moved to the country.

By Mr. Blue:

Q. Did you visit regularly with Mrs. Vann at that time?
A. Yes, sir.
Q. How often were you there?
A. There wasn't a week passed but what we visited each other.
Q. During that four years?
A. Yes, sir.
Q. Did she live in Fort Gibson?
A. Yes, sir.
Q. You were about a quarter of a mile apart?
A. I reckon it was that far, with there in sight; we were all in town; we call it
    a town.

■

14

Q. After you moved out to the bayou how often were you at Fort Gibson?
A. Not at all; I reckon I have been there less than anybody that ever lived
    there, after I moved away.

ELIZA ANDRE, being first duly sworn, testified as follows:

By the Commission:

Q. What is your name?

A. Eliza Andre.

Q. How old are you?

A. I will be 57, you ought not to ask people how old they are.

Q. What is your postoffice?

A. Fort Gibson.

Q. Are you a citizen by blood of the Cherokee Nation?

A. Yes, sir.

Q. Do you know the applicants in this case, Elizabeth Bowlin and her
mother, Georgeanna Thornton?

A. Yes, sir.

Q. How long have you known them?

A. Ever since I can remember.

By Mr. Davenport:

Q. Do you know whether or not Georgeanna Thornton went away from Fort
Gibson during or about the close of the war?

A. She left there time of the war; I never saw her when she come back; I
heard she come back; I never saw her.

Q. Did she go away again after that?

A. Yes, sir, she went away in 1866 she wasn't here; I was here off and on all
the time after '64.

Q. When did you first see or hear of Georgeanna Thornton after the war?

A. Here at this place in '78.

Q. Did you have any conversation with her about where she had been?

A. She said she had been in the states.

Q. Did she say how long she had been back?

A. Said she hadn't been back very long.

Q. From 1864 up until you saw her here in Muskogee in 1878, where had you
been living?

A. Part of the time in Canadian district and part of the time in Fort Gibson;
never been out of the Nation.

Q. You met Georgeanna Thornton here in 1878?

A. Yes, sir, at my house; her girl nursed my girl a while.

Q. What was her girl's name?

A. Lizzie.

Q. Where did she say she had been?

A. Just remarked that she had been in the states.

Q. How long did she say she had been back?

A. Said she had just got back.

Q. Where had she been living since that time?

A. She stayed with me a while in Fort Gibson; I haven't seen Lizzie at all.

By Mr. Blue:

Q. Where were you born?

A. In Tahlequah, Cherokee Nation.

Q. How long did you reside at Tahlequah?

A. Me? I couldn't tell you; I went to school there quite a while and lived over there at Fort Gibson was my principal home; my mother lived there.

Q. You went to school at Tahlequah?

A. Yes, sir.

Q. Did you have a home there, your parents?

A. They did at one time, a short time, when I was very small.

Q. When you went to school there did they reside there?

A. No, sir, I boarded.

Q. How long were you there?

A. I couldn't tell you, I was small.

Q. About how long?

A. A short time, I stayed with Mr. Foreman while I was going to school there.

Q. Where did your parents live then?

A. At Fort Gibson.

Q. When you quit school there where did you go?

A. To Fort Gibson.

Q. How long did you reside there until you changed to some other place?

A. Until I was about grown.

Q. That is indefinite time; I can't tell what that means, how many years did you stay?

A. Often and on all my life.

■

15

Q. When were you married?

A. I was married in 1865.

Q. When you married did you establish a home separate from your mother's home?

A. Yes, sir.

Q. Where was that?

A. In Canadian district.

Q. How far from Fort Gibson?

A. About twenty-five miles.

Q. Where do you live now?

A. In Fort Gibson.

Q. How long did you live in Canadian district?

A. About nine years.

Q. From sometime in 1865 until 1874 you must have been living there then where did you move?

A. Here to Muskogee.

Q. Then you were living here in 1878?

A. Yes, sir.

Q. Did you live in Muskogee from 1874 to 1878?

A. Yes, sir.

Q. How long did you continue to reside here after 1878?

A. I guess I lived here up till I don't remember, four or five years.

Q. That would make it about 1883 when you left here, then where did you go to?

A. I moved out to Brushy Mountain and from Brushy Mountain back to Fort Gibson.

Q. About how far is Brushy Mountain from here?

A. About ten miles.

Q. Do you know how long you resided there?

A. About five months.

Q. Then you moved to Fort Gibson to your mother's?

A. Yes, sir.

Q. In the house with her?

A. Yes, sir.

Q. And have resided there ever since?

A. Yes, sir.

Q. Have had no separate home?

A. She died soon after that and I remained in the same place.

Q. From 1865 to 1874 you didn't live at Fort Gibson?

A. No, sir, but I was there often; my mother lived there.

Q. From 1874 until 1883 you were either here or at Brushy Mountain?

A. I moved to Brushy Mountain, but didn't stay but a short time.

Q. How far is this place from Fort Gibson?

A. About eight miles.

Q. When you saw Georgeanna Thornton here at Fort Gibson, as you stated in what month in 1878 was it?

A. I don't remember, along in the spring.

Q. Of 1878?

A. Yes, sir.

Q. She was at your house at that time?

A. Yes, sir, I got her girl to nurse for me.

Q. Was she visiting at your house?

A. No, sir, she was hired out here in town.

Q. Did you ever have but the one conversation with her about when she had been?

A. Yes, sir.

Q. She told you she had just come from the states?

A. Yes, sir, when I first saw her.

Q. She didn't say about how long she had been away?

A. No, sir.

Q. She just simply told you that she had been away to the states?

A. Yes, sir.

Q. And had just come back?

A. Yes, sir.

Q. What state?

A. Said she went from here to Kansas.

Q. What other states?

A. I don't remember.

Q. Georgeanna did go to Kansas in 186[3], didn't she?

A. I don't know where she went from here.

Q. She went north in 1862 with the Thorntons didn't she?

A. I don't remember. Not that I know of, no, sir.

Q. And came back with them?

A. I wasn't there.

Q. Didn't she go with them and come back with them?

A. No, sir, she didn't come back with them; I heard she was there; she didn't go away with them; I was there then.

Q. You don't know what happened in Fort Gibson when you were not there?

A. No, sir.

Q. You are not pretending to swear about things that you don't know about?

A. No, sir, I wouldn't be guilty of that for nothing.

Q. And when you saw her in 1878 you hadn't seen her for sometime before that?

A. No, sir.

Q. Do you know where she is now?

A. No, sir.

Q. Have you seen her recently?

A. No, sir.

Q. Don't know where she resides now?

A. No, sir.

Q. How long has it been since you saw her?

A. Quite a while.

Q. About how long?

A. It has been 15 years, all of it.

■

16

Q. Do you know her little girl, Lizzie?

A. Yes, sir, when she was a girl.

Q. How long has it been since you saw her?

A. Not for a long time, when she nursed for me.

Q. Not since 1878?

A. No, sir.

Q. You don't know much about them now?

A. No, sir, not now, but I have known Georgeanna Thornton all my life.

Q. You haven't seen her for fifteen years?

A. No, sir.

Q. You were away from Fort Gibson for nine years at one time?

A. No, sir, off and on I was there; every year of my life; my mother lived
there, and I went there to see my mother.

Q. You didn't reside there for nine years?

A. No, sir, but I went there.

Q. You didn't reside there for five years after that?

A. No, sir, it wasn't my home, but that didn't keep me from going.

Q. You only visited there occasionally?

A. Yes, sir, I went often to see my mother.

Q. You stayed at home some of the time didn't you?

A. Yes, sir, of course I did.

FRANK SMITH, being sworn, testified as follow:

By the Commission:

Q. What is your name?

A. Frank Smith.

Q. How old are you?

A. 59.

Q. What is your postoffice address?

A. Braggs, I.T.

Q. You are a citizen by blood of the Cherokee Nation?

A. Yes, sir.

Q. Do you know the applicants in this case, Elizabeth Bowlin and her
mother Georgeanna Thornton?

A. I know Georgeanna Thornton.

Q. How long have you known her?

A. I knew her before the war.

Q. Ever since before the war?

A. Yes, sir.

By Mr. Davenport:

Q. Did you go out of the Cherokee Nation during the war?
A. Yes, sir.
Q. When did you come back to the Cherokee Nation?
A. In the Spring of 1866.
Q. To what point did you come?
A. Fort Gibson.
Q. How long did you live in or near Fort Gibson after you returned in 1866?
A. Until about 1875.
Q. Was Georgeanna Thornton living in Fort Gibson when you returned in 1866?
A. Not that I know of.
Q. Was Lewis or Amos Thornton living there at that time?
A. Yes, sir.
Q. Did you see her around their place at any time after you returned until Lewis moved to the country?
A. No, sir.
Q. Have you seen Georgeanna since the war?
A. Not until about a month ago.
Q. You lived in Fort Gibson from 1866 to 1875?
A. Yes, sir.
Q. You had known her before the war?
A. Yes, sir.
Q. She was grown at that time?
A. About 14 or 15 years old.

By Mr. Blue:

Q. When was she about 14 or 15 years old?
A. At the breaking out of the war.
Q. Do you know anything about when Elizabeth Thornton was born?
A. I remember the circumstance, yes, sir, when the child was born.
Q. You lived in Fort Gibson at that time?
A. Yes, sir.
Q. And you returned in 1865?
A. '66.

Q. What time?

A. Spring.

■

17

Q. What month?

A. It was April or May, I don't remember which.

Q. How long did you continue at Fort Gibson?

A. Mighty near all the time; went to the Choctaw Nation and was gone
about a month.

Q. When was that?

A. In the fall of 1866.

Q. What month?

A. Along in August.

Q. In what business were you engaged in Fort Gibson?

A. Nothing, my folks all lived there.

Q. Didn't have any particular business then?

A. No, sir.

Q. Had no occupation of any kind?

A. None.

Q. Did you work on anything?

A. No, sir.

Q. You were simply at leisure there in Fort Gibson?

A. Just simply loafing around town.

Q. Did you have a home of your own at that time?

A. I stayed first one place then another; once in a while at Thorntons; once
in a while with the Bean family; my mother was in the Choctaw
Nation.

Q. Did you have any home of your own at that time?

A. No, sir.

Q. How long did you live at Fort Gibson in that way?

A. I went down and brought my mother up to Gibson.

Q. When was that?

A. In 1856.

Q. Fall of 1856?

A. Yes, sir.

Q. Then you mean to say that you didn't have any home when you returned from the Army until you brought her?

A. Yes, sir.

Q. How long did you live there at Fort Gibson? After you came back from the war continuously?

A. Until 1875.

Q. About ten years?

A. Yes, sir.

Q. You say you knew Georgeanna Thornton before you went off in the war?

A. Yes sir.

Q. Did you come back during the war to stay?

A. Only a little while.

Q. Were you in the Army?

A. Yes, sir.

Q. Which Army?

A. Stand Watie Brigade.

Q. Confederate side?

A. Yes, sir, confederate soldier.

Q. You didn't come back, except to scout, from that time until the war was over?

A. Yes, sir.

Q. Did you know Georgeanna Thornton after the war was over?

A. I never saw her until here—

Q. Did you see her before the war?

A. Yes, sir.

Q. She was only about 14 or 15 years old then?

A. Yes, sir.

Q. You didn't see her when she came back?

A. No, sir.

Q. Would you have know her if you had seen her?

A. I guess so.

Q. Are you sure?

A. Yes, sir.

Q. Have you seen her since?

A. Not until about a month ago.

Q. You didn't see her there until after 1865 that you know of?

A. No, sir.

Q. Do you say that she wasn't there?

A. Yes, sir, she wasn't there.

Q. During the ten years that you were there you swear positively that she wasn't there?

A. Yes, sir.

Q. She couldn't have been about the Army post and you not have known it?

A. No.

Q. Couldn't have been there cooking for anybody and you not have known it?

A. No, sir.

Q. Did you travel around in the country anywhere?

A. Yes, sir, anywhere and everywhere, all over it.

Q. What was your business there?

A. Farmed at home and worked at home there for my mother.

Q. Do you know Bob Ross?

A. Yes, sir.

Q. Do you know whether he was in charge of the command there at any time at Fort Gibson?

A. Not after the war that I know of.

Q. During the war?

A. I don't know it; I wasn't there; couldn't tell you.

Q. Was he to your knowledge about there at any time after the war?

A. Bob Ross, yes, sir.

■

18

Q. You knew him well, didn't you?

A. Yes, sir.

Q. Have you testified in this case before?

A. No, sir.

Q. When were you first talked to about?

A. I don't remember now.

Q. Who first conversed with you concerning it?

By Mr. Davenport: Objected to as immaterial and not cross-examination.

Commission: Objection noted; witness will answer.

A. Mr. Keys.

Q. Who else talked with you about it?

A. Mr. Hoel [Bell].

Q. Who else?

A. That is all, I believe.

Q. Mr. Keys and Mr. Bell are attorneys for the Cherokee Nation, are they not?

A. Yes, sir.

Q. Did they come to see you about it or did you go to see them?

A. We were all here.

Q. Were you here as a witness in this case then?

A. No, sir.

Q. They pointed her out to you and asked you if you knew her?

A. Yes, sir.

Q. They first talked to you about it and asked you what you would swear?

A. They asked me what I knew about it.

Q. Were they together or separate?

A. Separate.

Q. When was that?

A. When we were here that evening.

Q. How long ago has that been?

A. Sometime last month; I don't recollect the date exactly.

BLUE THOMPSON, being first duly sworn, testified as follows on behalf of applicants:

By the Commission:

Q. What is your name?

A. Blue Thompson.

Q. How old are you?

A. 54.

Q. What is your postoffice address?

A. Chetopa, Kansas.

Q. Are you a Cherokee Freedman?

A. I am.

Q. Do you know the applicants in this case, Elizabeth Bowlin and her mother, Georgeanna Thornton?

A. Yes, sir.

Q. How long have you known Elizabeth Bowlin?

A. Since she was a girl.

Q. How long have you known Georgeanna Thornton?

A. Pretty near since after the war.

By Mr. Blue:

Q. Where did you first see her?

A. Fort Gibson.

Q. When was that?

A. I think in the fall of 1866 or spring, fall, I believe, when I went to Fort Gibson in the fall of 1866.

Q. You mean by that the fall of 1866 or the spring of 1867?

A. Yes, sir, somewhere along there.

Q. When did you go to Fort Gibson?

A. In the fall of 1866.

Q. How long did you remain there then?

A. I remained there permanently two or three years possibly; didn't stay all the time.

Q. Did you know Georgeanna Thornton all that time?

A. Yes, sir, I knowed her, but didn't see her all that time.

Q. How frequently did you see her during that time?

A. I might have seen her two or three times a month.

Q. Where was she to your knowledge from the time you went there in the fall of 1866 until you left there?

A. I didn't know who she was staying with; she was working there in town; I don't know whether with Mrs. Vann or up in the garrison.

Q. At Fort Gibson?

A. Yes, sir, might have been working for Mrs. Brown; I would see her in town from time to time.

■

19

Q. When did you leave there permanently?

A. I believe I left there between '69 and '70 to stay away from there; I used to go and come backwards and forwards home; I didn't stay there all the time.

Q. Did you know her daughter who married Mr. Bowlin?

A. Yes, when she was a girl.

Q. How big a girl when you first knew her, if you remember?

A. She must have been nine or ten years old, maybe; don't know for certain; didn't pay much attention to girls then.

Q. Where did you see Georgeanna Thornton last, if you remember?

A. Since when?

Q. When did you see her the last time that you remember?

A. Sometime in March last, I think.

Q. During all this the time that you were there at Fort Gibson state whether or not she was there also?

A. Couldn't say for certain; don't know.

Q. During the time you were there, as you stated, at different times?

A. Yes, sir.

Q. Did they continue there all the time that you were there?

A. No, sir, not continuously, but from time to time as I was passing.

Q. Since that time when you were there at Fort Gibson how frequently have you seen Georgeanna Thornton?

A. Since I left Fort Gibson I have seen her frequently.

Q. Where?

A. Sometimes at Vinita; sometimes out at Lightning Creek.

Q. Have you seen her outside of the Cherokee Nation since you saw her at Fort Gibson?

A. I believe I have, yes, sir.

Q. How often?

A. I used to visit the lodge every two weeks at Parsons; I would see her there.

Q. When was that?

A. Don't know, sir, what year it was.

Q. Where has her home been since you knew her in 1865?

A. '66, you mean?

Q. Yes, 1866?

A. Her home has been in the Cherokee Nation.

Q. Has she had any other home?

A. Not to my knowing.

Q. Do you know where she resides now?

A. Last time I saw her she resided at Lightning Creek.

Q. In the Cherokee Nation?

A. Yes, sir.

Q. Now, Lizzie Bowlin, since you saw her in 1866 how frequently have you seen her?

A. Sometimes twice a month; I go to their house and stay all night.

Q. Do you know where she lives now?

A. Yes, sir, I do.

Q. Where is that, please?

A. Out at Pryor Creek.

Q. In the country or village?

A. In the country, not a village, in the country.

Q. What was her husband's name?

A. John Bowlin.

Q. Is this him here?

A. Yes, sir.

By Mr. Davenport:

Q. Did I understand you to say that you visited a son-in-law, was it your son-in-law or hers?

A. Her son-in-law.

Q. What is his name?

A. John Bowlin.

Q. When was it you visited in Parsons?

A. I don't know what years.

Q. When did you first get acquainted with John Bowlin?

A. In Parsons.

Q. When was that?

A. Don't know what year.

Q. He had a home there?

A. No, not when I knowed him.

Q. Wasn't he keeping house in Parsons?

A. I visited him before he married.

Q. After he married Lizzie and was living in Parsons?

A. Yes, sir.

Q. He was keeping house?

A. Yes, sir.

Q. Had a house there?

A. He didn't have a house; he rented.

Q. Wasn't he keeping house and living in Parsons when you visited there?

A. Yes, sir.

Q. Wasn't Georgeanna living there at that time?

A. Sometimes, yes, sir.

Q. What year was this?

A. Don't know, sir, Mr. Davenport, I told you.

■

20

Q. Where was John Bowlin living in 1867?

A. In Michigan, I guess, that's what he told me.

Q. You never knew him then?

A. No, sir.

Q. Did you know Georgeanna Thornton before the war?

A. No, sir.

Q. You don't know to whom she belonged?

A. Not personally; only what I heard.

Q. After you returned to Fort Gibson after the war closed did you learn whom she claimed was her former owner?

A. I don't know whether it was Lewis Thornton or Thompson.

Q. Lewis Thornton was living in Fort Gibson?

A. He used to live there.

Q. In '66?

A. I don't know whether—he ran a butcher shop there.

Q. In 1866?

A. I don't know what year.

Q. Wasn't he running one there in 1865?

A. I don't know.

Q. Was he running one there in 1868?

A. Possibly might have been.

Q. Can you tell me a year in which you know of your own knowledge that Lewis Thornton was running a butcher shop there?

A. No, sir.

Q. Was you interested in the return and residence of Georgeanna Thornton in Fort Gibson?

A. Yes, sir.

Q. You had never seen her until you met her there?

A. No, sir.

Q. Did you remain in the Cherokee Nation during the war?

A. No, sir, left in '62.

Q. Where did you go?

A. Chickasaw Nation.

Q. Where else?

A. Couldn't mention the places; I was 11 years old couldn't mention all the places; was at Briartown; we left here when—

Q. Were you only 11 years old in '62?

A. Yes, sir.

Q. When did you join the Army after that?

A. Never joined the Army.

Q. I thought you said you left here with the Army?

A. Left here with my boss, John Allen Thompson.

Q. Did you return with Thompson?

A. No, sir.

Q. Who with?

A. Bell and some others.

Q. What point?

A. Sequoyah District.

Q. What year was that?

A. '65.

Q. How long did you remain in Sequoyah District?

A. I don't know.

Q. How long?

A. Two or three years off and on.

Q. Then where did you go?

A. From there to Fort Smith and from there to Fort Gibson.

Q. Had you been running on a boat when you met Georgeanna Thornton?

A. No, sir, I had been away here before and went back.

Q. How did you travel when you came to Fort Gibson the first time?

A. Come there over the mountain.

Q. By the water or by land?

A. Horseback.

Q. Who was living in Fort Gibson when you saw Georgeanna Thornton there in 1866?

A. I don't know, Mr. Ross, Meigs, Houston, Boan, Hickey, Silas McPherson, I don't know who all.

Q. Who, do you remember, was in command of the fort at that time, in 1866?

A. I don't know whether Col. Williams at that time or not.

Q. Where was General Forsythe at that time?

A. I don't know.

Q. Don't you know that Georgeanna left in 1864 and went with general Forsythe to Springfield, Missouri, and went from there to Fort Riley?

A. No, sir, I don't know; I don't know nothing about general Forsythe.

Q. If she says she left with general Forsythe and left him at El [Reno] is that true?

A. I don't know.

Q. Do you know, since you became acquainted with her, of her being with the United States Army at Springfield, Missouri, and from there transferred to Fort Riley or Fort El Reno in Oklahoma?

A. No, sir, I don't know that; she was out there, but I don't know how she got there.

Q. What years was she there?

A. I don't know.

Q. Was it before or after you met her at Fort Gibson?

A. It wasn't before, but I don't know what years after that.

■

21

Q. General Forsythe was in command of the post in Fort Gibson at that time, wasn't he?

A. No, sir, I don't know.

Q. After you claim to have seen her there in 1866 when was the next time you saw her?

A. In Parsons.

Q. How many years afterwards?

A. I don't know, after the railroad was there; I went there to work on the railroad.

Q. You can approximate it, can't you?

A. It was when the railroad was there; must have been 15 or 16 years ago, when I—-

Q. Then you didn't see her from 1866 until 16 years ago?

A. I seen her in Cooweescoowee District from time to time and was out at Bowlin's when Bowlin had a farm there.

Q. At whose house and at what year did you see Georgeanna Thornton in Cooweescoowee district up to the time that you say you saw her in Parsons 15 years ago?

A. I don't know in any particular house, excepting John Bowlin's.

Q. John Bowlin hadn't moved to the Cherokee Nation at all until after you saw her at Parsons, had he?

A. No, sir.

Q. Then how could you have seen her at John Bowlin's house before he moved there?

A. Didn't say that.

Q. Where and at whose house in Cooweescoowee district did you see Georgeanna Thornton from the time you saw her at Fort Gibson until you saw her about 15 years ago at John Bowlin's house in Parsons, Kansas?

A. I disremember whether I seed her at Mrs. Forman's house at Vinita or not, but from 1865 up to the time I told you I saw her in Parsons, then I saw her at John Bowlin's house on Pryor Creek.

Q. How long after you saw her at John Bowlin's in Parsons until you saw her at John Bowlin's on Pryor Creek?

A. It was that year that you run for Council, when was that?

Q. The first time was 1897.

A. Then you have got it.

Q. Then the first time that you ever saw Georgeanna Thornton in the Cherokee Nation from the time you saw her in 1866 was in 1867?

A. To the best of my knowledge. I might have seen her at Mrs. Foreman's.

Q. You don't know where she made her home from the time you saw her at Fort Gibson up until 1897?

A. No, sir, I don't know.

Q. She did live in Kansas?

A. Yes, sir, I saw her at John Bowlin's in Kansas.

Q. Where did she marry?

A. I don't know.

Q. John was living at Parsons before he married?

A. Yes, sir.

Q. Do you know whether Georgeanna and Lizzie had kept house in Parsons before John and Lizzie married?

A. I don't know.

By Mr. Blue:

Q. You spoke of Lewis Thornton, was there another Thornton there?

A. I believe there was one named Amos; I forget them fellows.

Q. Do you know what relation they were to each other?

A. I believe they said they were brothers.

Q. Do you know whether Georgeanna claimed to be the slave of Amos or Lewis?

A. No, sir, I never interrogated them in regard to their rights.

Q. You did understand that she had been the slave of some Thornton?

A. Yes, sir.

(Adjourned until nine o'clock A. M., July 16, 1904)

July 16, 1904. Appearances same as yesterday. Blue Thompson on the stand.

By Mr. Blue:

Q. What is your recollection as to what was the name of the Thornton whose slave she was?

A. Said Lewis Thornton; I don't know.

Q. Did you know anything about that, yourself?

A. No, sir.

Q. When you saw Georgeanna Thornton at Parsons, as you have stated, do
you know where her home was at that time?
A. Her home would have been here, but she was in Parsons when I saw her.

■

22

Q. Do you know where she claim her home from the time you first saw her
up to the present time?

By Mr. Davenport: Objected to as incompetent and immaterial as to where
she claimed.
Commission: Objection noted; witness will answer.

A. Claimed the Cherokee for her home.
Q. When you saw Mr. Bowlin at Parsons what was he doing there, if you
know?
A. He was porter at a hotel, Belmont Hotel, when I got acquainted with
him.
Q. How long have you known Mr. Bowlin?
A. I don't know; quite a while; ever since he worked at that hotel; I don't
know how long it has been.
Q. Where has he resided since he ceased to reside or work at Parsons?
A. He resided in the Cherokee Nation; that is to the best of my knowledge.
Q. About where, if you know?
A. On Pryor Creek.

By Mr. Davenport:

Q. Blue, any numbers of them claimed one thing and actually did another
with reference to their home didn't they?
A. Yes, sir.
Q. In what way did she claim the Cherokee Nation her home while in Kansas?
A. When we would be up there we would be asking where do you live, and
so on, Cherokee Nation.

Q. She actually lived in Kansas, matters not where she claimed?

A. Yes sir, she was in Kansas.

Q. Are you in the 1880 roll?

A. No.

By Mr. Blue:

Q. You say she was in Kansas do you know whether or not she was there as a visitor or staying with her daughter or did she have a permanent home there?

A. No, sir she didn't have a permanent home.

By Mr. Davenport:

Q. How do you know she didn't have a permanent home there?

A. She was staying from one place to another, working.

Q. Didn't you say yesterday they were keeping house there?

A. No, sir.

Q. Didn't you answer on yesterday afternoon in this case that Lizzie Bowlin and her husband rented a house in the city of Parsons, Kansas, and that Georgeanna Thornton was living with them?

A. Yes, sir.

Q. Where did either Lizzie Bowlin or Georgeanna Thornton have a home in which they lived during the time they were living and keeping house in Parsons, Kansas?

A. They lived right north of Dick Kennedy Livery stable.

Q. Then they didn't have any other home at the time they were living in Parsons, except in Parsons?

A. Not to my knowing; they were renting.

Q. They were keeping house there?

A. Yes, sir.

Q. Where did they keep house in the Cherokee Nation during the time they were keeping house in Parsons, Kansas?

A. I couldn't tell you where they kept house in Parsons and Cherokee Nation both. They were living on Pryor Creek.

Q. Did they to your knowledge have a home in which they lived in the

Cherokee Nation from 1866 up to and including the time you saw
them on Lightning Creek about seven years ago?

A. Not to my knowing.

By Mr. Blue:

Q. Do you know why Georgeanna Thornton and her daughter, Mrs. Bowlin,
and her husband, were in Kansas at the time you saw them there and
for what purpose they were there?

■

23

Mr. Davenport: Objected to as incompetent and immaterial and as not
cross-examination or in rebuttal.

Commission: Objection noted; witness will answer.

A. I don't.

Q. Do you know how they made their living at that time?

Mr. Davenport: Objected to as immaterial as to how they made their living;
they had a perfect right to follow any vocation.

Commission: Objection noted; witness will answer.

A. The old lady worked around; I don't know how she made it; the girl didn't
work I don't think, she might, I didn't see her; she wasn't healthy and I
don't think she worked.

Q. The question is as to all three?

A. I don't know anything about all three of them. John continued to work at
the hotel after I left; I don't know anything about his business.

Q. Was he at work there at that time?

A. Yes, sir, when I got acquainted and worked afterwards.

Q. As porter?

A. Yes, sir.

Q. Were they all there for the purpose of making a livelihood?

A. I suppose so; I didn't inquire as to the merits of their business.

WILLIAM HUDSON, being first duly sworn, testified as follows:

By the Commission:

Q. What is your name?
A. William Hudson.
Q. How old are you?
A. 58.
Q. What is your postoffice address?
A. Fort Gibson.
Q. Are you a citizen of the Cherokee Nation?
A. By intermarriage.
Q. Do you know the applicants in these freedman cases, Elizabeth Bowlin
    and Georgeanna Thornton?
A. I know Georgeanna Thornton; I don't know the other one by that name;
    she was a little girl when I saw her last.
Q. How long have you known Georgeanna?
A. I got acquainted with her in 1866.

By Mr. Blue:

Q. Where?
A. In Fort Gibson.
Q. What time in 1866?
A. Along about April, I think it has been quite a while ago; I arrived there
    the first of March, 1866, and I got acquainted with her in the spring.
Q. From what place did you come to Fort Gibson?
A. Augusta, Georgia.
Q. You reached there in March?
A. First day of March, 1866.
Q. Where have you resided since that time?
A. Right there in Gibson.
Q. Where did Georgeanna Thornton reside from the time you got
    acquainted with her?

A. She lived with Mollie Rankin a while and Nancy Thornton a while.

Q. How long did you see her and know of her about Fort Gibson from that time?

A. Up to June, 1867.

Q. 1867?

A. Yes, sir.

Q. About how frequently did you see her during that time?

A. I saw her every week or two, especially on Sunday going to Church. She used to wash and iron around there.

Q. What were you doing there about that time?

A. I was waiting on the officers in the 19th Infantry.

Q. During all of 1865?

A. '66; wasn't there in 1865.

Q. From the time you came there in March, 1864, to June, 1867, were you in the same business?

A. Yes, sir. Cholera broke out there and the government hauled them out from town four miles and give them tents, and I got missed of this woman then, and I was acquainted with her up to that time, and I got mistracked of her. The government people scattered the people out from town on account of being too thick.

■

24

Q. What do you mean when you say you got missed of her?

A. Out of town; I stayed in town.

Q. Do you mean she left at that time and you didn't see her for a while?

A. I didn't see none of them for a while after they left town.

Q. When after June, 1867, did you next see her?

A. I saw her passing through there going to the garrison where the soldiers were.

Q. When was that?

A. I couldn't tell you, but I saw her frequently.

Q. What year was that?

A. Latter part of '67.

Q. Where was that?

A. Fort Gibson.

Q. Now then how long did you continue to see her at Fort Gibson.

A. After the latter part of '67 I didn't see her then for quite a while.

Q. When did you next see her, if you remember?

A. Along about the census taking.

Q. Do you remember when that was?

A. No, sir, I don't.

Q. What census do you refer to?

A. Enrolling of the freedman.

Q. You don't remember what year it was?

A. No, sir, I don't know.

Q. Where did you see her then?

A. There in Fort Gibson.

Q. Did you know Elizabeth Bowlin before she was married?

A. Yes, sir, she was a little girl then.

Q. When did you first become acquainted with her?

A. In '66. She was with her mother then.

Q. How frequently did you see her?

A. Most every time I saw her mother I saw her.

Q. Where did you see them?

A. Passing backwards and forwards through the streets.

Q. At what place?

A. Fort Gibson.

Q. That was in what Nations?

A. Cherokee Nation.

Q. Now then since 1867, latter part of 1867, how often have you seen her?

A. Not but twice.

Q. Where did you see her then?

A. Fort Gibson.

Q. You say you have lived at Fort Gibson since 1866?

A. Yes, sir.

Q. And you are an adopted Cherokee?

A. No sir, adopted colored freedman. I married according to the Cherokee laws there in '67.

Q. Married a Cherokee Freedman?

A. Yes, sir, 22nd day of June, 1867, by Reverend John R. James; I have got my papers to show it.

By Mr. Davenport:

Q. You first met Georgeanna Thornton in what year?

A. '65.

Q. With whom was she living at that time?

A. She was living with a woman called Mollie Rankin; she is dead now; she was backwards and forwards with Aunt Nancy Thornton a part of the time; Aunt Nancy lived up in the southwest of the town and Aunt Mollie Rankin lived down on the river.

Q. To whom was Aunt Nancy Thornton related of the Thornton family?

A. Old Amos, I believe.

Q. What relation was she to Amos Thornton?

A. She was no relation to him; she was a colored woman. She used to belong to old Amos they tell me.

Q. You came to Fort Gibson from Georgia, you say?

A. Yes, sir.

Q. With whom did you come?

A. Dr. B. B. Herbert, Surgeon of the 19th Infantry

Q. You were stationed at the garrison?

A. Wasn't no garrison then; we were stationed down there in town; wasn't but two buildings up in the garrison.

Q. It had been a frontier post?

A. Yes, sir, right there on [Grand] river.

Q. Who of Cherokee by blood or of United States citizens were living in Fort Gibson at that time that you can now recall?

A. Canon Vann as a Cherokee and F. H. Nash, a White man and W. S. Nash, Henry Meigs; I believe all the balance of is dead.

■

25

Q. Was Lewis Thornton living there at that time?

A. Out in the country a piece, not far from there.

Q. I will ask you if you got acquainted with Georgeanna Thornton and her daughter, Lizzie Bowlin, before or after Lewis Thornton moved from Fort Gibson out to the bayou where he lived at the time of his death?

A. Before.

Q. How long before?

A. I couldn't tell you that, because I don't know exactly when he moved.

Q. Did you get acquainted with him while he lived at Fort Gibson?

A. Yes, sir.

Q. Why did you tell me he was living in the country?

A. He moved out there soon afterwards and might have been backwards and forwards.

Q. Is this the first time you have testified in this case?

A. Yes, sir.

Q. When were you first spoken to about what you know in this case?

A. Not until this morning, I was summonsed over here.

Q. Who summonsed you?

A. That man there come over and ask all I knowed and asked me to come over, Mr. Bowlin.

Q. You told him when you first met the woman?

A. Yes, sir.

Q. When did General Forsythe leave Fort Gibson?

A. I am not acquainted with him.

Mr. Blue: Objected to as incompetent, immaterial and not proper cross-examination.

Commission: Objection noted.

Q. Did you ever know such a man was in command of the post there after you got there?

A. Major Lugenbiel was in command when I came.

Q. I will ask you, Bill, if Georgeanna Thornton came back there in 1866 and lived with Amos and Lewis Thornton for three years?

A. I couldn't tell you that.

Q. Did you know Amos Thornton?

A. Yes, sir, as well as I know you.

Q. Did you know where Amos Thornton lived in 1866?

A. He was living there in Fort Gibson.

Q. What part of Fort Gibson?

A. He was living up there close to the new town; Mr. Hart is living at the place.

Q. Did Georgeanna Thornton live up in that part of town?

A. Not at that time; she was living down on the river with Aunt Mollie and was backwards and forwards with Nancy Thornton.

Q. You don't know where she lived in 1866, do you?

A. There in Fort Gibson.

Q. If she says she was living with Amos and Lewis Thornton, is that true?

A. I couldn't say.

Q. If she says she left with General Forsythe and went to Springfield and from there to El Reno, which is now part of Oklahoma Territory, is it true or not?

A. I couldn't tell that; I didn't keep track of where she went; I just know I saw her there in Gibson.

Q. You know if she stayed in Fort Gibson after you went there?

A. I saw her from April, 1866, to June, 1867, and then I didn't keep much track of anybody; the people scattered on account of cholera.

Q. Did the cholera break out in 1866 or 1867?

A. '67.

Q. What time of the year?

A. Along about the first part of June or July.

Q. Then L. D. Daniels, who has testified in this case, is mistaken when he says the cholera broke out in 1866?

By Mr. Blue: Objected to as incompetent, irrelevant and not proper cross-examination.

Commission: Objection noted; witness will answer.

A. It broke out in '67.

M. M. Vance, being first duly sworn, states that as stenographer to the Commission to the

26

Five Civilized Tribes, he reported the proceedings and in the above entitled cause and that the above and foregoing is a true and accurate transcript of his stenographic notes thereof.

//WM Vance//

Subscribed and sworn to before me this 20th day of July, 1904.

//Charles H. Sawyer//
Notary Public.

■

Transcript VI. Elizabeth Bowlin
[manuscript]
Filed by
Lizzie Bowlin
in case of
Lizzie Bowlin
vs
Joseph Hunt
this the 22nd day
of July 1889
Rev. V. Care[y] Clade
Cooweescoowee [dis/In]
C. N.

[stamped]
F I L E D
Jul 11 1904
COMMISSION TO THE FIVE TRIBES.

[verso?]

Pryor Creek Cherokee Nation

I. T. Cooweescoowee [district]
January 24th 1883
This 24th of January
I sell my claim on the West side of Prier Creek
which consist of a field
& to its limits running down the
creek south & north to a
sirtin blaze to Lizzie
Thornton or Mrs JL Bowlin
& her Airs for the sum of
twenty dollars

[fres mosta .   .]

■

Transcript VII. Henrietta Bowlin
Department of the Interior,
Commissioner to the Five Civilized Tribes,
Cherokee Land Office,
May 30, 1906

Roll no. 3990.
Cherokee Freedman Card Nos. 936 and 1444.

In the matter of the application of Henrietta Davis, enrolled as Henrietta Bowlin, to select and allotment and designate her homestead in the Cherokee Nation.

Joseph Davis, being first duly sworn by John D. Tidwell as notary public, was examined on behalf of the Commissioner and testified as follows:

Q. What is your name?
A. Joseph Davis.
Q. How old are you?
A. 24 years old.
Q. Where do you live?
A. Hayden, Indian Territory.

Q. Are you a Cherokee Freedman?

A. Yes, sir.

Q. What is the name of you mother?

A. Emma Davis.

Q. Did you marry Henrietta Bowlin?

A. Yes, sir.

Q. When?

A. June 30, 1904.

Q. Is she a Cherokee Freedman?

A. Yes, sir.

Q. What is the name of her mother?

A. Elizabeth Bowlin.

Q. Are you and your wife living together at the present time?

A. Yes, sir.

Q. Your purpose in appearing at the Cherokee Land Office is to file for Henrietta Davis?

A. Yes, sir.

Q. Have you land selected for her allotment?

A. Yes sir.

Q. Are there any improvements on it?

A. No, sir.

Q. All public domain, is it?

A. Yes, sir.

Witness Excused.

I George A. Lowell, being first duly sworn, state that as stenographer to the Commissioner to the Five Civilized Tribes, I recorded the testimony in the foregoing and that the above is a true and correct transcript of my stenographic notes thereof.

//Geo A. Lowell//

Transcribed and sworn to be before on this 6 day of June, 1906.

//Chas E. Webster//
Notary Public

■

Transcript VIII. Helen F. Nail
Department of the Interior,
Commission to the Five Civilized Tribes,
Muskogee, Oklahoma, June 29, 1908

In the matter of the application for the enrollment of Elizabeth Bowlin, et al, as Cherokee Freedmen.

Helen F. Nail, being first duly sworn by Notary Public, Walter W. Chappel, and examined testified as follow:

By J. O. Rosson On Behalf of Commissioner:

Q. What is your name?
A. Helen F. Nail.
Q. How old are you?
A. 17 years.
Q. What is your postoffice?
A. Parsons, Kansas.
Q. Are you a Cherokee Freedman?
A. Yes sir.
Q. What is the name of your mother?
A. Elizabeth Bowlin.
Q. What is the name of your father?
A. John Bowlin.
Q. Are you married?
A. Yes sir.
Q. When were you married?
A. 8th of December.
Q. Last year?
A. Yes sir.
Q. What is the name of your husband?
A. Albert Nail.
Q. Is he a Cherokee citizen?
A. No sir.

Q. Are you and he living together now?
A. Yes sir.

Witness Excused.

Louise Smith, being first duly sworn, states that as stenographer to the Commissioner to the five Civilized Tribes, she reported the proceedings had in the above entitled cause and that the foregoing is a true and correct transcript of her stenographic notes thereof.

//Louise Smith//

Subscribed and sworn to before me this July 2, 1908.

// Walter W. Chappel //
Notary Public

APPENDIX B
Chronology

1990. Native American Graves Protection and Repatriation Act recognizes federal responsibility to protect Native American culture

1975. Indian Self-Determination and Education Assistance Act provides funds for some social services to federally recognized tribes plus authority over their administration

1971. Willie Adams participates as the Indians of All Tribes "liberate" Alcatraz

1949. Termination policies curtail federal obligations to tribes, reorganize, decentralize the Bureau of Indian Affairs

1936. Oklahoma Indian Welfare Act or Thomas-Rogers Act extends the Indian Reorganization Act to tribes within the boundaries of the state

1934. Wheeler-Howard Act or Indian Reorganization Act ends the Allotment Era but exempts indigenous groups in Oklahoma and Alaska

1934. Washington, Lewis, and Thomas Adams, as members of the Organization of Unrestricted Indians of the Muscogee Creek Nation, petition John Collier at a conference for the Five Civilized Tribes

1933. Franklin Delano Roosevelt, president, supports some autonomy for Indians

1929. Great Depression, Indians suffer more than general population

1908. Land allotments are granted to Georgeanna Thornton and Elizabeth Bowlin

1907. Indian Territory becomes the state of Oklahoma, Indian rolls are closed

1906. John Bowlin's application for Cherokee Freedman status is denied

1905. Ethel is born to Lewis and Annie Adams, the last Adams granted an allotment

1904. Hearings are completed in the applications of Georgeanna Thornton and Elizabeth Bowlin for Cherokee Freedman status

1903. Andrew (Crugee) is born to Lewis and Annie Adams

1901. Preliminary hearing for Georgeanna Thornton and Elizabeth Bowlin application for Cherokee Freedman status—doubtful card granted

1901. Theodore Roosevelt, president, has knowledge of, and interest in, the West

1899. Creek Census, Field Cards completed

1899. Thomas Jefferson Adams signs Red Fork Oil Lease

1898. Curtis Act amendment to Dawes Act, extends allotment policies to Five Civilized Tribes

1897. Former Cherokee slaves petition for full citizenship

1896. Kern-Clifton Roll for Cherokee Strip payments, fills Wallace Roll omissions

1895. Adams and Sepulpa Mining Company established

1893. Dawes Commission empowered to establish rolls of Five Civilized Tribes

1890. The Wallace Roll lists Cherokee Freedmen

1889. Sale of Creek and Seminole land opened to settlement begins series of Oklahoma land rushes

1887. The Dawes Severalty Act or General Allotment Act launches the Allotment Era (1887–1934)

1885. Thomas Jefferson Adams elected speaker of the House of Warriors, Creek Nation

1883. Henrietta Bowlin born (died 1966)

1882. Joseph Davis born (died 1966)

1880. Cherokee Census

1880. John Bowlin marries Elizabeth Thornton

1880. Lewis born to Thomas and Mahala Adams

1879. Carlisle Indian Industrial School established

1872. Bureau for Refugees, Freedman, and Abandoned Lands defunded

1871. Anne Chamberlain born in Illinois

1869. Andrew Jackson rescinds Field Order No. 15, denying compensation to former slaves who fought in the Civil War

1867. Tompkins Roll includes Cherokee residing in northeastern Oklahoma, also a Freedman index

1867. Cholera outbreak in Fort Gibson

1866. Treaty of 1866 puts an end to slavery in Indian Territory, e.g., treaty with the Cherokee, 14 Stat. 799, former slaves returning within six months to have all the rights of Cherokee citizens

1865. Civil War ends

1865. General Sherman proposes forty acres to freed slaves serving under his command in Field Order No. 15

1865. April 14, Lincoln assassinated, Andrew Johnson becomes president

1863. Elizabeth Thornton born to Georgeanna Fields (Thornton) and her owner Amos Thornton

1863. Bureau for Refugees, Freedman, and Abandoned Lands created by Congress

1863. George Washington born to Thomas and Mahala Adams

1861. Thomas Jefferson Adams marries Mahala Grayson

1861. Civil War declared

1861. Abraham Lincoln voted to a second term as president

1851. Cherokee Old Settlers Census

1850. John Leonard Bowlin born in Boliver, Tennessee; arrived in Indian Territory (Oklahoma) in 1880, died August 24, 1934

1845. Thomas Jefferson Adams born at the old Creek agency

1838. First wave of Indians set out on the Trail of Tears

1836. Voluntary Cherokee removal begins

1835. Treaty of New Echota signed by sham representatives relinquishes Cherokee land

1833. Cherokee Emigration Roll

1831. Georgeanna Thornton born to Hanna Hamilton and John Fox Fields

1830. Indian Removal Act

1829. Andrew Jackson elected president of the United States until 1837

1827. Cherokee adopt constitution mirroring US sovereignty rights

1825. Second Treaty at Indian Springs cedes Creek lands to Georgia

1823. Supreme Court declares Indians cannot hold title to the land they occupy

1821. Treaty at Indian Springs cedes Lower Creek lands

1817. Treaty establishes a Cherokee Nation in Arkansas

1817. Emigration Rolls of those who wish to emigrate
1814. Defeated Creeks sign Treaty of Peace at Fort Jackson, ceding 23 million acres
1813. Creek civil war as Red Stick Rebellion culminates with their defeat in Battle of Horseshoe Bend
1810. Amos Thornton born in Tennessee
1803. Louisiana Purchase
1801. Thomas Jefferson, president, considers potential of commercial agriculture for Indians
1790. Naturalization Act, only White males qualify for citizenship

APPENDIX C

List of Documents from the National Archives, Fort Worth, Preliminary Inventory of the Office of the Five Civilized Tribes Agency, Muscogee Area of the Bureau of Indian Affairs, Record Group 75, Records Relating to Allotment, Retrieved November 2004

The following list comprises the documents found among the original hard-copy files contained in the Western Collection of the Commission of the Five Civilized Tribes, National Archives, Fort Worth, Texas.

Adams (1–142)

1. a. Creek Allotment Card, Thomas J. Adams
   b. Tax exemption for Martha Adams
2. Application for Allotment, No. 2460, Thomas J. Adams, October 5, 1899
3. Application for Allotment, No. 5069, Martha Adams, June 7, 1900
4. Application for Allotment, No. 3430, Thomas J. Adams, January 13, 1900
5. Application for Allotment, No. 1680, Thomas J. Adams, August 8, 1899
6. Application for Allotment, [no number], Thomas J. Adams, July 12, 1902
7. Application for Allotment, No. 1680, Thomas J. Adams, Cancelled, July 11, 1900
8. Application for Allotment, No. 5214, Thomas J. Adams, July 12, 1900
9. Certificate: listed for enrollment as a citizen, Thomas J. Adams, December 29, 1904
10. Letter from Thos. Ryan, Commission of the Five Civilized Tribes, approving the removal upon alienation of a portion of Mary Boon, nee Adams, December 14, 1905
11. Case dismissal of Contest No. 109, Hepsey Adams, Guardian of Daniel Adams v. Thomas J. Adams, Guardian of Mary Adams
12. Notice of noncompletion of selection of land, Thomas J. Adams for Martha Adams, June 12, 1902

13. Letter from John Collier, regarding investigation of tax exempt land, March 21, 1934

14. Allotment application testimony of Thomas J. Adams, January 13, 1900

15. Allotment application testimony of Thomas J. Adams, August 8, 1899 (1)

16. Allotment application testimony of Thomas J. Adams, August 8, 1899 (2)

17. Allotment application testimony of Thomas J. Adams, July 11, 1900

18. Application for Homestead Allotment, Thomas J. Adams, March 16, 1903

19. Certificate that Thomas J. Adams represents Mary Adams re 1680, re field no. 653, August 8, 1899

20. Certificate that Martha Adams represents William Washington, re field no. 653, June 7, 1900

21. Certificate that Thomas J. Adams represents Mary Adams, re field no. 653, August 8, 1899

22. Land plat, Township No. 15 N, Range No. 12 E (1)

23. Land plat, Township No. 15 N, Range No. 12 E (2)

24. Land plat, Township No. 15 N, Range No. 12 E (3)

25. Land plat, Township No. 16 N, Range No. 12 E

26. Land plat, Township No. 14, Range No. 12 (1)

27. Land plat, Township No. 14 N, Range No. 12 E (1)

28. Land plat, Township No. 15 N, Range No. 12 E (4)

29. Certificate 1830, Designating Lands Exempt from Taxation, Martha Adams, August 19, 1930

30. Letter from Adlai S. Baker, Okmulgee Building & Loan Assn., to Congressman W. W. Hastings, requesting clarification on land restrictions removal, March 15, 1934

31. Letter from Superintendent to Martha Adams, re change in tax exemption certificate No. 1830, May 8, 1934

32. Order of Cancellation, re certificate No. 1830, April 19, 1934

33. Letter from Superintendent to Okmulgee Building & Loan Association, April 28, 1934

34. Letter from A. G. William to Commissioner, re certificate No. 1830, April 12, 1934

35. Letter from Superintendent to Okmulgee Building & Loan Association, April 8, 1934

36. Enrollment and Allotment Record, Martha Adams, April 3, 1934

37. Dr. DuBoise, certifies that Martha Boon is not physically able to travel to Muskogee, August, 5, 1907
38. Certificate: William Washington, deceased, re field card 653, August 9, 1907
39. Power of Attorney from Martha Boon (nee Adams) to Peter Boon to complete allotment selection, August 5, 1907
40. Notice to Martha Boon from the Chairman that an additional selection of land should be made for William Washington, July 9, 1907
41. Land plat, Township No. 14, Range No. 12 (2)
42. Application for Homestead Allotment, Martha Boon nee Adams for William Washington, August 12, 1907
43. Testimony by Peter Boon, re William Washington allotment, August 9, 1907
44. Memoranda, re Martha Adams allotments
45. Notice of noncompletion of selection of land, to heirs of William Washington, May 25, 1904
46. Allotment of land and homestead designation, William Washington (Dead), August 9, 1907
47. Note 9509, re homestead 6402, William Washington, November 10, 1901
48. Land plat, [no township or range], William Washington
49. Certificate: Thomas J. Adams appears on Census Card of the Creek Nation, Field No. 653, January 13, 1900
50. Testimony by Thomas J. Adams, re Martha Adams, June 12, 1902 (1)
51. Notice of noncompletion of selection of land, to Thomas J. Adams for Martha Adams, July 12, 1900
52. Land plat, Township No. 14 N, Range No. 12 E (2)
53. [duplicate see 55 below]
54. Certificate: Mahala Adams (represented by Thomas J. Adams) appears on Census Card of the Creek Nation, Field No. 653, October 5, 1899
55. Testimony by Thomas J. Adams, re Martha Adams, June 12, 1902 (2)
56. Notice of Dismissal of Contest, in Hepsey Adams, Guardian of Daniel Adams v. Thomas J. Adams, Guardian of Mary Adams, Contestee, November 24, 1900
57. Land plat, Township No. 14 N, Range No. 12 E (3), Thomas J. Adams for wife
58. Testimony by Thomas J. Adams for Mahala Adams, October 5, 1899

59. Testimony by Thomas J. Adams, re application to relinquish land for Martha Adams, June 12, 1902

60. Testimony by Martha Adams for William Washington, June 9, 1900

61. Allotment of land and homestead designation, heirs of William Washington, May 25, 1904

62. Notice of noncompletion of selection of land, to Martha Adams, December 29, 1904

63. Letter to Martha Boon from Commissioner, re completion of designation of homestead for William Washington, July 9, 1907

64. [duplicate of 40 above]

65. Notice to Martha Adams Boon from the Chairman that an additional selection of land should be made for William Washington, November 30, 1904

66. Notice to Thomas J. Adams from the Chairman that an additional selection of land should be made for Martha Adams, November 30, 1904

67. Letter to Mary Adams cancelling and indicating a new deed, October 15, 1903

68. Allotment application file pocket for George W. Adams, 3780–3786

69. Application for allotment, George W. Adams, No. 4258A, March 26, 1900

70. Application for allotment, George W. Adams, No. 3272, December 8, 1899

71. Application for allotment, George W. Adams for Willie Adams, No. 5379, September 6, 1900

72. Testimony by George W. Adams, March 26, 1900

73. Application for homestead allotment by George W. Adams for Heirs of Fred Adams, January 26, 1904

74. Notice to George W. Adams from the Chairman that an additional selection of land should be made for Sarah Adams, No. 7835, November 30, 1904

75. Certificate: Sarah Adams (represented by George W. Adams) appears on Census Card of the Creek Nation, Field No. 1173, December 8, 1899

76. Land plat, Township No. 14, Range No. 12 (3)

77. Testimony by George W. Adams, December 8, 1899

78. Testimony by George W. Adams, March 26, 1900

79. Notice of noncompletion of selection of land to George W. Adams, August 17, 1901

105. Testimony by George W. Adams for himself and his wife Sarah Adams, March 26, 1900

106. Application for allotment by George W. Adams for Benjamin Adams, John Adams, and Robert Manuel, No. 4270, March 26, 1900

107. Application for allotment by Lewis Adams, No. 4267, March 26, 1900

108. Testimony by Lewis Adams, September 13, 1902

109. Notice of noncompletion of selection of land to Lewis Adams, September 13, 1902

110. Land plat, Township 14, Range No. 12 (5)

111. Application for allotment, Lewis Adams, September 13, 1902

112. Application for homestead allotment, Lewis Adams, January 22, 1903

113. Certificate: Leo Adams is represented by Lewis Adams, Creek Census Card, Field No. 1175, March 1900

114. Land plat, Township 14 N, Range No. 12 E (6)

115. Land plat, Township 17, Range No. 17

116. Testimony by Lew Adams for his son Leo Adams, March 26, 1901

117. Testimony to relinquish land by Lewis Adams, February 13, 1902

118. Letter to Lewis Adams from Tams Bixby divesting a portion of his allotment to make way for the town of Beggs, May 7, 1901

119. Testimony by Lewis Adams, March 26, 1900

120. Certificate: Washington Adams is represented by Lewis Adams, Creek Census Card, Field No. 1175

121. Land plat, Township 15, Range No. 11

122. Land plat, Township 14, Range No. 12 (6)

123. Land plat, Township 15, Range No. 12

124. Notice of noncompletion of selection of land to Austin Chissoe for Taylor Chissoe, November 30, 1901

125. Application for allotment, Lewis Adams for Hepsa Adams, No. 6666, March 26, 1901

126. Application for allotment, Lewis Adams for Leo Adams, February 13, 1902

127. Application for allotment, Lewis Adams for Leo Adams, No. 6667, March 26, 1901

128. Certificate: Hepsa Adams is represented by Lewis Adams, Creek Census Card, Field No. 1175

129. Land plat, Township 17 N, Range No. 17 E

150. Letter from the Acting Commissioner to Cherokee Land Office re land contested by Georganna Thornton, dismissed, March 8, 1906

151. Letter from the Acting Commissioner to Cherokee Land Office, re land contested by Georganna Thornton, reinstated, December 7, 1906

152. File receipts for the family of John Bowlin, July 29, 1909

153. Notice of noncompletion of selection of land to Helen F. Nail, Freedmen, July 20, 1908

154. Land plat, Township 12 N, Range No. 19 E Section 25

155. Application for described land, Helen F. Nail, July 20, 1908

156. Notice of noncompletion of selection of land to Helen F. Nail, Freedmen, June [29?], 1908

157. Land plat, Township 27 N, Range No. 24 E Section 20

158. Application for described land, Helen F. Nail, June 29, 1908

159. Testimony by Helen F. Nail, June 29, 1908

160. Testimony by John L. Bowlin for Leonard Elmer Bowlin, May 15, 1908

161. Application for described land, Leonard Elmer Bowlin, May 15, 1908

162. Notice of noncompletion of selection of land to Leonard Elmer Bowlin by John L. Bowlin, May 15, 1908

163. Land plat, Township 20 N, Range No. 19 E Section 36

164. Notice of noncompletion of selection of land to Elizabeth, Sophia A., and Doda C. Bowlin by John L. Bowlin, May 15, 1908

165. Land plat, Township 13, Range No. 23 Section 2

166. Land plat, Township 14, Range No. 23 Section 3

167. Request by John L. Bowlin for arbitrary allotment by the Commissioner for completing selections for Elizabeth, Sophia A., and Doda C. Bowlin, May 15, 1908

168. Letter from the Commissioner to John L. Bowlin, land allotment re May 15, 1908 request, May 27, 1908

169. Allotment and homestead designations for Elizabeth, Sophia A., and Doda C. Bowlin, May 16, 1908

170. Certificate from the Cherokee Enrollment Office that Helen F. Bowlin represented by John L. Bowlin appears as a citizen of the Cherokee Nation, September 21, 1907

171. Land plat, Township 25, Range No. 18 Section 20 (1)

172. Allotment and homestead designations for Helen F. Bowlin, September 21, 1907

191. Land plat, Township 25, Section 27 Range No. 18, Leonard Elmer Bowlin

192. Land plat, Township 25, Section 28 Range No. 18 Section 27, Sophia A. Bowlin

193. Testimony by John L. Bowlin for Elizabeth Bowlin, January 17, 1906

194. Testimony by John L. Bowlin for William Henry Bowlin, January 17, 1906

195. Testimony by John L. Bowlin for Eunice Cornelius Bowlin, January 17, 1906

196. Testimony by John L. Bowlin for Leonard Elmer Bowlin, January 17, 1906

197. Testimony by John L. Bowlin for Sophia A. Bowlin, January 17, 1906

198. Order of allotment to John L. Bowlin for Elizabeth, William Henry, Eunice Cornelius, Leonard Elmer, and Sophia A. Bowlin, January 20, 1906

199. Testimony by John L. Bowlin for Doda C. Bowlin, July 16, 1905

199a. Allotment and homestead designation for Doda C. Bowlin, July 16, 1905, citizenship approved November 15, 1905

199b. Testimony by John L. Bowlin for Doda C. Bowlin, July 13, 1905

199c. Allotment and homestead designation for Doda C. Bowlin, July 13, 1905

200. Certificate from the Cherokee Enrollment Office that Doda C. Bowlin appears as a citizen of the Cherokee Nation, November 15, 1905

APPENDIX D

Adams Land Allotments

Muscogee Creek Nation Land Allotments to Thomas Jefferson Adams and His Descendents

	Application Date	Township	Range	Section	Acres	Allottee	Roll No.	Notes
1	1-13-1900	14	12	26, NE ¼	160	Thomas J. Adams	2145	Ap. for allotment no. 3430, approved 10-11-1901, FWA 4
2	3-16-1903	14	12	26, S ½ of NE ¼ of NE ¼ and N ½ of SE ¼ of NE ¼	40	Thomas J. Adams	2145	Ap. for homestead Allotment, FWA 18 (see item 4 for homestead applications filed in 1902)
		14	12	23, NE ¼ of SE ¼	40	Mahala Adams	2146	
		14	12	26, NE ¼ of NW ¼	40	Martha Adams	2147	
		15	12	4, SE ¼ of NW ¼		Mary Adams	2148	
3	10-5-1899	14	12	23, SE ¼	160	Mahala Adams	2146	Ap. for allotment no. 2460, approved 10-5-1899, FWA 2
4	7-12-1902	14	12	26, NE ¼ of NW ¼	40	Martha Adams	2147	Ap. for allotment, FWA 6
5	8-8-1899	16	12	31, SE ¼	160	Martha Adams	2147	Ap. for allotment no. 1680A, canceled 7-11-1900, FWA 7

	Application Date	Township	Range	Section	Acres	Allottee	Roll No.	Notes
6	7-12-1900	15	12	32, E ½ of SW ¼	120	Martha Adams	2147	Ap. for allotment no. 5214, FWA 8
				30, SW ¼ of SE ¼				Attestation: sells 40 acres for town site, 12-14-1905, FWA 1, 10
								Tax exemption letter, 4-10-1934, FWA 29
7	12-29-1904	15	12	33, NE ¼ of NW ½ of NW ¼ of NW ¼	2.50	Martha Adams	2147	Acknowledgment of enrollment and ap. for allotment, FWA 9
8	8-8-1899	15	12	4, S ½ of NW ¼; Lot 3 and Lot 4	159.87	Mary Adams	2148	Ap. for allotment no. 1680, approved 7-12-1900, FWA 5
								Contested by Hepsy and Daniel Adams, 12-6-1900 (dismissed), FWA 11
9	8-12-1907	14	12	17, SE ¼ of NW ¼	40	William Washington (son of Martha)	2149	Ap. for homestead allotment, FWA 42
10	5-25-1904	15	12	31, E 5 acres of NW 10 acres of Lot 1; SW 9.06 acres of Lot 1; and Lot 4	52.08	William Washington (heirs of)	2149	Allotments of land and homestead designations described and made, FWA 61
		14	12	17, S ½ of NW ¼	80			

	Application Date	Township	Range	Section	Acres	Allottee	Roll No.	Notes
11	6-7-1900	14	13	18, NE ¼	160	William Washington	2149	Ap. for allotment no. 5069, canceled 10-11-1901, FWA 3
12	8-9-1907	14	12	19, S ½ of SE ¼ of SE ¼ and $2.40; S ½ of NE ¼ of SE ¼ of SE ¼ and $2.40; and SE ¼ of NW ¼ of SE ¼ of SE ¼	27.5	William Washington (Deed)	2149	Allotments of land and homestead designations described and made, FWA 46
13	12-8-1899	14	12	9, W ½ of NW ¼	80	George Washington Adams	3780	Ap. for allotment no. 3272
		14	12	8, E ½ of NE ¼; 5, Lot 4; 6, Lot 1	161	Sarah Adams (wife)	3781	Cancelled for Sarah Adams 3-26-1910, FWA 70
14	12-6-1904	14	12	6, E ½ of E ½ of SE 10 acres of Lot 4	2.50	George Washington Adams	3780	Acknowledgement of enrollment and ap. for allotment, FWA 85
15	8-17-1901	15	12	31, SE ¼ of NE ¼	40	George Washington Adams	3780	Ap. for allotment, FWA 86
16	12-6-1904	14	12	6, E ¾ of NE; 9/64 acre of Lot 4	3.04	Sarah Adams	3781	Acknowledgement of enrollment and ap. for allotment, FWA 97
17	3-26-1900	15	12	32, SW ¼ of NW ¼	40	George Washington Adams	3780	Ap. for allotment no. 4258, FWA 98, 105

	Application Date	Township	Range	Section	Acres	Allottee	Roll No.	Notes
		14	12	8, E ½ of NE ¼	80	Sarah Adams	3781	
		15	12	31, E ¼ of SE ¼	80	Sarah Adams	3781	
				32, NW ¼ of SW ¼				
18	9-6-1900	15	12	20, SE ¼	160	Willie Adams	3785	Ap. for allotment no. 5379, approved 9-20-1901, FWA 71
19	1-26-1904	14	12	6, Lot 3	40.19	Fred Adams (heirs of)	3786	Ap. for homestead allotment, FWA 73, Died August 10, 1899
20	2-3-1902	15	12	31, SW ¼ of NW ¼ and W ½ of SE ¼	160.19	Fred Adams (heirs of)	3786	Ap. for allotment, approved 2-19-1902, FWA 91
		14	12	6, Lot 3				
21	1-17-1903	14	12	9, NW ¼ of NW ¼	40	George Washington Adams	3780	Ap. for homestead, FWA 99, (see items 13 and 22 for homestead applications filed in 1900)
		15	12	32, NW ¼ of SW ¼	36.94	Sarah Adams	3781	
		15	12	29, NW ¼ of NE ¼	40	Benjamin Adams	3782	
		15	12	20, SE ¼ of SW ¼	40	John Adams	3783	
		15	12	29, NE ¼ of NW ¼	40	Robert Manuel	3784	
		15	12	20, SW ¼ of SE ¼	40	Willie Adams	3785	

	Application Date	Township	Range	Section	Acres	Allottee	Roll No.	Notes
22	3-26-1900	15	12	29, NE ¼	160	Benjamin Adams	3782	Ap. for allotment 4270, FWA 92, 106
		15	12	20, SW ¼	160	John Adams	3783	
		15	12	29, NW ¼	160	Robert Manuel	3784	
23	3-26-1900	14	12	9, N ½ of SW ¼	80	Lewis Adams	3790	Ap. for allotment no. 4267, FWA 107
		14	12	9, E ½ of SW ¼; W ½ of SE ¼	160	Washington Adams (Stripet)	3791	
		15	12	30, SE ¼ of SE ¼	40	Lewis Adams	3790	
		15	11	1, NE ¼ of SE ¼	40	Lewis Adams	3790	
24	9-13-1902	14	12	9, SW ¼ of SE ¼ of NW ¼	40	Lewis Adams	3790	Ap. for allotment, FWA 111
				8, W ½ of NE ¼ of SW ¼ and SE ¼ of NW ¼ of SW ¼				
25	1-22-1903	14	12	9, NW ¼ of SW ¼	40	Lewis Adams	3790	Ap. for homestead allotment, FWA 112 (see item 23 for homestead applications filed in 1900 and item 27 for 1902)
		14	12	9, NE ¼ of SW ¼	40	Washington Adams	3791	
		14	12	8, W ½ of NW ¼ of SE ¼ and E ½ of NE ¼ of SW ¼	40	Leo Adams	3792	

	Application Date	Township	Range	Section	Acres	Allottee	Roll No.	Notes
		17	17	14, NW ¼ of SW ¼	40	Hepsa Adams	3793	
26	3-26-1901	17	17	14, SW ¼	160	Hepsa Adams	3793	Ap. for allotment no. 6066, approved 10-22-1901, FWA 125
27	2-13-1902	14	12	8, W ½ of NW ¼ of SE ¼ and E ½ of NE ¼ of SW ¼	40	Leo Adams	3792	Ap. for allotment, cancelled 2-14-1902, FWA 126, 127
28	3-26-1901	17	17	14, W ½ and SE ¼ of SE ¼	120	Leo Adams	3792	Ap. for allotment no. 6067, FWA 127
29	12-8-1905	14	12	4, Lot 1	41.53	Andrew Adams	NB 786	Ap. for allotment, FWA 138, 139
				3, S 20 acres of Lot 4	20			
				3, S 15 acres of N 21.48 acres of Lot 4	15			
				8, W ½ of E ½ of W ½ of NE ¼	20			
				8, W ½ of W ½ of NE ¼	40			
				8, N ½ of NW ¼ of SW ¼	20			
				8, N ½ of N ½ of SW ¼ of NW ¼ of SW ¼	2.50			
30	12-8-1905	14	12	Portions of 8 NW, 5 SW, and 17 NE	160	Ethel Adams	N.B. 787	Allotment entitlement certificate, FWA 141, 142

Note: Accessed from the Okmulgee County Courthouse, August 2006 (see Appendix C for list of National Archives, Fort Worth, FWA, documents)

NOTES

Chapter 1

1. Debo, *Road to Disappearance*, 99; Strum, *Blood Politics*, 174.
2. See Catherine Royce's interview for NPR's series, *This I Believe*, from December 4, 2004 (http://www.npr.org/templates/story/story.php?storyId=6560320), and her book, *Wherever I Am, I'm Fine*.
3. See, for example, Chang, *Color of the Land*; Miles, *Ties That Bind*; Naylor, *African Cherokees in Indian Territory*; Perdue, *Mixed Blood Indians*; May, *African Americans and Native Americans*; Saunt, *Black, White, and Indian*; and Strum, *Blood Politics*.
4. The need for a new taxonomy of race is discussed in the section Terms and Trends. I use the terms *Red*, *White*, and *Black* to stress the broad meanings of these social constructs. *Colored*, though socially weighted, is used in the same manner as it was at the time described (the term is used throughout the appended Cherokee application transcripts), as is *people of color*. *Native American* and *Indian* are used interchangeably, as are *Creek* and *Muscogee*. Similarly, I use the term *mixed-blood* in a colloquial sense, rather than the more contemporary *multiracial*, recognizing the metaphorical, symbolic, political, and literal abuses of the former. For other views, see Chang, *Color of the Land* (15), and especially his discussion of "full blood" as a description of dedication to tradition more than actual ancestry (47). He notes, as well, the erasure of any racial distinctions between freedmen associated with tribes and African Americans who were newcomers to the area at the advent of the state of Oklahoma in 1907. Likewise, the new state assigned all people not of African descent— including Indians—in the group "white race" (160–61). Also see May, *African Americans and Native Americans*, 13; Perdue, *Mixed Blood Indians*, 90; Root, *Within, Between, and Beyond Race*, 11; Strum, *Blood Politics*, 33, 213; and Yarbrough, *Race and the Cherokee Nation*, 6.

5. For ways in which Indians have been lumped together, see the introduction to Mihesuah, *Natives and Academics*. Mihesuah also raises the challenge of interrogating sources whose research or interpretations may be biased. In the preface to that volume, she suggests ways that contentious points of view might be handled when Native and non-Native scholars differ on the value or interpretation of sources such as oral histories (x).

6. See, for example, Jacobs, *Incidents in the Life of a Slave Girl*.

7. As examined in *Grandchildren of the Buffalo Soldiers*, a play by William S. Yellow Robe Jr., produced at the National Museum of the American Indian, 2010.

8. See, for example, Blackmon, *Slavery by Another Name*, on the forced labor of southern Blacks; Katznelson, *When Affirmative Action Was White*, on inequitable treatment of Blacks in New Deal policies; or Thistlethwaite, *Great Experiment*, on the American experiment in equality.

9. See F. Davis, *Who Is Black?*, 12.

10. Armstrong, *In Search of Civilization*, 187.

Chapter 2

1. Strum, *Blood Politics*, 71–74.

2. Wickett, *Contested Territory*, 7.

3. To smooth the transition from slavery to freedom beyond the southern states, the Commissioner for Indian Affairs appointed a special commissioner of the Freedmen's Bureau to Indian Territory (Krauthamer, *Black Slaves, Indian Masters*, 110).

4. See Ronda, "We Have a Country," for Thomas Jefferson's early ideas about removal that were finally put into place under Jackson's administration (740–45) and Wickett, *Contested Territory*, 206.

5. See Appendix A for the complete transcript.

6. Kehoe, *North American Indians*, 195.

7. "Evidence demonstrates that when people of African descent have greater access to education they are better placed to participate in political, economic and cultural aspects of society and to defend their own interests." "Righting Past Wrongs," International Year for People of African Descent 2011, http://www.un.org/en/events/iypad2011/background.shtml.

8. Blackmon, *Slavery by Another Name*; Katznelson, *When Affirmative Action Was White*.

9. See Mihesuah, *Cultivating the Rosebuds*, 43, for a ranking of racial superiority among Cherokee in the later half of the nineteenth century.

10. Hernando de Soto led an expedition that explored the Southeast in 1539. Kehoe, *North American Indians*, 178–79; Green, *Politics of Indian Removal*, 12.

11. See Appendix B for a chronology.

12. Perdue, *Mixed Blood Indians*, 15.

13. Debo, *And Still the Waters Run*, 5; Kehoe, *North American Indians*, 201.
14. Chang, *Color of the Land*, 112.
15. Chang traces the transformation among the Creeks as their practice of making property on commonly held tribal lands shifts under pressure from Whites to individuals having property in the service of commercial agriculture, tenancy, and ranching (31). Chang goes on to link control of land use with social and political development, race, and power. See also the section on Revisiting History.
16. "In the nineteenth century, at least, there was no concept of a truly pluralistic society." Prucha, *Great Father*, 64.
17. Prucha, 65.
18. Debo, *Road to Disappearance*, 5; Chang, *Color of the Land*, 25.
19. Debo, *History of the Indians*, 121–22; Moulton, *John Ross*, 44–45. Also see the trio of judgments handed down by Chief Justice John Marshall in Johnson v. McIntosh, 21 U.S. 543 (1823), Cherokee Nation v. Georgia, U.S. 1 (1831), and Worcester v. Georgia, 31 U.S. 515 (1832).
20. Debo, *History of the Indians*, 105, 111–12; Prucha, *Great Father*, 28.
21. Saunt, *Black, White, and Indian*, 21.
22. Removing the Indians from the East was his "first goal as president." McLoughlin, *After the Trail of Tears*, xii.
23. Kehoe, *North American Indians*, 199; Perdue, *Mixed Blood Indians*, 97.
24. Debo, *And Still the Waters Run*, 95–103; Debo, *History of the Indians*, 117–26.
25. Kehoe, *North American Indians*, 200.
26. For the contrasts between the pro- and antitreaty factions among Cherokees that culminated in the signing of the New Echota treaty, see Moulton, *John Ross*, 56; and Strum, *Blood Politics*, 63.
27. Moulton, Letter from Chief John Ross.
28. See Foreman, *Indian Removal*, 281–82, and the entire volume for an additional, although dated, account of Removal; also see Moulton, *John Ross*, 99–101.
29. See Moulton, *John Ross*, 100, for estimates of the total number lost prior to and during the journey. He sets the total at about four thousand.
30. Naylor, *African Cherokees in Indian Territory*, 1.
31. Debo, *History of the Indians*, 122, 127; Moulton, *John Ross*, 132.
32. See McLoughlin, *After the Trail of Tears*, 22–31, for the forging of an uneasy unity among the three Cherokee factions following Removal.
33. Kehoe, *North American Indians*, 201–2.
34. For the antecedents of the Scottish Diaspora see Lynch, *Scotland*, and Macinnes, *A History of Scotland*.
35. Wickett, *Contested Territory*, 23. The interrogation of outmoded or hackneyed terms used to describe indigenous peoples has been the focus of more recent historical queries. A number of scholars caution against conflating abstract notions of race or culture with terms such as *full-blood, half-breed,* and

mixed-blood (Strum, *Blood Politics*, 56). Among the Five Tribes, these terms have often been conflated with retention or loss of traditional cultural beliefs and practices (Mihesuah, *Cultivating the Rosebuds*, xi). For more on the fluidity and shifts in the meaning and significance of these terms over time, see Chang, *Color of the Land*; Krauthamer, *Black Slaves, Indian Masters*; Miles, *Ties That Bind*; Perdue, *Mixed Blood Indians*; Saunt, *Black, White, and Indian*; and Yarbrough, *Race and the Cherokee Nation*. For example, Strum notes the Cherokees use of *full-bloods* in describing religious officials who represent core cultural beliefs, regardless of their actual racial mixture or blood quantum (*Blood Politics*, 121).

36. Chang, *Color of the Land*, 119–20; F. Davis, *Who Is Black?*, 9.
37. McLoughlin, *After the Trail of Tears*, 234.
38. Chang, *Color of the Land*, 212; Perdue, *Mixed Blood Indians*, 3–4; Strum, *Blood Politics*, 105; Yarbrough, *Race and the Cherokee Nation*, 25.
39. The *Phoenix* used a syllabary of the Cherokee language developed by Sequoyah (Wickett, *Contested Territory*, 2).
40. Debo, *And Still the Waters Run*, 5; Wickett, *Contested Territory*, 42.
41. Moulton, *John Ross*, 166–75.
42. Strum, *Blood Politics*, 71–73. See McLoughlin, *After the Trail of Tears* (esp. 214–17), for the contrast between Ross and his nemesis Stand Watie, whose treaty party faction sided with, and fought for, the South.
43. Chang, *Color of the Land*, 42; Wickett, *Contested Territory*, 43.
44. Yarbrough, *Race and the Cherokee Nation*, 89.
45. McLoughlin, *After the Trail of Tears*, 304.
46. Indian Territory was not open for White settlement until 1890 (Yarbrough, *Race and the Cherokee Nation*, 59). Also see Chang, *Color of the Land*, 76; McLoughlin, *After the Trail of Tears*, 234, who mentions the thousands of Red, White, and Black squatters on Neutral Lands; and Wickett, *Contested Territory*, 47.
47. Prucha, *Great Father*, 142.
48. Chang, *Color of the Land*, 112; Perdue, *Mixed Blood Indians*, 52.
49. Wickett, *Contested Territory*, 59–61.
50. Prucha, *Great Father*, 256–58.
51. Debo, *History of the Indians*, 307.
52. Debo, 330; Strum, *Blood Politics*, 79.
53. US Senate Committee on Indian Affairs, "Amending the Indian Land Consolidation Act," 3.
54. See Miles, *Ties That Bind*, for the story of the different fates of siblings.
55. Wickett, *Contested Territory*, 53–54.
56. Appendix A contains a complete transcript of the testimony.
57. Appendix A, Transcript I, Elizabeth Bowlen, 4.
58. Appendix A, Transcript III, John L. Bowlin, 1.

59. Appendix A, Transcript IV, Georgeanna Thornton, 1.
60. O'Beirne and O'Beirne, *Leaders and Leading Men*, 310–11; Stahura and Gibson, *Sons of Union Veterans*, 104.
61. Stahura and Gibson, *Sons of Union Veterans*, 104. The dates here contradict the testimony given by Ellen Thornton, which states: "In '62 they returned when the Army came back they all returned to Gibson." Appendix A, Transcript V, Elizabeth Bowlin et al., and Georgeanna Thornton, 9.
62. Appendix A, Transcript II, Georgeanna Thornton, 1.
63. Much of the information about John Leonard Bowlin is from the papers, personal correspondence, and conversations I had over the years with my aunt, Hazel Armstrong (nee Davis) and her daughter, Frances Lax (nee Armstrong).
64. See McLoughlin, *After the Trail of Tears*, esp. 84, 100, 213, and 235.
65. Saunt, *Black, White, and Indian*, 45, 54.
66. See Article 1, Section 2; also Debo, *And Still the Waters Run*, 46.
67. Krauthamer, *Black Slaves, Indian Masters*, 113.
68. Quoted in Katz, *Black Indians*, 147; a similar quote is attributed to Choctaw Freedmen in Krauthamer, *Black Slaves, Indian Masters*, 146.
69. Appendix A, Transcript III, John L. Bowlin, 3. One Cherokee citizen, Aleck Nivens, was an eyewitness to her travels with his regiment.
70. Kosmerick, "Hastings, William Wirt."
71. Appendix A, Transcript V, Elizabeth Bowlin et al., and Georgeanna Thornton, 3.
72. Hanneman, "Davenport, James Sanford."
73. Stahura and Gibson, *Sons of Union Veterans*, 104.
74. Appendix A, Transcript IV, Georgeanna Thornton, 2.
75. Appendix A, Transcript V, Elizabeth Bowlin et al., and Georgeanna Thornton, 12.
76. Appendix A, Transcript V, Elizabeth Bowlin et al., and Georgeanna Thornton, 3.
77. Appendix A, Transcript V, Elizabeth Bowlin et al., and Georgeanna Thornton, 23.
78. McLoughlin, *After the Trail of Tears*, chronicles the inconsistency in the application of Cherokee laws, noting at least one instance in which a former Cherokee slave married to a Cherokee citizen was granted citizenship (356).
79. Lambert, "Historical Sketch of Col. Samuel Checote," 276.
80. Searching references to them among the National Archives Cherokee applications files, their names appear in several other application hearing transcripts.
81. Appendix A, Transcript V, Elizabeth Bowlin et al., and Georgeanna Thornton, 17.
82. Appendix A, Transcript V, Elizabeth Bowlin et al., and Georgeanna Thornton, 22.
83. This information was conveyed in a personal conversation with African American genealogist, Angela Y. Walton-Raji, September 2004.

84. Appendix A, Transcript V, Elizabeth Bowlin et al., and Georgeanna Thornton, 25.
85. Appendix A, Transcript V, Elizabeth Bowlin et al., and Georgeanna Thornton, 1.
86. Appendix A, Transcript V, Elizabeth Bowlin et al., and Georgeanna Thornton, 13.
87. Blackmon, *Slavery by Another Name*, 18.
88. King, "I Have a Dream." Dr. King notes that African Americans still did not enjoy the same measure of freedom, security, and justice as Whites.
89. Sixteen-page letter to the author from Hazel Armstrong (nee Davis), dated August 30, 1992, author's collection.
90. Appendix A, Transcript V, Elizabeth Bowlin et al., and Georgeanna Thornton, 7, 12, and Transcript VI, Elizabeth Bowlin.
91. The land may have been leased, as discussed by Chang, *Color of the Land*, 110.
92. Appendix A, Transcript V, Elizabeth Bowlin et al., and Georgeanna Thornton, 12.
93. Appendix A, Transcript V, Elizabeth Bowlin et al., and Georgeanna Thornton, 22.
94. Elizabeth had to reside in the Cherokee Nation for six months before she and John could be wed under tribal law. Thus, according to family lore, they married in Kansas in 1880 and in the Cherokee Nation in 1885.
95. I am grateful to Frances Lax (nee Armstrong) for the newspaper clipping of John Bowlin's obituary; however, it does not include a citation.
96. Unfortunately, all contact with Julia Kidd was lost following our last email exchange in 1998. She died in 2014 and despite many subsequent attempts to find and contact her descendants, the trail has run cold.
97. Debo, *And Still the Waters Run*, 42; also see Krauthamer, *Black Slaves, Indian Masters*, 147.
98. Debo, *And Still the Waters Run*, notes that unlike other tribes, Creek and Creek Freedmen were given the same size allotments. Thus, at the time there was no incentive for the Freedmen to claim a degree of Indian blood (45).
99. May, *African Americans and Native Americans*, 102.
100. See Hedtke, *Freckleton, England*.
101. Among the many documents contained in the National Archives at Fort Worth, records appear incomplete or inconsistent as to the exact acreage that Georgeanna, Elizabeth, and the seven Bowlin children were granted. Allotments were made to them from July 1905 to May 1908, with numerous reminders that their various selections were not complete. The total land allotted to each individual (which was rarely larger than 40-acre noncontiguous plots) appears to have ranged from 80 to 130 acres. However, the values for their individual allocations are close to $325 dollars. Only one of the Bowlin children received land valued at $285, one got land valued at $320, one at $321, and five at $325. Similarly, the number of separate parcels of land ranged from 2 to 5 (See Appendix C for a list of Fort Worth documents including 143, 153, 155, 156, 161, 169, 172, 178, 180, 186, 199a, and 199c).

102. McLoughlin, *After the Trail of Tears*, 253.
103. See Chang, *Color of the Land*, 151; Krauthamer, *Black Slaves, Indian Masters*, 143.
104. Appendix A, Transcript III, John L. Bowlin, 1.
105. Appendix A, Transcript III, John L. Bowlin, see testimony by Aleck Nivens, 2.
106. McLoughlin, *After the Trail of Tears*, 282.
107. Nieves, "Putting to a Vote."
108. See Carlson, *Indians, Bureaucrats, and Land*, for a study of economic projections comparing farming under Allotment with the trajectory of farming prior to the Dawes Act. Carlson concludes that Allotment likely decreased productivity because it disrupted farmers at a crucial period.
109. Chang, *Color of the Land*, 119.
110. F. Davis, *Who Is Black?*, 11.
111. Bronfenbrenner, "Ecology of the Family."
112. See Gibson, "Promoting Additive Acculturation in Schools," on Mexican immigrant children.
113. Bronfenbrenner, "Ecology of the Family."
114. Deyhle, "Navajo Youth and Anglo Racism."
115. Mihesuah, in *Cultivating the Rosebuds*, reports that some Cherokee Female Seminary alumnae "were able to slip back and forth between the white and Cherokee cultures" (105). Perdue, *Mixed Blood Indians*, notes that in the early 1800s, ferries or taverns were often run by mixed-bloods (63).
116. "It is not uncommon for groups identified by race, gender, class, ethnicity, sexual orientation, disability, or age to call themselves 'cultures' and to be so called by others, despite the fact that their members also reside in and partake in the 'culture' of the larger society and despite the fact that members of these groups do not necessarily share distinctive histories, languages, rules, beliefs, or an inclusive array of cultural practices." Veroff and Goldberger, "What's in a Name?," 11. See also, Krauthamer, *Black Slaves, Indian Masters*, on "affective citizenship" and "imagined community" (124–25).
117. See the Descendants of Freedmen of the Five Civilized Tribes website at www.freedmen5tribes.com for a history and the individual lawsuits. Also see Strum, *Blood Politics*, 178.
118. Debo, *History of the Indians*, 338–39; Prucha, *Great Father*, 321–25.
119. See Chaudhuri, "American Indian Policy," 19; and O'Brien, "Federal Indian Policies," 44; as well as Prucha, *Great Father*, 340.
120. Prucha, *Great Father*, 379.
121. Schmidt, "American Indian Identity," 21.
122. Reportedly, the Cherokee Nation grew from 50,000 in 1980 to over 250,000 by 2005. Koerner, "Blood Feud," 120.
123. The Indian Gaming Regulatory Act, Pub. L. 100–497, 25 U. S. C. Section 2701 et seq.
124. See Strum, *Blood Politics* (183), for a discussion of the 1983 election for Cherokee Nation principal chief and deputy chief.

125. Koerner, "Blood Feud," 122.

126. Vann, interview.

127. Hembree, "Cherokee Nation."

Chapter 3

1. Debo, *Road to Disappearance*, ix.

2. Debo, x.

3. See Wright, *Creeks and Seminoles*, 1–5.

4. For example, Krauthamer, *Black Slaves, Indian Masters*, seeks to resurrect the messy, complicated, and largely unwritten past of Black Americans among the Choctaw and Chickasaw (153); Strum, *Blood Politics*, sets the objective of extending the literature on multiracial populations in the United States that are bypassed because of racial typological boundaries (17); and Yarbrough, *Race and the Cherokee Nation*, sheds light where other historians neglected the fact that groups other than Whites have developed their own racial ideologies (3).

5. See Wright, *Creeks and Seminoles*, for a history of how various indigenous groups came to be known as Creeks. Muskogee, the language spoken by Creeks today, is used here interchangeably with "Creek." Wright refers to the Creeks, some of whom spoke Muskhogean languages and some of whom did not, as "Muscogulges" (xi).

6. Under the Dawes Act, and the subsequent Curtis Act, most full-blood Indians were restricted from selling allotment land as they were deemed less competent to manage business transactions. For example, see Chang, *Color of the Land*, 119. Of course, the blood quantum required for citizenship today (a separate issue) is designated by each individual tribe.

7. Wright, *Creeks and Seminoles*, 1–3.

8. Green, *Politics of Indian Removal*, 2, 4.

9. The work of both Foreman and Debo was meticulous but also reflected the biases of the period in which they worked and, in the case of Debo, a pessimism that colored her conviction that tribes would soon disappear. For example, see May, *African Americans and Native Americans*, 5. Also see Littlefield, *Africans and Creeks*.

10. Littlefield and Petty Hunter, *Fus Fixico Letters*, 56.

11. Saunt, *Black, White, and Indian*, seeks to fill the gaps left when George Washington Grayson's autobiography was purged of references to their Black relations that would have been objectionable to his immediate descendants (viii).

12. Littlefield, *Africans and Creeks*, xi.

13. Chang notes that by 1902, ten thousand Creeks and five thousand Creek Freedmen had selected allotments (Chang, *Color of the Land*, 231n60). Also see Taylor, "Native Americans and African Americans," 3.

14. According to Debo, *And Still the Waters Run*, that is 6,858 full-bloods and 6,809 freedmen (47).
15. Chang, *Color of the Land*, 40.
16. See Mihesuah, *Cultivating the Rosebuds*, for a discussion of White aspirations among Cherokee Seminary students (4).
17. See the General Allotment Act of 1887 (Dawes Act), Chapter 119, Laws 1887, 24 Stat. 388, 25 U.S.C., section 331.
18. Chang, *Color of the Land*, 94, 124; Krauthamer, *Black Slaves, Indian Masters*, 25; Strum, *Blood Politics*, 55; and Yarbrough, *Race and the Cherokee Nation*, 37; have given attention to gender in the cultural transformations seen in Indian Territory.
19. See Mihesuah, *Cultivating the Rosebuds*, 7; as well as Wright, *Creeks and Seminoles*, 29, for naming traditions, and 229 for English names given to Creek students.
20. O'Beirne and O'Beirne, *Leaders and Leading Men*, 242–43.
21. *The Chronicles of Oklahoma* 13, no. 4, December 1934, 408–10.
22. Mihesuah, *Cultivating the Rosebuds*, notes that the school was the largest of the Creek Nation schools (34).
23. The W. H. Heydrick Collection contains an unpublished and incomplete manuscript, "History of Early Oil Development in Oklahoma," penned by John W. Flinner in 1931 or 1932. He died in 1935. This section draws from those materials, especially chapter 13, "Oil Excitement at Red Fork," and chapter 14, "A Profitless Venture Ends" (295–358).
24. Evidence of the official role that Thomas Adams played in signing the oil lease is based on a 1952 newspaper article, materials from the Heydrick Collection mentioned above, and family accounts.
25. Personal conversation with Willie Adams, September 2010.
26. This photo graces the cover of Chang, *Color of the Land*, and appears on page 56 but is labeled "Creek National Council members" rather than Tom Adams, his two sons, the two prospectors, and other witnesses.
27. 153 P. 65, 52 Okla. 495, Case Number 5845.
28. Krauthamer, *Black Slaves, Indian Masters*, details the discussion of land distribution by race among the Choctaw and Chickasaw Nations. Their legislators also proposed that "Indian" allotments would be 160 acres while those of "Negroes" would be 40 (115). May, *African Americans and Native Americans*, among others, notes that Isparhecher actually championed the equality of Reds, Whites, and Blacks (110).
29. Chang, *Color of the Land*, 83, 95–96.
30. Chang notes that taxes had been imposed on a racially graduated basis, with Blacks and "Indians by Blood" of more than half White ancestry the first to be taxed (136). The Allotment Period ran from 1887 to 1934, when the Indian Reorganization Act put an end to allotment policies. Although some states were

initially exempt, Oklahoma was added in 1936 with the Oklahoma Welfare Act (Debo, *History of the Indians*, 339).

31. See Appendix D for a list of Adams family allotments.

32. Fort Worth Archives (FWA) document 14. References denote documents from the files of the Western Collection of the National Archives. Numbers have been assigned by the author. Descriptions of referenced documents appear in Appendix C.

33. See Appendix C, FWA document 18.

34. O'Beirne and O'Beirne, *Leaders and Leading Men*, 243.

35. See Chang, *Color of the Land*, 119, Table 1, "Race and Restrictions on Allotments in the Act of May 27, 1908," which is compiled from "An Act for the Protection of the People of the Indian Territory, and for Other Purposes" (30 Stat. 495; Act of June 28, 1898 [the Curtis Act]), in Lawrence Mills, The Lands of the Five Civilized Tribes (St. Louis: F. H. Thomas Law Book Co., 1919), 538–41.

36. Mihesuah, *Cultivating the Rosebuds*, reports of similar discrepancies among Cherokee Female Seminar alumnae when some who had married Whites claimed a lesser degree of Cherokee blood on the Dawes Rolls than their siblings (106).

37. Mary Adams recalled the names of this particular delegation in a personal communication. Willie Adams remembered that Stripet received the *Congressional Record* weekly (personal conversation, September 2010).

38. See Appendix C, FWA document 89.

39. Thomas Jefferson Adams has the Dawes Roll number 2145 with the numbers of his wife and minor daughters running sequentially. The same is true for his adult sons, George Washington (3780 etc.) and Lewis (3790 etc.), while Thomas Jr.'s number is 2998 with no apparent progeny.

40. See Appendix C, FWA document 111.

41. See Appendix C, FWA document 116.

42. With his claim to citizenship through his mother, Lewis should have solidified his status with her clan. In marrying Annie, he ensured that any link to a Creek clan by their progeny was severed.

43. Appendix C, FWA document 136.

44. I am indebted to Francis Flavin, who suggested I spend yet more time in the Reading Room at the National Archives in Washington, perusing the correspondence files covering the Indian Reorganization Act. There I found a folder containing the Proceedings of the Conference for the Indians of the Five Civilized Tribes of Oklahoma, Held at Muskogee, Oklahoma, March 22, 1934, to discuss the Wheeler-Howard Indian Bill, Box 3, Entry 1011, Record Group 75, Bureau of Indian Affairs, National Archives and Records Administration, Washington, DC, retrieved July 28, 2016.

45. *Proceedings of the Conference for the Indians of the Five Civilized Tribes*, 11.

46. See Cottle, "Indian Land Reform," 77.

47. Hampton, "We Have to Think of the Indian People Themselves."
48. Creek Correspondence, Box 6, Entry 11E3 12/16/1, Record Group 75, CCF #62028–1936-Creek-050.
49. The information in the following sections was largely shared over the course of this project by my mother, Mary Louise Adams, except as noted.
50. Handwritten transcription recorded by an unidentified member of the Adams family and found among the papers of Leo Adams, who died in 1999, author's collection.
51. "Interviewer W. T. Holland, June 21, 1937, John Charles Chamberlain, Cherokee Old Timer, 720 South St. Louis Avenue, Tulsa, Oklahoma," handwritten transcription by an unidentified member of the Adams family, author's collection.
52. Dickinson College houses the Carlisle Indian School Digital Resource Center containing a searchable database of student files at http://carlisleindian.dickerson.edu.
53. According to a personal conversation with Crugee's daughter, Vanessa Adams, September 29, 2010, Tom Adams was a speaker of the House of Warriors when the school was founded.
54. Chang, *Color of the Land*, cites the town of Muskogee as a magnet for Blacks going west (132).
55. Still, the second set of children, who are my maternal aunts and uncle, because of their mother's status, belong to a tribal clan.
56. In 2010, African Americans made up 18.2 percent of the population of Beggs compared with 13 percent at the national level. "Race and Hispanic or Latino Origin: 2010, 2010 Census Summary File 1," Beggs, Oklahoma, United States Census Bureau, retrieved December 7, 2017, from factfinder.census.gov/faces/tableservices/jsf/pages/produtview.xhtml?src=CF, and "2010 Census Shows America's Diversity," United States Census Bureau, March 24, 2011, https://www.census.gov/newsroom/releases/archives/2010_census/cb11-cn125.html.
57. Chang, *Color of the Land*, notes a number of shifts in the town of Beggs. He writes that tensions following the influx of outsiders brought on by an oil boom in 1918 made the site a gathering point for a major Ku Klux Klan presence that was directed more at Blacks than at Indians (197–200).
58. Mihesuah, *Cultivating the Rosebuds*, cites a former teacher at the Cherokee Female Seminary as implying that lice were in evidence only among the more "traditional" students who were either indigent or more likely to be full-blood (80–81, 86).
59. According to Mary Adams (personal communication, September 9, 2010), when her mother died, her affluent aunt Lula Allison offered to raise her and the rest of Crugee's children in the all-White section of Muskogee where she lived, but bad blood flowed between Lula's near-White "Negro" relations and the "wild Indian" family that her sister Connie Allison had married into. Mary noted some evidence of Lula's color: When her nephew (the son of Lula's

maternal uncle and a bomber pilot) died in South Africa, the family used his "death" money to disappear into the White world.

60. Appendix C, FWA document 39.
61. Chang, *Color of the Land*, notes that in the second decade of the twentieth century, farm mortgage rates in Oklahoma were among the highest, if not the highest, in the nation (135).
62. Green, *Politics of Indian Removal*, 15–16.
63. Perdue, *Mixed Blood Indians*, 52. Also see Wulf, *Founding Gardeners*.
64. Public Law No. 360—70th Congress.
65. See Appendix C, FWA document 29.
66. Prior to Allotment, when tribes relinquished lands to the federal government through outright sale or treaties, the proceeds were generally held in trust, guaranteeing a fund for payment of tribal annuities. Under Allotment, plots allocated to full-bloods but restricted for a given time period were also held in trust. The result has been an arrangement by which the federal government has a responsibility to tribal communities for the property it holds in trust, rendering these communities dependent on a paternalistic system in which each side has been reluctant to end the relationship. See Prucha, *Great Father*, 296–98.
67. The title of her book on the history of the Creeks, *Road to Disappearance*.
68. Leo and Chester Adams were my mother's paternal cousins. Their mother was part Creek, providing them with the traditional matrilineal tie to her clan. Rather than calling them our cousins once removed, or our second uncles, to us they were "Uncle Leo" and "Uncle Chester."
69. Our Creek forebears, including Tom Adams, are listed on the Dawes Rolls as Indian by blood, not freedmen. See May, *African Americans and Native Americans*, for a discussion of Creek inclusion of African-descended citizens in relation to the other nations comprising the Five Civilized Tribes (255). Also see Chang, *Color of the Land*, on the close alliance of traditional Creeks and Black Creeks in resisting Allotment policies as defying US standards (69).
70. Saunt, *Black, White, and Indian*, 108–10.
71. Handwritten in May 2010, author's collection.

Chapter 4

1. McBride, *The Good Lord Bird*, reading and musical performance, Politics and Prose Bookstore and Coffeehouse, Washington, DC, December 2, 2013.
2. Nieves, "Putting to a Vote."
3. See Strong and Van Winkle, "Indian Blood," for a discussion of the meaning of "part Indian" (550).
4. Davis, "Federal Indian Education Policy Implementation."
5. Another atypical aspect of my family heritage is that I could trace more of my Cherokee Freedmen relatives than my maternal Muscogee Creek relations.

Names that existed in the original Muskogee Creek may account for the gaps I could not fill in the Adams lineage.

6. Helpful Oklahoma Historical Society staff pointed me to the invaluable materials contained in the Heydrick Collection. I have drawn heavily on that manuscript's chapters covering the Red Fork oil strike recounted above.

7. Women's Caucus for Art, annual meeting, Chicago, Illinois, 1991.

8. See McLaughlin, *After the Trail of Tears*, on the Delaware presence in Indian Territory and the polyglot makeup of the Cherokee Nation (260–61).

9. See Root, *Within, Between, and Beyond Race*, who raises the question "Who are we?" (3) and discusses the impact of self-naming among multiracial persons as a declaration of visibility. Also see Strong and Van Winkle, "Indian Blood," for a discussion of self-identification, attributed identity, and the official discourse of identity (558).

10. Klinkenborg, *Several Short Sentences*, 7.

11. Limerick, Milner, and Rankin, preface to *Trails*, x.

12. See Limerick, Milner, and Rankin (xi) and Napier, "Rethinking the Past," for a discussion of revisionist history in the American West.

13. Napier, "Rethinking the Past," 247.

14. Wilson, *Blood Quantum*, 110.

15. Napier, 221.

16. See Strum, *Blood Politics*, on the conflation of blood, color, and race (2) or race and ethnicity (15).

17. Yarbrough, *Race and the Cherokee Nation*, 7, 99.

18. McLoughlin, *After the Trail of Tears*, 123.

19. Chang, *Color of the Land*, 6.

20. Chang, 1; also see May, *African Americans and Native Americans*, on the transition where "Indian Territory rapidly developed from a triracial almost egalitarian into a rigid triracial caste society" (26).

21. See Strum's note to the reader, *Blood Politics*, xvii–xviii.

22. See Strum, 18.

23. Limerick, "Unleashing of the Western Public Intellectual," 65–67.

24. Limerick, 86.

25. Tayac, *Indivisible*.

26. I am fortunate to have been interviewed for the exhibit catalogue and to have one of my paintings reproduced there in full color (Tayac, 167–68).

27. Limerick, "Unleashing of the Western Public Intellectual," 72.

28. Quindlen, College Commencement Address. Also see Penha-Lopes, "What Next?," on race, assimilation, and the absence of prejudice (821).

29. Koerner, "Blood Feud," 146.

30. These small percentages could be erased by the large margin of error among the analyses (Koerner, 145).

31. Koerner, 145; Tallbear, *Native American DNA*, 3.

32. Koerner, "Blood Feud," 146.

33. F. James Davis, *Who Is Black?*, argues that Blacks condone the one drop rule as a means of increasing their numbers and thereby consolidating political power, which would, as a consequence, be reflected in government recognition and support (179). On use of the term *Negro*, the discontinuation of the word *mulatto*, and the admission of more than one choice in the US Census, see pages 11, 12, and 196, respectively. Also see Root, *Within, Between, and Beyond Race*, on race and the distribution of resources (8).

34. See McLoughlin, *After the Trail of Tears*, for milestones in the development of Cherokee "citizenship" (87, 105, 112, and 355–60).

35. See Mihesuah, *Cultivating the Rosebuds*, for a discussion of both traditional and progressive Cherokees considering themselves "more Cherokee" than the other (109).

36. Farris-Dufrene, *Voices of Color*, 139.

37. Schmidt, "American Indian Identity," 22.

38. Paul Spruhan quoted in Schmidt, 15. Also see Mihesuah, *Cultivating the Rosebuds*, on identifying features among the Cherokees prior and subsequent to the imposition of federal blood quantum designation policies (109–10).

39. F. Davis, *Who Is Black?*, 6.

40. Saulny, "Black? White? Asian?," A1.

41. Haney-Lopez, "The Social Construction of Race." Also see Yarbrough, *Race and the Cherokee Nation*, 5.

42. Gloor, "From the Melting Pot to the Tossed Salad Metaphor."

43. Mitchell, "Geographies of Identity," 641; Sleeper, "Review."

44. Mitchell, "Geographies of Identity," 647.

45. Sleeper, "Review."

46. Mitchell, "Geographies of Identity," 648.

47. May, *African Americans and Native Americans*, 260–61; McLoughlin, *After the Trail of Tears*, 376, 433n16.

48. McLoughlin, *After the Trail of Tears*, in reference to the Cherokees, notes "the inability of white America to accept the fact that the United States was, had always been, and would always be a multiracial and multicultural nation" (380).

49. For a discussion of the unique American practice of hypo-descent, see F. Davis, *Who Is Black?*, 5, and on America's provincialism, 172.

50. Penha-Lopes, "What Next?," 823.

51. See F. Davis, *Who Is Black?*, for a discussion of equalitarian pluralism (180).

52. See Penha-Lopes, "What Next?," on racial taxonomy in Brazil (818–19).

53. "Barack Obama's Speech on Middle East, full transcript," *Guardian*, May 19, 2011, http://www.guardian.co.uk/world/2011/may/19/barack-obama-speech-middle-east.

54. For an example, see Saunt, *Black, White, and Indian*, 15.

55. See the work of Ron Welburn for his research on the Indian roots of American jazz, as well as his efforts to foreground past history in *Hartford's Ann Plato*.

56. "Brandeis and the History of Transparency," Sunlight Foundation, May 26, 2009, https://sunlightfoundation.com/2009/05/brandeis-and-the-history-of-transparency.

57. Quoted in Schudel, "Michael Kammen," B5.

58. Penha-Lopes, "What Next?," discusses the promise of universal ideals embodied in the decline of racial and ethnic prejudices and the acceptance of other cultures in the pursuit of equality (809).

59. Armstrong, *In Search of Civilization*, 140.

60. See Smith, *Everything You Know about Indians*.

61. Obama, "Remarks by the President."

62. See Ronda, "We Have a Country," on Removal as a means of weakening and eliminating native nations (743–44).

63. See above for Cherokee Rising section covering Vann et al. v. Salazar and the Cherokee Nation v. Nash decision.

64. See May, *African Americans and Native Americans*, on the particular clannishness of the Creeks (5) and when Creeks of African descent had clan or town affiliations, they fit in because "the individual was nothing and the family was everything" (100).

65. Marable, "Escaping from Blackness."

Appendix A

1. References within the text to pages for each of the eight documents transcribed here refer to the original pagination. Also note that in some instances, "Fort Gibson" appears to be used as a synonym for the Cherokee Nation.

BIBLIOGRAPHY

Armstrong, John. *In Search of Civilization: Remaking a Tarnished Idea*. Minneapolis, MN: Greywolf, 2011.

Blackmon, Douglas A. *Slavery by Another Name: The Re-Enslavement of Black Americans from the Civil War to World War II*. New York: Doubleday, 2008.

Bronfenbrenner, Urie. "Ecology of the Family as a Context for Human Development: Research Perspectives." *Developmental Psychology* 22, no. 6 (1986): 723–42.

Carlson, Leonard A. *Indians, Bureaucrats, and Land: The Dawes Act and the Decline of Indian Farming*. Westport, CT: Greenwood, 1981.

Chang, David A. *The Color of the Land: Race, Nation, and the Politics of Landownership in Oklahoma, 1832–1929*. Chapel Hill: University of North Carolina Press, 2010.

Chaudhuri, Joyotpaul. "American Indian Policy: An Overview." In *American Indian Policy in the Twentieth Century*, edited by Vine Deloria Jr. Norman: University of Oklahoma Press, 1992.

Cottle, Melissa. "Indian Land Reform: Justice for All? An Examination of Property Laws Pertaining to the Five Tribes Indians and a New Call for Reform." *Oklahoma City University Law Review* 39, no. 1 (Spring 2014): 71–103.

Davis, Darnella. "Federal Indian Education Policy Implementation: A Comparison of Educators' Perceptions in Rural and Urban School." Ann Arbor, MI: UMI, 1998.

Davis, F. James. *Who Is Black? One Nation's Definition*. University Park: Pennsylvania State University Press, 2001.

Debo, Angie. *And Still the Waters Run: The Betrayal of the Five Civilized Tribes*. Norman: University of Oklahoma Press, 1989.

———. *History of the Indians of the United States*. Norman: University of Oklahoma Press, 1989.

———. *The Road to Disappearance: A History of the Creek Indians*. Norman: University of Oklahoma Press, 1989.

Deyhle, D. "Navajo Youth and Anglo Racism: Cultural Integrity and Resistance." *Harvard Educational Review* 65, no. 3 (Fall 1995): 403–45.

Farris-Dufrene, Phoebe, ed. *Voices of Color: Art and Society in the Americas.* Atlantic Highlands, NJ: Humanities Press International, 1997.

Flinner, John W. "History of Early Oil Development in Oklahoma." Unpublished manuscript. W. H. Heydrick Collection, Western History Collection, University of Oklahoma, 1931–1932.

Foreman, Grant. *Indian Removal.* Norman: University of Oklahoma Press, 1932.

Gibson, Margaret A. "Promoting Additive Acculturation in Schools." *Multicultural Education* 3, no. 1 (Fall 1995): 10–12.

Gloor, LeAna B. "From the Melting Pot to the Tossed Salad Metaphor: Why Coercive Assimilation Lacks the Flavors Americans Crave." *Hohonu* 4, no. 1 (2006), http://www.uhh.hawaii.edu/academics/hohonu/writing.php?id=91.

Green, Michael D. *The Politics of Indian Removal: Creek Government and Society in Crisis.* Lincoln: University of Nebraska Press, 1985.

Hampton, Neal M. "'We Have to Think of the Indian People Themselves': Oklahoma Indians and the Congresses of October 1934." In *Native Ground: Protecting and Preserving History, Culture, and Customs,* proceedings of the Tenth Native American Symposium, Southeastern Oklahoma State University, November 14–15, 2013, edited by Mark B. Spencer, 73–81. Durant: Southeastern Oklahoma State University, 2015. http://www.se.edu/nas/files/2015/08/A-NAS-2013-Proceedings-Hampton.pdf.

Haney-Lopez, Ian F. "The Social Construction of Race: Some Observations on Illusion, Fabrication, and Choice." 29 Harv C.R.-C. L. L. Rev. 1, 1994.

Hanneman, Carolyn G. "Davenport, James Sanford (1864–1940)." Encyclopedia of Oklahoma History and Culture, Oklahoma Historical Society, http://digital.library.okstate.edu/encyclopedia/entries/D/DA013.html.

Hedtke, James R. *The Freckleton, England Air Disaster: The B-24 Crash that Killed 38 Preschoolers and 23 Adults, August 22, 1944.* Jefferson, NC: McFarland, 2014.

Hembree, Todd. "Cherokee Nation: Extending Citizenship to Descendants of Slaves Is 'the Right Thing to Do.'" *Washington Post,* September 15, 2017, https://washingtonpost.com/news/post-nation/wp/2017/09/15-why-the-cherokee-nation-is-ending-its-decades-old-fight-to-deny-citizenship-to-descendants-of-its-former-slaves/.

Hogan, Linda. *Mean Spirit.* New York: Ballantine, 1990.

Jacobs, Harriet. *Incidents in the Life of a Slave Girl Written by Herself,* edited and with an introduction by Jean Fagan Yellin. Cambridge, MA: Belknap, 2009.

Katz, William Loren. *Black Indians: A Hidden Heritage.* New York: Ethrac, 1986.

Katznelson, Ira. *When Affirmative Action Was White: An Untold History of Racial Inequality in Twentieth-Century America.* New York: W. W. Norton, 2005.

Kehoe, Alice B. *North American Indians: A Comprehensive Account.* Englewood Cliffs, NJ: Prentice Hall, 1992.

King, Martin Luther Jr. "I Have a Dream." Martin Luther King's Address at March on Washington, August 28, 1963. Martin Luther King Jr., http://www.mlkonline.net/dream.

Klinkenborg, Verlyn. *Several Short Sentences about Writing*. New York: Vintage Books, 2013.

Koerner, Brendan I. "Blood Feud." *Wired*. September 2005, 118–46.

Kosmerick, Todd J. "Hastings, William Wirt (1866–1939)." Encyclopedia of Oklahoma History, Oklahoma Historical Society, http://digital.library.okstate.edu/encyclopedia/entries/H/HA051.html.

Krauthamer, Barbara. *Black Slaves, Indian Masters: Slavery, Emancipation, and Citizenship in the Native American South*. Chapel Hill: University of North Carolina Press, 2015.

Lambert, O. A. "Historical Sketch of Col. Samuel Checote, Once Chief of the Creek Nation." *The Chronicles of Oklahoma* 4, no. 3 (September 1926): 276.

Limerick, Patricia Nelson. "The Unleashing of the Western Public Intellectual." In *Trails: Toward a New Western History*, edited by Patricia Nelson Limerick, Clyde A. Milner II, and Charles E. Rankin. Lawrence: University Press of Kansas, 1991.

Limerick, Patricia Nelson, Clyde A. Milner II, and Charles E. Rankin, eds. *Trails: Toward a New Western History*. Lawrence: University Press of Kansas, 1991.

Littlefield, Daniel F. Jr. *Africans and Creeks: From the Colonial Period to the Civil War*. Westport, CT: Greenwood, 1979.

Littlefield, Daniel F. Jr, and Carol A. Petty Hunter, eds. *The Fus Fixico Letters: Alexander Posey, A Creek Humorist in Early Oklahoma*. Norman: University of Oklahoma Press, 2002.

Lynch, Michael. *Scotland: A New History*. London: Century, 1991.

Macinnes, Allan I. *A History of Scotland*. London: Palgrave Macmillan, 2017.

Marable, Manning. "Escaping from Blackness: Racial Identity and Public Policy." Along the Color Line, syndicated column. September 2000. http://www.jacksonprogressive.com/issues/civilliberties/marable/blackness.html.

May, Katja. *African Americans and Native Americans in the Creek and Cherokee Nations*. Berkeley: University of California Press, 1996.

McBride, James. *The Good Lord Bird*. New York: Riverhead, 2013.

McLoughlin, William G. *After the Trail of Tears: The Cherokee Struggle for Sovereignty 1839–1880*. Chapel Hill: University of North Carolina Press, 1993.

Mihesuah, Devon A. *Cultivating the Rosebuds: The Education of Women at the Cherokee Female Seminary, 1851–1909*. Chicago: University of Illinois Press, 1998.

———, ed. *Natives and Academics: Researching and Writing about American Indians*. Lincoln: University of Nebraska Press, 1998.

Miles, Tiya. *Ties That Bind: The Story of an Afro-Cherokee Family in Slavery and Freedom*. Berkeley: University of California Press, 2005.

Mitchell, Katharyne. "Geographies of Identity: Multiculturalism Unplugged." *Progress in Human Geography* 28, no. 5 (2004): 641–51.

Moulton, Gary E. *John Ross: Cherokee Chief.* Athens: University of Georgia Press, 1978.

———, ed. Letter from Chief John Ross, "To the Senate and House of Representatives," Cherokee Nation, September 28, 1836. In *The Papers of Chief John Ross, vol. 1, 1807–1839.* Norman: University of Oklahoma Press, 1985.

Napier, Rita G. "Rethinking the Past, Reimagining the Future." *Kansas History* 24 (Fall 2001): 218–47.

Naylor, Celia E. *African Cherokees in Indian Territory: From Chattel to Citizens.* Chapel Hill: University of North Carolina Press, 2008.

Nieves, Evelyn. "Putting to a Vote the Question 'Who Is Cherokee?'" *New York Times*, March 3, 2007.

Obama, Barack. Remarks by the President at a Memorial Service for the Victims of the Shooting in Tucson, Arizona, January 12, 2011. http://www.whitehouse.gov/the-press-office/2011/01/12/remarks-president-barack-obama-memorial-service-victims-shooting-tucson.

O'Beirne, Harry F., and E. S. O'Beirne. *Leaders and Leading Men of the Indian Territory, with Interesting Biographical Sketches.* Chicago: American Publishers Association, 1891.

O'Brien, Sharon. "Federal Indian Policies and the International Protection of Human Rights." In *American Indian Policy in the Twentieth Century*, edited by Vine Deloria Jr. Norman: University of Oklahoma Press, 1992.

Penha-Lopes, Vania. "What Next? Race and Assimilation in the U. S. and Brazil." *Journal of Black Studies* 26, no. 6 (July 1996): 809–26.

Perdue, Theda. *Mixed Blood Indians: Racial Construction in the Early South.* Athens: University of Georgia Press, 2003.

Proceedings of the Conference for the Indians of the Five Civilized Tribes of Oklahoma. Held at Muskogee, Oklahoma, March 22, 1934, to discuss the Wheeler-Howard Indian Bill. Box 3, Entry 1011, Record Group 75, Bureau of Indian Affairs, National Archives and Records Administration, Washington, DC.

Prucha, Francis Paul. *The Great Father: The United States Government and the American Indians.* Lincoln: University of Nebraska Press, 1986.

Quindlen, Anna. "Grinnell College Commencement Address," May 23, 2011, http://www.grinnell.edu/offices/confops/commencement/quindlen.

Ronda, James P. "'We Have a Country': Race, Geography, and the Invention of Indian Territory." *Journal of the Early Republic* 19, no. 4, Special Issue on Racial Consciousness and Nation-Building in the Early Republic (Winter 1999): 739–55.

Root, Maria P. P. "Within, Between, and Beyond Race." In *Racially Mixed People in America*, edited by Maria P. P. Root. Newbury Park, CA: Sage, 1992.

Royce, Catherine. *Wherever I Am, I'm Fine: Letters about Living While Dying.* Bloomington, IN: Xlibris, 2009.

Saulny, Susan. "Black? White? Asian? More Young Americans Choose All of the Above." *New York Times*, Sunday, January 30, 2011.

Saunt, Claudio. *Black, White, and Indian: Race and the Unmaking of the American Family*. New York: Oxford University Press, 2005.

Schmidt, Ryan W. "American Indian Identity and Blood Quantum in the 21st Century: A Critical Review." *Journal of Anthropology* (2011), http://dx.doi.org/10.1155/2011/549521.

Schudel, Matt. "Michael Kammen: Historian Looked Deeply into American Identity." *Washington Post*, December 4, 2013, B5.

Sleeper, Jim. "Review of Samuel Huntington's Who Are We?: The Challenges to America's National Identity." *George Mason University's History News Network*, August 8, 2005, http://hnn.us/articles/4987.html.

Smith, Paul Chaat. *Everything You Know about Indians Is Wrong*. Minneapolis: University of Minnesota Press, 2009.

Stahura, Barbara, and Gary L. Gibson. *Sons of Union Veterans of the Civil War*. Paducah, KY: Turner, 1996.

Strong, Pauline Turner, and Barrik Van Winkle. "'Indian Blood': Reflections on the Reckoning and Refiguring of Native North American Identity." *Cultural Anthropology* 11, no. 4, Resisting Identities (November 1996): 547–76.

Strum, Circe. *Blood Politics: Race, Culture, and Identity in the Cherokee Nation of Oklahoma*. Berkeley: University of California Press, 2002.

Tallbear, Kim. *Native American DNA: Tribal Belonging and the False Promise of Genetic Science*. Minneapolis: University of Minnesota Press, 2013.

Tayac, Gabrielle, ed. *Indivisible: African-Native American Lives in the Americas*. Washington, DC: National Museum of the American Indian, Smithsonian Institution, 2009.

Taylor, Quintard. "Native Americans and African Americans: Interactions Across Time and Space in the West." Presented at the Shifting Borders of Racial Identity Workshop 1, February 23, 2004, University of Kansas, Lawrence, Kansas.

Thistlethwaite, Frank. *The Great Experiment: An Introduction to the History of the American People*. Cambridge: Cambridge University Press, 1969.

U.S. Senate Committee on Indian Affairs. "Amending the Indian Land Consolidation Act to Improve Provisions Relating to Probate of Trust and Restricted Land, and for Other Purposes." Senate Report 108–264, 2004, 3.

Vann, Marilyn. Interviewed in "Court Victory for Cherokee Freedmen." Native AmericaCalling.com, Wednesday, September 6, 2017, podcast, soundcloud.com/native-america-calling/09-06-17-court-victory-for-cherokee-freedmen.

Veroff, Jody Bennet, and Nancy Rule Goldberger. "What's in a Name? The Case for 'Intercultural' Psychology." In *The Culture and Psychology Reader*, edited by Nancy Rule Goldberger and Jody Bennet Veroff. New York: New York University Press, 1995.

Welburn, Ron. *Hartford's Ann Plato and the Native Borders of Identity*. Albany: State University of New York Press, 2015.

Wickett, Murray R. *Contested Territory: Whites, Native Americans, and African Americans in Oklahoma, 1865–1907*. Baton Rouge: Louisiana State University Press, 2000.

Wilson, Terry P. *Blood Quantum: Native American Mixed Bloods, in Racially Mixed People in America*, edited by Maria P. P. Root. Newbury Park, CA: Sage, 1992.

Wright, Jr., J. Leitch. *Creeks and Seminoles*. Lincoln: University of Nebraska Press, 1986.

Wulf, Andrea. *Founding Gardeners: The Revolutionary Generation and the Shaping of the American Nation*. New York: Knopf, 2011.

Yarbrough, Fay A. *Race and the Cherokee Nation: Sovereignty in the Nineteenth Century*. Philadelphia: University of Pennsylvania Press, 2008.

INDEX

Page numbers in italic text indicate illustrations.

12/26/18